DATE DUE

SFPL JAN 13 '81

S0-EMF-163

66 '79

792.094
P834s **Porter, Hal.**
  Stars of Australian stage and screen. Adelaide, Rigby;
San Francisco, Tri-Ocean Books [1965]
  304 p. illus., ports. 23 cm.

  1. Theater—Australia—Biog. I. Title.

PN3017.P6   792.0994   540
                  65–19136

 Library of Congress   [3]

STARS OF
AUSTRALIAN
STAGE AND SCREEN

Also by Hal Porter

STARS OF
AUSTRALIAN
STAGE AND SCREEN

HAL PORTER

RIGBY LIMITED
ADELAIDE

Rigby Limited   James Place   Adelaide
Sydney   Melbourne   Brisbane   Perth

First published 1965

Copyright 1965 by Hal Porter
Library of Congress Catalog Card Number: 65-19136
All rights reserved

792.094
P834e

San Francisco Public Library

AUG   1965

Registered in Australia for transmission by post as a book
PRINTED IN AUSTRALIA BY HALSTEAD PRESS, SYDNEY

*For Patricia Reynolds and
Patricia Rolfe, with
affectionate gratitude*

ACKNOWLEDGMENTS

Thanks are offered to James McAuley
for permission to reproduce his
prologue to *The Sleeping Prince*.

CONTENTS

ILLUSTRATIONS

9

Illustrations

10

CHAPTER ONE

INTRODUCTORY

THE first play seen in Australia was produced almost two centuries ago. Although rawly presented in a thatched mud shack it was less uncouth entertainment than what had served as such in the penal settlement of Sydney Town. Bestial stuff had served before: it was, after all, the eighteenth century.

In London, the *bon ton* was dressing and over-scenting its ill-bathed self to tour the sights: the manacled lunatics of Bedlam, the fetid malefactors in Newgate Prison, the stripped drabs being flogged at Bridewell, the cages of delinquent boys at Mansion House. There were, of course, more elegant forms of entertainment: ballet, *opéra bouffe*, five-act tragedies, bawdy *commediette*. It was, however, the less elegant and more barbarous amusements for the English exiles in early New South Wales. They did the rounds of the cat-o'-nine-tails floggings, the stocks, the treadmill, criminal corpses strung up to rot in chains, seven-at-one-blow hangings. Public hangings were, indeed, not abolished in New South Wales until 1853, nor until 1854 in Victoria.

The birth of a less unseemly form of entertainment took place on June 4, 1789, in honour of George the Third's birthday, with a production of Farquhar's *The Recruiting Officer*. The cast, spiced (or leavened) by soldiers, contained eleven convicts. Although rice, Irish beef, Cape wine, or Jamaican rum bought admission to later eighteenth-century productions, £20 in cold cash was, this first time, taken from the audience of sixty—Governor Arthur Phillip and his officers, among them being Captain Watkin Tench. Australian "theatre" was born.

Since that eighteenth-century première of premières there have been Australian theatrical ventures and experiments without number. These, hit or miss shows produced lavishly or on a shoe-string, have covered every conceivable and inconceivable aspect of public entertainment. The gross total of performances from 1789 to this very day is great. The sum total of performers must be uncountably greater.

It is a total which includes those whose fame was as glittering and short-lived as a catherine wheel; those who sweated by centimetres to a summit of skill, and remained defiantly aloft, overpowering, and glamorous despite their farded wrinkles; those who achieved a too easy renown which vanity destroyed, or money, or debt, or drink; those who were loved for a scant week by the turncoat public; those who enchanted generations into fidelity; those who died wealthy, conspicuous, and glorious; those who died forgotten, owing the rent of a seedy back-street bed-sitter.

Hunting each to earth is a fascinating chore. Old one-page theatre programmes, brittle as autumn leaves, and nearly as brown; fringed satin programmes headed and footed by VIVAT REGINA; glazed and gilded programmes gaudy as cathedral stained-glass and thick as literary periodicals; movie magazines; gossip columns; tomes of Press cuttings; acidulous or facetious "jottings" by chatterbox raconteurs; theatre and film histories; arch memoirs and mock-modest autobiographies chock-a-block with distortions of fact—from these and elsewhere the entertainers show forth as inhabitants of overlapping worlds: the everyday one, and the one of illusion. Well cast as they may have been as characters in the province of artificial light and canvas landscapes, how miscast many were in the rôle of a human being. Therein lies much of their double-sided fascination. Let us, then, briefly track a few of the multitude that have teased the emotions of Australian audiences throughout nearly two hundred years.

They range from the convict actors and Coppin and Cinquevalli and Clyde Cook, to Diane Cilento and Zoe Caldwell; from Melba, whose baptismal name was as flatly Australian as Nellie Mitchell, to Mo, whose name was as un-Australian as Harry van der Sluys; from Eliza Winstanley (Mrs O'Flaherty), the first Australian-born actress to be world-famous, to Errol Flynn; from Bernhardt—"the divine Sarah" who adorned all she touched even when, as an old woman with one leg amputated, she played the part of Napoleon's youthful son in *L'Aiglon*—to Dan Barry, Australia's best showman and worst actor during the Edwardian era, who butchered everything *he* touched.

Engaging and all-too-human individuals appear briefly, then step back into the wings of the past.

There is Batters the Tinker, an actor who owned a small tin-shop in Collins Street, Melbourne. On May 25, 1843, he was playing the part of Hardcastle the gaoler in a melodrama called *Guilderoy*. Guilderoy, the hero, escaping from gaol, was required to fire at and wound Hardcastle. The pistol, as stage pistols will at moments of climax, jammed. With a self-possession that must have startled and chilled the tinker-actor, Guilderoy drew a dagger, and stabbed him —just like that! Batters fell heavily, copiously bleeding, for he was a full-bodied, full-blooded man, and the curtain also fell upon his cries of pain and astonishment—and his minuscule immortality.

There is Sir William Henry Don, a baronet six feet six inches tall, given to wearing nail-can toppers, and trousers of blinding plaid. A ludicrous female impersonator popular in the 1850s, he and his wife, Lady Don, appeared in many Australian theatres. He had been obsessed with the limelight since childhood, and remained so until his death in Hobart

Town in 1862. He fervently desired that his name should be remembered. It is. The Sir William Don is a well-known Hobart tavern.

There is Blondin, the incomparable wire-walker, born Jean François Gravelet, on February 24, 1824. By 1859 this ungiddiest of Frenchmen was walking the eleven-hundred-foot rope stretched from shore to shore a hundred and sixty feet above Niagara Falls. In 1861 he performed at not so great a height near the none the less dizzily high glass ceiling of the Crystal Palace. On the afternoon of Wednesday, November 24, 1874, in a huge fenced-in marquee on the Government Domain, Melbourne, the fifty-year-old Blondin danced on the high-wire, knelt on it, stood on his head, lay on his back, crossed it blindfolded with his body enclosed in a sack. High-wire still, but not so high as in his youth, for the trampled Domain grass within the marquee was now no more than thirty feet below Blondin's antics.

There is John Barrymore, loudly announcing in the Melbourne of 1906 that it was the only place on earth where a crime was made of being happy. He had come straight from the San Francisco earthquake, which Marion Marcus Clarke and the already perennial Nellie Stewart from Woolloomooloo had also experienced, to make his appearance on the Melbourne stage. For being "happy" at ten-thirty at night in Bourke Street he had to make an appearance also in Melbourne's Russell Street lock-up. It is common knowledge what this stylish actor with the cameo profile and the flawless legs meant by happy. It was an administered happiness that more and more impaired his performances and, as though by heredity, decades later, and in Australia too, the performances of his daughter Diana.

There is Dolores Eliza Rosanna Gilbert who, as Lola Montez, had been the cigar-smoking mistress of several somebodies of European court society before becoming the mistress of Franz Liszt and, with ruinous results, of King Ludwig I of Bavaria. Her feckless machinations were

14

directly responsible for the revolution that unseated this absurd monarch. Her riproaring decline had begun by the time she reached Australia and Ballarat in the heady gold-digging era. She matched, almost outmatched, that era. She defied the law, tied her Chinese servant to a door-knob by his pigtail so that she could slap him and beat him, and danced her provocative Spider Dance for the miners, before disappearing into shabby obscurity.

It is not too surprising to find the catalogue of those who entertained Australia showing the names of such people as Lola Montez and Batters the Tinker—although merely minor ones they were indisputable entertainers. As Bernhardt did, they prepared an act, however wretched it was, and presented the outcome, however wretchedly, to an audience. They have their positions among the ever-enshrined, the half-remembered and the almost-unrecallable who, in this, that, or the other year, displayed themselves in Australia; Batters and Montez occupy their minute places among such varied and variously gifted artists as Ada Reeve, W. C. Fields, George Wallace, Ristori, Judy Garland, Little Tich, Sir Laurence Olivier, Fay Compton, Frank Thring, Carrie Haase, Mischa Auer, Barrie Humphries, Sylvia Breamer, Dame Sybil Thorndike, Diana Parnham, Peter O'Shaughnessy, Beppie de Vries, Irene Vanbrugh, Theo Shall, Sir Seymour Hicks, Snowy Baker, Eve Grey, Lily Brayton . . . the catalogue has no end. Import, home-grown, expatriate on a money-making visit, ex-star in an attempted comeback, the range of their personal abilities, eternally magnificent to fashionably and momentarily so-so, is as wide as the range of their media of expression—vaudeville, opera, musical comedy, tea-cup comedy, high tragedy, kitchen-sink drama, bell-ringing act, ballet, chatauqua, the *tableau vivant*. One and all they are entertainers, "stage people".

In the infinite catalogue it is interesting to find one's eye catching on the names of those whose more resounding fame is in other fields—David Low, the cartoonist, playing the ferocious father, Rory Megan, in Galsworthy's *The Pigeon*; Hugh McCrae, the poet, as the wrestler in *As You Like It*; Blamire Young, the water-colour artist, as playwright of *The Children's Bread*.

On a Saturday night in March 1901 a man walked from the wings in the Bijou Theatre, Bourke Street, Melbourne. In Year One of the twentieth century a Bourke Street Saturday night was uproarious with the racket of a happy-go-lucky city on the tiles, with everyone alert for devilment or be-devilling. As the man on the Bijou stage began to orate, there was pandemonium. "Ananias!" shouted the audience. "Ananias! Ananias!" The name was apt. The man, who billed himself in South Africa in 1899 as The Greatest Liar On Earth, had printed the truth. In 1898 *Wide World* magazine had published some astounding travel articles. The writer, whose real name was Henri Grien, was born in Yverdon, Switzerland, in 1844, and died in a Kensington, England, workhouse on June 10, 1921. The travel articles about an incredible Australia were soon proved fabrications. On his way to the workhouse and death he was shouted off the Bijou stage, for he was truly one of the most infamous liars of all time—Louis de Rougemont.

Between 1880 and 1900 one of the actor-managers dominating the Australian theatre was George Rignold. In private, in dressing room, and in green room, he was noted for his use of Eliza Doolittle's adjective. Publicly, he was noted for his melodramas, and particularly for his Shakespearian characterizations—Hamlet, Mark Antony, Caliban, Falstaff, Bottom, Macbeth, Othello, and Henry the Fifth—all plum parts, all actor-manager's parts. As Henry, in 1886, he ranted mellifluously before a painted Harfleur, and a group of supernumeraries who were each paid two shillings nightly. One of these spear-holders, a small pantryman with a large nose, born in London in 1864, had been christened William Morris Hughes.

The hero of *Honest Hands and Willing Hearts*, a moral

16

melodrama especially written for him, was not unused to public appearances, but on a more boisterous stage which he had arrogantly dominated for ten years as Champion of the World. He was a burly Irish braggart, a boxer of the days before gloves were used. His name was John L. Sullivan.

When Gregan McMahon founded the Melbourne Repertory Company in 1911, and produced Ibsen's *John Gabriel Borkman* at the Old Turn Verein Hall in East Melbourne, critics lauded the performance of the young man who played Borkman, and foretold a great future on the stage for him. He had a great future, but elsewhere than on the stage, for he became Major-General Sir Frank Kingsley Norris.

A professional liar, a politician, a world-champion boxer, a soldier . . . why not a short story writer? After all, the inspired and dedicated short story writer from New Zealand, Katherine Mansfield, when she first went to England, appeared in films there. Why not an Australian writer in an Australian film? Henry Lawson? In 1921, when Australian film-making was at its busy height, Henry Lawson appeared in the film *While the Billy Boils*.

An examination of the vast field of entertainment makes it obvious that nothing except a monumental encyclopaedic work could deal with everything and everybody.

The intention of this book is much less far-reaching, and most modest: to make a survey, and a broad one, of those Australians who have left some mark, vivid or pallid, on the legitimate theatre and the film, and to indicate the fluctuating climate in these two areas from 1789 to the present. Later books intend to deal with Melba's world, Mo's world, the world of Josie Melville and Gladys Moncrieff. Other books will deal with ballet, and the "little theatres".

To define *Australian* in these worlds poses something of a problem. For instance, James Cassius Williamson and his wife Maggie Moore were Americans, yet their largest contribution to theatre must be rated as Australian. Cecily

B

Courtneidge and Marie Löhr were born Australians; in the theatrical sense they are English. How is one to pigeonhole Peter Finch, English-born, who founded his career in Australia, and built on it elsewhere? What of the delightful American, Tittell Brune, adored by gallery girls, who made her name in Australia before going on to greater things in England—where she insisted that she was Australian? In selecting from the edgeless confusion of voices, faces, and bodies which bewitched, amused, thrilled to terror, or moved to tears successive publics, the problem of weighing Australianism will keep cropping up. It does not occur in the selection of the first notable performer this book is to deal with.

Australia has bred many daughters who have made their names on the stage or before the movie camera, but the first of them to make a powerful impression on England, Europe, and America was born more than a century and a half ago. In later life she was editor of *Bow Bells*, and author of numerous novelettes and other works including *Shifting Scenes in Theatrical Life* (1859), *Twenty Straws* (1864), and *What is to be, will be* (1867). First and foremost she was a brilliant actress, and it is fitting the book begins with her— Eliza Winstanley.

CHAPTER TWO

EARLY THEATRE

By the time Eliza Winstanley was fifteen, in 1833, Sydney had a Theatre Royal. It was in George Street, near where Dymock's Book Arcade is now.

This was not Sydney's, nor Australia's, first playhouse. Thirty-seven years earlier, on January 16, 1796, Robert Sidaway, a baker who had the Government's bread contract, had suffered entrepreneur yearnings, and had opened a playhouse in Bell Row, now Bligh Street, with a flaccid drama, *The Revenge*, and a boisterous "entertainment", *The Hotel*. The cast, according to Lieutenant-Colonel Collins, comprised "some of the more decent class of prisoners, male and female". The double-barrelled programme was the custom of the day. *The Revenge* was an unfortunate work in verse by Edward Young, the poet of *Night Thoughts*. The playhouse cost £100 to build, and was perilously ill-lit by fat-lamps, and rushlights made from the rushes of Rushcutters' Bay.

Theatres of that era, even in London, were eschewed by the more circumspect as disreputable, and were indeed so. They were stamping-grounds for pickpockets, criminal beggars, drunkards, and immoral women. Moreover, a family at the theatre meant an empty house at the mercy of thieves. Sidaway's, therefore, functioned on sufferance. The authorities warned the proprietor that "the slightest impropriety would be noticed, and a repetition punished by banishment of the company to the other settlements". Admission prices were: Boxes 5/-, Front Boxes 4/-, Pit 2/6, and Gallery 1/-. Currency being short in the raw colony, salt beef, flour, Irish pork, Bengal rum, and tobacco were accepted in lieu. To get in, one drama-crazy rascal sold the flesh of an esteemed and stolen greyhound as kangaroo meat at ninepence a pound. This was one of the numerous improprieties noticed as resultant on the theatre's existence, and helped shorten that existence. In 1798 Governor Hunter ordered Sidaway's closed. By 1800 it was defunct.

The next playhouse, the Theatre Royal, had been open a year when Eliza Winstanley made her début there on October 31, 1834.

She made this début in a Sydney that was still eighteenth-century and Hogarthian in tone. Convicts, nicknamed "canaries" because of their yellow uniforms, were chained and yoked to drag wagons of gravel and stone. Streets were filled with dungaree-men, the poorest settlers, dressed in the cheapest blue cotton from India; low-grade Chinese from Amoy; shepherds in smocks and cabbage-tree hats; kangaroo-skin-hatted gully-rakers who raked the gullies for strayed and scabby sheep; harridans smoking Brazil twist in short clay pipes called dudeens. For entertainment there were cock-fights, bull-baiting, women wrestlers, knuckle-fighting, rat-ting, cricket with ironbark bats, skittles, and public hangings of bushrangers—as many as nineteen in one session.

Blow-me-skull-off was a popular stimulant for those who could afford it. This satanic nostrum, at 2/6 a wine-glass, contained spirits of wine, rum, opium, *cocculus indicus*, and cayenne, and was sold at the Sheer Hulk and the Black Dog, taverns standing in a sort of Limehouse above King's Wharf, to the reeking riff-raff—prostitutes, fences, blackbirders, cashiered army men, hut-keepers, wood-splitters of the red beefwood of Botany Bay, and those who had been transported for stealing oysters, poaching, duelling, damaging trees, forming combinations, and the unlicensed selling of butcher's meat.

On the other hand, there were the drawing-room people, physically cleaner, and seemingly morally cleaner: the merchants in plum-coloured swallow-tails and nankeen tights, and their women in high-waisted dresses and elaborate heelless sandals. There were the Government officials, magistrates, officers of regiments, and civil functionaries. There were neat windmills, thatched cottages, and gardens, shops with parrots or cockatoos swinging in cages outside their doors, and small but elegant mansions enclosing the objects and evidences of culture. There was the Theatre Royal with its dimly classic exterior, and its boxes lined with crimson, and lavishly spangled with brass-headed nails.

This building, capable of holding a thousand people, was the objectified dream of Barnett Levey, host of the Royal Hotel, George Street, which was the only completed part of a five-storeyed warehouse designed by Francis Greenway, and to be topped by a windmill. In 1828 the eager, thirty-year-old Levey importuned for shareholders in his dream theatre. It was easy to sell two hundred shares at £5 each; it was difficult, at first, to get a Government licence.

Ultimately, however, under the patronage of the Governor, Sir Richard Bourke, on September 10, 1832, Levey was permitted to hold the first of a series of At Homes in the saloon of the Royal Hotel. Thirteen sketches and nine songs were presented. A programme note requested no encores; a not unreasonable plea since, although accompanied on the pianoforte by a nameless "professional Gentleman", and the band of the West Middlesex Regiment, Levey was the sole performer. As the result of his unfaltering enthusiasm, his amiable nagging, and his pioneer astuteness, the playhouse was built, inevitably slap-bang behind his own hotel, which got its foreseen rake-off by providing cold collations and drinks during intervals.

The Royal opened on October 5, 1833, with a mediocre melodrama *The Miller and His Men*, by I. Pocock, and a farce *The Irishman in London*. Critics pronounced the show "a complete failure", and advised "All the actors should go to school before they act again." Critical brutality notwithstanding, Sydney had a proper theatre, and a company of players that included the "mischievously fascinating" Mrs Taylor, Mr and Mrs Mackie, Mrs Dawes, the fidgety Mr Peat, and the handsome Conrad Knowles, whose later career was to be dashing though frustrating. The company was required to play anything. During the next few years its repertoire was frighteningly large and variegated: burlesques, extravaganzas, tragedies, dramas of every sort—domestic, serio-comic, romantic, nautical, historical, operatic, balletic, and bombastic, as well as comic operas, Shakespeare, and the expected farces which ended each night's presentation, and diplomatically sent the audience home in fits of uncultured laughter. In this *milieu* Eliza Winstanley began her incredible career, at the age of sixteen, in the title rôle of Sir Henry Bishop's *Clari; or The Maid of Milan*, Australia's first operatic production.

She was born in Kent Street, Sydney, on September 1, 1818, and educated at Sydney College, where Sydney Grammar School stands today. This education was thorough enough to be of value to her as a classic actress, and of equal value when she left the stage to be a writer. Her father, as Barnett Levey did, kept a tavern, the Blue Lion Tavern in Pitt Street. One suspects that Mrs Winstanley did most of the keeping, as she was to do in other public-houses they later owned—the Currency Lass, and the Nag's Head. Mr Winstanley painted scenery for Mr Levey's theatre.

In those days, and far into the twentieth century, Benefits were frequently held. A Benefit was an occasion when the complete proceeds of a theatrical performance were given to one particular actor or actress, to some deserving widow or orphan, and even, sometimes, to the prompter or one of the back-stage staff. It was at a Benefit for her scene-painting papa that Eliza Winstanley first played Clari. Critics and audience were taken with the tall, dark-eyed, lively, comely, and intelligent girl. With her "agreeable form", "rich voice", "graceful deportment", and "countenance susceptible of strong expression", she became Sydney's favourite actress, replacing, in their treacherous affections, the overworked and hitherto omnipresent Mrs Taylor. There were, of course, less dazzled critics who wrote, "Miss Winstanley is too affected, and making improper use of the letter 'h' ", and, "if she had not displayed such a wish to be in heroics she would have succeeded better".

Despite these shafts she went successfully on to give the first performances ever in Australia of many leading-lady parts: Desdemona in *Othello*, Rosalind in *As You Like It*, Mistress Page in *The Merry Wives of Windsor*. She starred also in blood-streaked melodramas: *Madeleine the Maniac*, and *The Whistler; or The Lily of St Leonard's*. Her singing voice was fine enough to earn her, years later, in Birmingham, praise from Mendelssohn. In Sydney she took part, as did her sister Anne, in a *Grand Oratorio* at St Mary's Cathedral, where seats in the transept cost 15/-, and in the western end 10/-. Anne Winstanley later married Señor Ximenes. As Madame Ximenes, she too trod the boards as singer and comedienne and dancer. She was plump, the "most spherical of sylphides", and, though she did "bounce like an Indian-rubber [*sic*] ball", was never to bounce metaphorically so famously high as her sister Eliza.

Actors and actresses then, even more than now, were more likely, by having extra strings to their bows, to bring down that elusive animal, Success. Indeed, versatility was a *sine qua non*. Eliza Winstanley's leading man in Sydney, Conrad Knowles, was as multi-gifted as she. Not only was he acting manager of the Theatre Royal, and later manager of the Victoria Theatre, Sydney, but in one evening, for example, he played Shylock, sang "Pretty Polly Perkins", delivered a comic recitation in broken English, and acted Mazzeroni in *The Italian Brigand*. Shows ran from seven p.m. until midnight. Audiences expected non-stop entertainment: the *chef d'œuvre*, the concluding farce, and generous interlarding of *divertissements*—songs, recitations, dances.

In 1841, Eliza Winstanley found time to marry Henry Charles O'Flaherty, an Irish musician in a theatre orchestra. As the husbands of many coruscating public women do, he remained so much in the background of her recorded life that the date of his death is uncertain. In March 1846, having been a prominent member of the *corps dramatique* of Sydney's three theatres, the Royal, the Royal Victoria, and the Olympic in Pitt Street, she and her husband set sail on the barque *Kinnear* for the Old World. She was twenty-eight. During her twelve years on the colonial stage she had gained enough experience, and saved enough money, to attempt London.

In London a theatrical reformation was taking place. By the 1840s London had twenty theatres and two opera houses, but, for two hundred years, three only of these—Covent Garden, Drury Lane, and Haymarket theatres—had had the monopoly of playing legitimate drama; that is, works with literary and theatrical merit. In 1843 the Theatres Act rescinded this right of monopoly, so that all London theatres, if so minded, could offer works of dramatic and artistic value. This was a fillip to the high-minded, and enticed to the fore such talented actor-managers as Samuel Phelps and Charles Kean.

At the same time, the prudish but gay young Queen Victoria and her arts-cultivating Albert not only began to attend the theatre, but revived, in 1848, the lapsed custom of Command Performances at Windsor Castle. The playhouse, for so long a scandalous, uncomfortable, and depraved place, became acceptable to the prudent middle class, became comfortable and profitable. Into this transmuted theatrical landscape Eliza Winstanley, Mrs O'Flaherty, stepped from the *Kinnear*.

After proving herself in the provinces, at Newcastle-on-Tyne, and the Royal Theatre, Manchester, she achieved London, the first Australian actress to appear there. Later, she acted in the New Broadway, and Astor House, New York, the first Australian actress to appear in America, being considered great enough to act opposite America's finest Shakespearian actor, James Hackett, especially distinguishing herself in one of her own favourite parts, Mistress Quickly.

In 1850 she returned to Drury Lane, from which she was lured to join Charles Kean's theatrical company. Now that the three-theatre monopoly was broken, Samuel Phelps was presenting estimable works at Sadler's Wells, while Kean was able to fulfil himself aesthetically at the Princess Theatre, Oxford Street. Signal of Kean's distinction was the fact that Queen Victoria engaged a permanent box at the Princess to witness his overwhelming Shakespearian productions. These were tastefully opulent, archaeologically correct to the minutest detail, with hundreds of supernumeraries including horses and hounds, spectacular scenery, and hand-picked casts in which Eliza Winstanley shone.

It was with Kean's company that she recorded yet another of her many *firsts*, as the first Australian actress to take part in a Command Performance. This was as Mrs Malaprop, in *The Rivals*. She also appeared at Windsor Castle as Lady Freelove, Lady Franklin, and Mrs Subtle. Possessed of inexhaustible vitality, without which no actress in that age of body-breaking stage labour and grisly travelling facilities could have survived, she toured widely: Melbourne, Hobart, Launceston—playing the Cape as she came out, and Canada as she returned—France, Germany, Italy, and even Russia, enacting the Shakespearian rôles by which she had earned her fame.

In 1865, at the age of forty-seven, a stately, handsome woman with large, intense eyes, she abruptly retired to become a writer. Her educated intelligence, which had much to do with her stage superiority, again served her well. In the next fifteen years she wrote thirty-three novels: *Desmoro; or, The Red Hand, Twenty Straws, Bitter Sweet, For Her Natural Life* among them. Most of these, like her numerous short stories, were set in the land of her birth, and dealt with bushrangers, convicts, the environs of Sydney, the characters she must have observed in her parents' taverns or in the more genteel streets of Wynyard. About 1880 she returned to Australia, and stayed awhile with her sister Anne, who had also retired to live in Geelong. Finally, she went back to Sydney, where she died in a house in Clarence Street on December 2, 1882.

She is buried in Waverley Cemetery beneath a decorous slab of red sandstone. Beside her grave is that of another famous Australian, Henry Lawson.

Before Eliza Winstanley's death Australian theatre had reached a peak of such vigour and zest that, in these effete, neuroses-ridden, and theatrically decadent days, it seems a golden Everest. To observe how this height was attained, it is necessary to circle back in time to when Eliza Winstanley was preparing to test her abilities abroad. Her path out crossed the path in of a man of almost her own age who was to be active and prominent in laying down the more solid foundation stones of Australian theatre. If Barnett Levey be called the Patriarch of Australian Theatre, this new arrival in Sydney, on March 10, 1843, can be called—as he often is—the Father of Australian Theatre. George Selth Coppin was a man of manifold activities which included twenty-six years as a Member of Parliament, the inauguration of the Royal Humane Society of Victoria, of the Old Colonists' Homes, of the Musical and Dramatic Association, and of Post Office Savings Banks, and the founding of the town of Sorrento as a watering-place. He owned the schooner *Apollo*, which traded along the coast of Victoria, and after which Apollo Bay was called. He introduced numerous stage notabilities to Australia—and thrushes and white swans. His life was so jam-packed and many-faceted that it is relaxing to note that, in October 1863, he and Mr and Mrs Charles Kean were seen picking wildflowers in St Kilda Park. As a boy, Coppin played with Kean in *The Hunter of the Alps*. When the turntable of time found Kean in low finances after his extravagant Shakespearian seasons at the Princess, London, the now powerful Coppin brought him to Australia. Before dealing with George Selth Coppin, who had eloped to Australia in the *Templar* with an American actress, a skeleton summary of the situation as it concerned early nineteenth-century playhouses in Australia will point up the value of his contribution.

HOBART. On December 17, 1833, at the Freemasons' Tavern, a company formed by Samson Cameron gave the first of a series of Dramatic Amusements. This offering was Kotzebue's Teutonically romantic *The Stranger; or, Misanthropy and Repentance*. The accompanying farce was *The Married Bachelor*.

From 1834 the Argyle Rooms, later the Argyle Theatre, with accommodation for five hundred, became the best-attended playhouse. Here Samson Cameron and Mrs Cameron presented plays; and Miss Reman, who became famous later as Mrs Clarke, made her Tasmanian début.

On March 6, 1837, Colonel Arthur, Lieutenant-Governor of Van Diemen's Land, graced the opening of the Royal Victoria Theatre, Campbell Street, when *Speed the Plough* and *The Spoiled Child* were presented. This theatre, Australia's oldest, and most elegantly furbished, is now the Theatre Royal, a Government-subsidized theatre. Here, Mr and Mrs Clarke (*née* Reman) strove to improve the taste of Hobart Town while keeping their heads above financial water. In 1845 they gave up the struggle. It was Mrs Clarke who brought back from London, in 1842, the kaleidoscopically gifted Mrs Stirling. In Hobart, Mrs Stirling married

27

Mr Guerin who, like Eliza Winstanley's husband, played in the theatre orchestra, and who, also like him, slipped unrecorded from the scene. Mrs Guerin became Mrs Stewart, mother of Nellie Stewart. Since the thrice-married Mrs Stewart had been Theodosia Yates, brilliant descendant of the brilliant Mary Ann Yates of Garrick's day, it is scarcely surprising that Nellie Stewart became an actress. Theodosia Yates had trained rigorously at Drury Lane, and was an outstanding comedienne, tragedienne, and *prima donna*.

ADELAIDE. On Monday, May 28, 1838, a Mr Bonnar opened his Theatre Royal, "a small, unique and commodious theatre", in the ballroom above the Adelaide Tavern, in Franklin Street, with *Mountaineers; or, Love and Madness*; the usual appendage of a farce, *The Lancers*; and the usual comic songs sandwiched in.

On November 27, 1839, Kotzebue's *The Stranger* appeared in South Australia, at a stringybark and paling edifice, a disused warehouse with the conventional but unwarranted name of the Royal Victoria Theatre. The actor-manager was Samson Cameron from Hobart; hence *The Stranger*. He and Mrs Cameron were the stars, and also played *Othello* with a cast of amateurs who paid for the privilege of mouthing and strutting with the canny professionals.

PERTH. On Tuesday, July 9, 1839, a group of Perth amateurs presented "the Petite Comedy, in two Acts", *Love à la Militaire*, in "Mr Leeder's large room". Intentions to gentility are suggested by the absence of a vulgar farce to top off the evening, the printing of the programme on fringed satin, the late hour of starting—"Half-past Eight precisely", and the programme note: "No Person will be admitted whose name does not appear on the Ticket."

By 1842, a subscription audience was admitted to the amateurs' plays in a room larger than Mr Leeder's, at Hodge's Hotel.

MELBOURNE. The playhouse history of Melbourne began in 1841 in a lofty weatherboard barn of a place, roofed in leaky shingles, and surrounded by a whitewashed paling fence.

It was the Pavilion. Later, with singular lack of originality, it was pretentiously renamed the Theatre Royal. It had been built in Bourke Street, next door to the Eagle Tavern, at the cost of £1,000, by the proprietors of the tavern, a Mr Jamieson and his notorious wife, Mother Jamieson. Their barman, Thomas Hodge, who had previously had some menial connection with the London stage, was the impulse behind the venture. The reputations of Mother Jamieson and the Eagle Tavern being what they were, Hodge was refused a licence to run a theatre, but was allowed to hold "concerts". The nature of these was so crude that Hodge was convicted in 1842. During its four years of existence a succession of experienced professionals tried, and failed, to impose some order on the ebullient audiences, but they persisted rowdy and bawdy. George Buckingham from Adelaide, Conrad Knowles and Mrs Knowles from Sydney, the Samson Camerons, and finally the striking tragedian Francis Nesbitt, all were forced to abandon the thought of making either cultural contact or money.

In April 1845 the Pavilion closed with a Nesbitt production; on April 21 Nesbitt opened Melbourne's second theatre, the Queen's Theatre Royal, with *The Bear Hunters; or, The Fatal Ravine,* and Douglas Jerrold's "admired nautical drama" *Black-eyed Susan; or All In The Downs.* To enliven this inauguration, music of a moral sort was provided by the brass band of the Port Melbourne Branch of Father Mathew's Total Abstinence Society, even though the Queen's Theatre Royal was no more than a rather baroque addition to the Adelphi Hotel, on the corner of Queen Street, and had been built with drinkers' money by John Thomas Smith, the licensee. The new company was richly veined with talent; Mrs Knowles (Conrad Knowles had died in 1844), Mr and Mrs Samson Cameron, Richard Capper, Mr and Mrs C. Boyd, Messrs Cochrane, Lee, Miller, and Jacobs. In the *dramatis personae* of the opening night appeared the name of Mr Batters—Batters the Tinker whose *contretemps* with the dagger in *Guilderoy* assured him of a curious and minute immortality.

It was at this stage that Coppin first descended on Melbourne with another talent-veined company, and the unique ability to succeed forcefully where others had failed dismally.

The above summary of the first Australian playhouses reveals that most were allied to grog-houses. By 1845, only Sydney, the eldest settlement, had broken this design of a too close marriage between alcohol and art. Admittedly the relationship was to last for years longer: the bars, the vestibules, and the promenades of later theatres were to be railed against by dourer and more virtuous citizens, but at least they were amenities of the theatre proper. They were adjuncts to the stage; the stage was no longer a mere adjunct to sozzling.

The Royal Victoria Theatre, Campbell Street, Hobart, had been built above The Shades, an underground gin-crib frequented by old lags (the Penitentiary was just a block away), street-women, pig-tailed sailors, shepherds on the loose, and the pock-marred and cat-o'-nine-tails-scarred dregs of Hobart. Players had to suffer the overflow from The Shades, along with the town's larrikins—The Bricks; with brandy-sodden bloods; and also with the more uncouth of the assistant surgeons from the Penitentiary Hospital just across Campbell Street.

In Adelaide, free-for-alls frequently occurred in the pit between ruffianly Tiersmen down from the Mount Lofty Ranges, and tough-as-nails whalers on the spree.

In Melbourne, the police were continually bursting into the Pavilion to reduce brawls between dress circle and pit, between the drunken Corinthians of the Melbourne Club with their curly-brimmed beavers, brass-buttoned swallow-tails, and high rolled collars, and the equally drunken pitites. A drunken actress once fell head-over-turkey into the double bass. Often enough, dress circle and pit combined, perhaps justifiably, to hurl fruit, heavy Georgian pennies, fireworks, and obscenities at the players. In September 1844 the Melbourne Irish rioted at *The Jewess* in which, Samson Cameron advertised, there was to be "a splendid procession of Cardinals to celebrate High Mass".

In short, most Australian audiences of the time were untrained, undisciplined, and uncouth. The effect of vegetable-chucking and loud-mouthed, drink-crazed audiences on the nerves of players was ruinous. It was financially ruinous too: staider elements of the community stopped at home reading Charles Dickens or Sir Walter Scott, and kept their money. A much more serious effect was that on the material presented. Ribald audiences demanded ribald fare: hornpipes, dirty songs, coarse buffoonery, debased farces.

All this is, of course, an over-simplification of the situation, but it contains enough of the truth.

The mere presence of playhouses, no matter how rough-as-bags, revealed the desperate and inborn need of people to be entertained. Not only did the new settlers hanker after what they had left behind in the old country; not only did they need to be diverted from their own fumbling humanness, and their own inconsequential daily lives; they needed also to turn their minds away from what could lie behind the ramparts of the bush, and behind the mountains, and beyond the horizon—an unguessable interior, sinister, comfortless, and immeasurable. What had been set up may have reproduced, in spirit, a sort of colonial Alsatia alive with spivs and molls and pickpocket street-arabs, but something had been set up. A force was needed to work on the shoddy ingredients. George Selth Coppin's arrival was fortuitous—it could even be said, Coppin being what he was, that it was perfectly timed. In London, as we have seen, the theatre was becoming respectable, and fashionable in the middle-class manner. This meant that it would attempt moralization, that it would be, at least, inclined to didactic "uplift".

In Australia, the gold rush was just around the next corner.

George Selth Coppin was born at Steyning, Sussex, on April 8, 1819. His father was manager of a small theatrical enterprise. He was trained from the cradle in the tricks of the trade. At the age of seven he made his first public appearance, standing on a table on the stage to play "Cuckoo Song" on the violin.

At nine he was second violin in his father's orchestra, and a child actor. His first part was as the little boy in *The Hunter of the Alps*, with the virtuous Charles Kean, son of the debauched Edmund Kean.

When Coppin was seventeen, his father retired from theatre management, and the youth and his violin set out to conquer. His energy was undiminishable, his cheek notable. He was a gambler: nothing daunted him. Known as "fiery Coppin" when young, he was short and stocky, with the bold but shrewd blue eyes of one of the yokels he was to make his name in playing.

His first years were ones of polychrome experiences. As Coppin himself wrote: "I then commenced the world upon my own account, with my fiddle under my arm, and went through strange vicissitudes that would be considered quite sensational in description."

He played walk-on parts. He played his violin. He played Polonius, as a low comic, in *Hamlet*. When theatre parts gave out, he earned money as a piano-tuner.

He was nineteen when he was given steadier employment in the Woolwich Theatre and, in one season, progressed from second violinist in the orchestra, and second low comedian, to stage manager and first low comedian at twenty-one

32

"The Merry Wives of Windsor"—Nancye Stewart and Neva Carr Glyn with William Rees

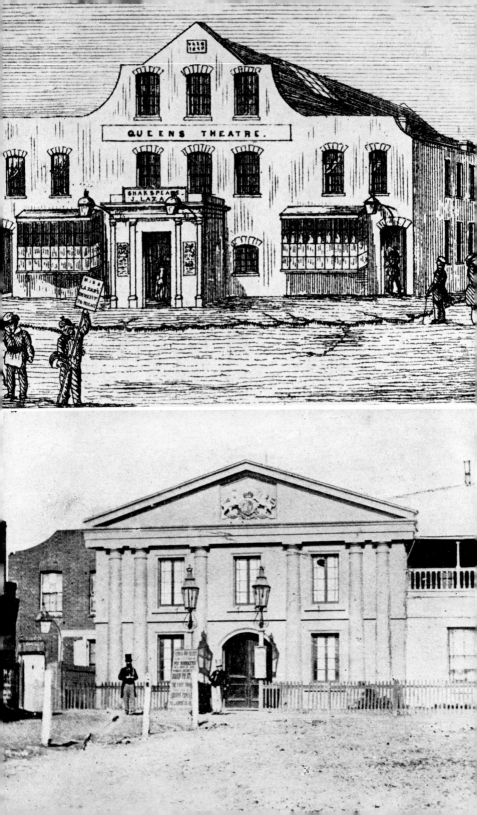

shillings a week. Next, he was engaged by T. D. Davenport, the original of Vincent Crummles in Dickens's *Nicholas Nickleby*. With Davenport, he decidedly earned his twenty-five shillings weekly—as violinist in the orchestra, second low comedian, dancer and singer during the *entr'actes*, and dancing-master to his employer's eight-year-old daughter Jean, "the infant phenomenon".

He advanced on London, where he played minor parts that led to his doing the York Circuit, a period of activity during which he played with Charles Kean, Ellen Tree (Mrs Kean), the Kembles, and Charles Dickens's actor friend, Macready, the Shakespearian tragedian. At twenty-two, he was well enough known to be given the important part—he and his "fiddle"—of Jem Baggs in *The Wandering Minstrel*. This opened at the Abbey Street Theatre—which became the Abbey—Dublin, on August 7, 1841. He was a success. Jem Baggs was one of the sorts of characters Coppin was to excel in—Daniel White, Paul Pry, Mr Mould in *Not Such a Fool As He Looks*, Trotter Southdown, Tony Lumpkin, Launcelot Gobbo, Chrysos in W. S. Gilbert's *Pygmalion and Galatea*, Crack the Cobbler in *The Turnpike Gate*—a musical farce first produced at Covent Garden in 1799, and Bob Acres in Sheridan's *The Rivals*. The public loved, and the critics praised, his portrayal of "the ponderous and impenetrable stupidity of certain types. The voice, the gait, the movements, the expression of the actor's features were all in perfect harmony with the mental and moral idiosyncrasies of the person he represented. . . ." He played Mawworm in *The Hypocrite*, Jacques Strop in *Robert Macaire*, Jeremy Twitcher in *The Golden Farmer*, Aminadab Sleek in *The Serious Family*, Stolbach (the Comedian) in *The King and the Comedian*, and Don Caesar in *Don Caesar de Bazan*.

After Belfast, Dublin, and a tour of Ireland, a Glasgow season, and an English tour, in *The Wandering Minstrel*, Coppin, motivated by ambition and amour, eloped with an

The old Queen's Theatre, near Light Square, Adelaide

The Queen's Theatre, dignified with a new front in 1850 and renamed the Royal Victoria

C

American actress, Mrs Watkins Burrows, comedienne and tragedienne, in S.S. *Templar,* which left Liverpool on November 17, 1842, and berthed in Sydney one hundred and thirteen days later—March 10, 1843. This first Mrs Coppin died in Adelaide in 1846. The second Mrs Coppin, *née* Harriet Bray, married him in 1855. In 1861 Lucy Hilsden became the third Mrs Coppin.

In Sydney, Coppin set two patterns he was to follow throughout a long life. First, he put the faltering Victoria Theatre, Sydney, on its financial feet. His share of the takings, £50 nightly, he invested in the Clown Tavern, 285 Pitt Street. He lost his money. This was the start of the pattern of rich-again, broke-again, rich-again, that was to continue until the end. The failing of investments, followed by explosively successful plunges, followed by financial misfortune, were never to faze the irrepressible Coppin.

Secondly, as early as 1843, when he was twenty-four, and barely a year in Australia, be began his curious custom of Final Appearances, which were to be as frequent as Dame Nellie Melba's Farewell Performances. He made one in 1843, another in 1846. He was still making one in Melbourne Cup Week, 1877, and also in 1881, "Most Positively the LAST APPEARANCE he will ever make as an Actor on the Melbourne Stage". It was not, however, until 1901 that he did make the final Final Stage Appearance he had begun fifty-eight years earlier.

He died on March 14, 1906, at Richmond, Melbourne, when he was eighty-seven. During a long life he had done so much that, for the purpose of this small book, it is necessary to select in miserly fashion.

On January 5, 1845, he was at the Royal Victoria Theatre, Hobart, and by March 3 was managing the Olympic, Launceston, with a new company including Mr and Mrs G. H. Rogers, Mr and Mrs Charles Young (later Mrs Herman Vezin), William and Alfred Howson, Mr and Mrs J. Hambleton, and Mrs Coppin. The company moved to the

Queen's Theatre Royal, Melbourne, opening on June 21, 1845, with *The Lady of Lyons*; the Petite Comedy, *The Four Sisters*; and the Musical Farce, *The Turnpike Gate*. In 1846, after a "Most Positively Final Appearance On Any Stage", he went to South Australia, and built a theatre in Adelaide (in five weeks), and another in Port Adelaide. He made a fortune; invested it in copper mining; lost it when gold was found in Victoria; became insolvent; attempted a fortnight's unsuccessful gold-mining—"blistered hands, a backache, and no gold"—and joined a go-getting actor, Mr Deering, in the control of the better of two Geelong theatres. After eighteen months and five hundred works, Coppin had made another fortune. Braced by this, he sailed for England in January 1854; ordered his prefabricated Iron Pot theatre; and then returned to Melbourne with the first of his notable imports, Gustavus Vaughan Brooke, a flamboyant Shakespearian from Dublin; and a conjurer, the Wizard Jacobs. While in London, billing himself as "the celebrated Australasian comedian", Coppin held a Benefit for Crimean soldiers, and orphans of Crimean soldiers, at the Royal Haymarket Theatre, on June 26, 1854, playing Crack the Cobbler in *The Turnpike Gate*, and Monsieur Putzi (Maire of Nevers) in *The Young King*.

The Dramatic Season of the Iron Pot opened on July 30, 1855, with Bulwer Lytton's five-act *The Lady of Lyons*, and *To Oblige Benson*. The Iron Pot, on the corner of Lonsdale Street and Stephen (now Russell) Street, was the affectionately sardonic name for the Olympic Theatre. Prefabricated buildings were the mode. Lieutenant-Governor La Trobe's house, still partly standing in Agnes Street, Jolimont, Melbourne, was wooden prefab; several of Bishop Perry's churches, and the Olympic, were of iron. Bellhouse and Company, Manchester, had built it to hold audiences worth £350 per sitting. The white-painted ceiling was sprinkled with gilt stars. The walls and dress circle balustrade were enlivened with circular oil-paintings of G. V. Brooke as Othello, Hamlet, Shylock, and Richelieu.

By 1856, George Selth Coppin and Gustavus Vaughan Brooke were virtually in control of the Australian theatre world. Writing to his mother in Dublin, in 1856, Coppin states, "We now have the Theatre Royal, the Olympic, Astley's Amphitheatre, Cremorne Gardens, and four very large hotels in full swing." The broad strokes of power are in that sentence.

Coppin was, however, to have wanings as well as waxings of fortune many more times. He was an incurable gambler; anything was to be grist to his dogged mill: Melbourne and Suburban Railways, roller-skating, coastal trading, and hotels were among his extra-theatrical speculations. It may endear the man to us to know that he picked wildflowers with the Keans in St Kilda Park, and introduced English thrushes as well as English actresses to Australia: it is fascinating to see what direct power he wielded, and what a chain-reaction effect many of his money-pursuing flutters had on the development of Australian theatre.

In 1862, during one of his financial crises, Coppin engaged Mr and Mrs Charles Kean to appear in his newly opened Haymarket Theatre in Melbourne. The fastidious Shakespearians had been reduced to relative near-penury with their lavish productions at the London Princess. When they left Australia for America, in 1864, Coppin went with them. He returned in January 1866 to play Melbourne and Sydney with *Coppin in California,* and a programme of low comedy characters. As well, he had engaged the famous Frenchwoman, Madame Celeste, who played in *The Woman in Red* at the Victoria Theatre, Sydney, which Coppin had taken. In a short time, he was again cock of the theatrical walk. In 1873 he made the move that was ultimately to have a profound effect on theatre management. He began astute inquiries about an American couple, one of whom, he could not have foreseen, was to inherit his crown. He had addressed his inquiries to Andrew Birrell of 1223 Mason Street, San Francisco. Birrell replied, "They are young, handsome, sober, sing *and* dance good." Coppin engaged the young, newly married couple, a Mr and Mrs James Cassius Williamson: J. C. Williamson and Maggie Moore. Whatever errors in speculation Coppin made, he made none in the choice of players. His boyhood apprenticeship, his years on circuit, his own meticulously presented plays, his association with so many of the great, all helped to sharpen that extra sense which made him an infallibly felicitous judge of star material.

In 1880, riding one of his crests, he cabled to a twenty-two-year-old Australian actress on tour in America, offering her the part of Principal Boy in *Sinbad the Sailor*. She accepted, and returned, and immediately became a star— Nellie Stewart.

It is curious that a man who, as Coppin did, spoke fervently against "the pernicious star system", and who, in fact, invented this bandied-about term, should thus lure such luminaries as J.C.W., Maggie Moore, and Nellie Stewart to his banner. Before attention is given to these shining mortals, it will be well to pay brief attention to some of the other stars who had flashed across the scene before 1880, and to indicate those dyed-in-the-wool Australians who were beginning to stand shoulder to shoulder with the gifted imports.

In 1831 Conrad Knowles came to Western Australia, moving thence to Tasmania, where he picked up a living by teaching Greek, Latin, French, and drawing. He joined Barnett Levey's company in Sydney as acting manager and leading man. Here he married the Mrs Jones with whom he had sung "Pretty Polly Perkins". Handsome, and an all-rounder, he was, says the *Sydney Morning Herald* of February 2, 1842, "undoubtedly the most clever performer in the colony, whether in tragedy or genteel comedy". He overcame an early inability to remember his lines, and was as impressive in *Richard the Third* and *Hamlet* as he was in lighter vehicles like *Isabelle; or, Woman's Life*. On August 24, 1842, he presented Melbourne's first really professional programme, *Monsieur Jacques* and *Naval Engagements*, at the turbulent Pavilion. He followed this in September with *Othello*, he in the lead, with Mrs Knowles—who also played anything from farce to tragedy—as Desdemona. The odds were stacked against him; the Pavilion audiences were intractable to the point of brutality. Even Coppin, who had successfully insisted on No Smoking in his Launceston theatre, was unable to quell these audiences, and was showered with halfpennies and apples. Knowles was far less hard-bitten than Coppin. Badgered and in debt, he died on June 19, 1844. An attractive man who had once studied for the ministry, he appeared with all the notables of that crude era: Eliza and Anne Winstanley, the merry Mrs Taylor, Mrs Larra, Gordon Griffiths, Joseph Simmons, George Buckingham, and Mr Deering.

In 1841 Francis Nesbitt (Francis Nesbitt M'Cron), an Irishman who had acted in London with Gustavus Vaughan Brooke, Gordon Griffiths, and Barry Sullivan, came to Sydney, and was immediately popular as Rolla in Joseph Simmons's production of *Pizarro*. He was a tragedian of dramatic appearance, and had an electrifying stage manner. In April 1845 he played the last season, a Shakespearian one, in the Pavilion, before it closed for ever. He became manager of Queen's, Melbourne, before joining with Coppin's company. In 1849 he went to California, but gold eluded him. Returning to Australia and Coppin, he followed where the energetic and tubby Coppin led: Adelaide, Hobart, Launceston, and Geelong, where he died in harness in 1853. He was buried there under a tombstone raised by Gustavus Vaughan Brooke "as a last tribute to a brother tragedian".

Other imports of the 1840s were Mrs Stirling (later Mrs Guerin, later Mrs Stewart), an incredible woman who was the original *Maritana*, some of which had been written by William Vincent Wallace in 1838, at the Bush Inn, which is still standing at New Norfolk, Tasmania; G. H. Rogers; Charles Young, who married Miss Jones, who was a Coppin player and an Australian. She later went overseas, appeared in productions by Samuel Phelps at Sadler's Wells, and divorced Charles Young to become Mrs Herman Vezin.

During the fifties and sixties, dress circles were crammed with red-shirted gold-diggers and their painted lights-o'-love whose pink bonnets were the badges of their profession. The earlier insults of flung fruit and halfpennies were frequently replaced by a flattering rain of small nuggets. Among those who benefited from this form of audience reaction were Lola Montez, Fanny Cathcart, the sisters Adelaide and Joey Goughenheim, the comedian John Drew, Kemble Mason, Mr and Mrs Charles Poole, Richard Younge, and Mr and Mrs Starke (*The Lady of Lyons; The Stranger; Ingomar the Barbarian;* and *Hamlet*). Provincial theatres proliferated. There were three in Bathurst and three in Bendigo. Theatres in Sandhurst, West Maitland, Ballarat, and Geelong ran non-stop.

There was an invasion of Americans skilled in raucous hyperbole; their advertisements were not one lying superlative less vulgar than now. The trans-Pacific players who attempted to act up to the king-size claims made for them included Mr and Mrs C. B. Thorn, Kate Denin, Mr and Mrs Waller, M'Kean Buchanan, Miss Goddard (who played a female Hamlet and Romeo), Mary Provost, and Miss Avonia Jones, who married Gustavus Vaughan Brooke. Laura Keene and Edwin Booth also came. Booth, whose Hamlet-playing was a record in his day, with one hundred successive performances, was the brother of Abraham Lincoln's assassin, John Wilkes Booth. Laura Keene, acting in *Our American Cousin*, was on the stage at the moment Lincoln was shot.

The showiest importations of this uproarious gold-rush era were, of course, Lola Montez and Gustavus Vaughan Brooke.

Lola Montez's *affaires de lit* were a European scandal,

which reached its zenith when King Ludwig I of Bavaria abdicated at her insistence during the 1848 insurrections. She may have been a successful enough courtesan. She was inspired neither as an actress nor a dancer, although her indelicate Spider Dance brought down houses in goldfields theatres and in Sydney. The inferior quality of her performances was stringently impugned by newspaper critics. She horsewhipped one, a Ballarat editor, Harry Seekamp, and defied others to step on to the stage and take up her glove, which she had flung down as a challenge to her detractors. There is no chronicle of any critic being unwary enough to take up the glove and the challenge—the cigar-smoking virago had, after all, unseated a king. On one occasion she was pursued on board a ship in which she was leaving Sydney for Melbourne, by a sheriff's officer, whose intention was to detain her because she had so many debts. Lola Montez removed all her clothes, and then taunted the officer to arrest her and drag her from the ship in this natural state.

She executed her Spider Dance during a dramatic hodge-podge intended to portray her life. Called *Asmodeus; or, The Little Devil*, it was composed of scenes such as Lola Montez in Bavaria, Lola Montez the Countess, Lola Montez the Patrician, and Lola Montez the Revolutionary. Hardly a work of great literary or dramatic importance, it appealed to the "half-tipsy, half-strumpet" audiences she catered for.

Lola Montez (1818-1861) was always disconcerting. After having warmed the beds of two husbands and a number of the lechers of European court society, including that of Franz Liszt the composer, she married a cornet of the Life Guards, George Heald, in 1849. She died in Ireland, puritanically regretting her gay life.

Gustavus Vaughan Brooke was the first of the Coppin importations, and one of the most consequential figures in that long line.

He was born in Dublin on April 25, 1818. He received a solid education, the first of his schoolmasters being Lovell Edgeworth, brother of the novelist Maria Edgeworth. From earliest boyhood he displayed a precocious ability in the art of self-expression, and a hankering for a career in the centre of the stage. This hankering quickened to a passion when he was taken to see Macready perform in Dublin in 1832. Brooke, who possessed the unquivering self-possession of the perfect extrovert, had earned a reputation as a prodigy in the Dublin world of private theatricals. When, in 1833, the brandy-sodden Edmund Kean failed to fulfil an engagement at the Dublin Theatre he was replaced by "a young gentleman not yet fourteen" who played William Tell. The young gentleman was Brooke, who was actually fifteen.

By October 1834 he was playing the lead in *Virginius,* at the Royal Victoria Theatre, London. For the next seven years he played in the English provinces, Manchester, Liverpool, and so on, and in Dublin and Belfast.

In 1841 Macready invited Brooke to join his London company. When Brooke arrived in London he discovered that Macready was offering small parts only. He refused, and returned to the provinces. His voice had matured to an instrument of sonorous quality, and his interpretations had gained in depth. Although his Romeo was not outstanding, his Macbeth and Othello were so magnificent that critics lauded him as the greatest tragedian of the day.

On January 3, 1848, he had a triumph as Othello at the Olympic Theatre, London. His one laxity was his love of alcohol. By the early 1850s, dissipation had begun to leave its marks, not only on Brooke's handsome face, but also on the voice of fire and passion which had given a flaunting beauty to his conception of the tragic heroes. When Coppin was in England in 1854 to order his Iron Pot theatre, Brooke was still drawing large houses, but was willing to follow Coppin back to Australia. They left England in November

1854, and arrived in Melbourne on February 22, 1855. Four days later, Gustavus Vaughan Brooke was launched by Coppin at the Queen's Theatre, Melbourne.

Although visibly granulated by mosquito bites, Brooke was a momentous Othello, and gave, said the Melbourne *Argus* critic, "a performance such as on leaving our English home we never expected again to witness".

Desdemona was played by Fanny Cathcart, and Iago by Richard Younge, both from Drury Lane. Emilia was played by the Australian Mrs Charles Young, who was to become Mrs Herman Vezin, and one of the notable actresses on the London stage of the middle and late Victorian age. Mrs Vezin's first part on the English stage was that of Julia, supporting Mrs Phelps in *The Hunchback* at Sadler's Wells Theatre. Also in the *Othello* cast for Brooke's Australian début was G. H. Rogers, who had come to Van Diemen's Land as a common soldier. Although he had never set foot inside a theatre, his performances in garrison entertainments were so good that a subscription was taken up to buy his discharge. He was taken up by Coppin.

The remainder of Brooke's first Melbourne season included *Hamlet, Richard the Third, Macbeth*, and works of a lower order: *Rob Roy, The Bride of Lammermoor, The Stranger; or, Misanthropy and Repentance*, and Sheridan Knowles's *The Hunchback*.

Brooke's voice recovered its beauty, and his art matured. He gave probably his best performances in Australia, and was immensely popular. At Ballarat the gold-diggers presented him with four large nuggets. In Melbourne he was given a cup, a salver, and a statuette of Shakespeare, all in gold; in Sydney a silver candelabrum weighing two hundred and seventy ounces.

Brooke was no business man. His close relationship with Coppin in many a reckless investment was unwise. In Melbourne alone the partnership had money in the Royal, the Olympic (the Iron Pot), Queen's, Astley's Amphitheatre (the nucleus of the later Princess), the Cremorne Gardens in Richmond, as well as in four hotels. In Hobart they had taken over the Argyle Rooms, and in Geelong the Theatre Royal.

Brooke had a repertoire of forty parts, mainly from Shakespeare, judiciously laced with Irish ones. Between his Melbourne seasons, he played Sydney, Hobart, Geelong, and the goldfields, where he was particularly popular in *O'Callaghan*, and as Captain Murphy Maguire in *The Serious Family*. Aminadab Sleek, in this latter play, was one of Coppin's parts.

Despite Brooke's undoubted popularity, his powerful acting, and his hard work, he was frequently in financial hot water. He did not have the resilient nature of Coppin. He began to drink too heavily again; his work and his morale deteriorated. While Coppin was in England in 1860, Brooke, who had been left the management of the Royal Theatre, Melbourne, lost thousands of pounds which even a season of the hop-pole Sir William Don, and Lady Don (Emily Saunders), did little to recoup.

In 1861 Brooke returned to England. Here, he discovered that theatrical taste had veered from ranting actors of his type, however mellifluous the ranting. He struggled on, but not with the former outrageous self-confidence. He became more and more dissipated. He had married Avonia Jones, the actress from America, who overworked herself into a consumption to try to bolster their diminished resources. While on an American tour, she wrote to Coppin, imploring help. Coppin persuaded Brooke to pull himself together and return to Australia on a two-year contract.

On December 23, 1865, Gustavus Vaughan Brooke gave his last performance. He had pulled himself together so successfully that the Belfast audience received his Richard the Third with tumultuous enthusiasm.

On January 9, 1866, he sailed from Plymouth in the iron screw steamship *London*. Two days later it foundered in the

Bay of Biscay. Of the two hundred and fifty passengers, nineteen only were saved in the one boat that was launched. Brooke was seen working at the pumps, and was heard crying out farewell messages to Melbourne friends.

When, a little later, Avonia Jones died of consumption, it was said, of course, to be of a broken heart.

Brooke was well built, five feet ten inches tall, and handsome, even with receding dark hair, and pouches of dissipation under his eyes. His voice had always been his cardinal magic, and had added dimension to his portrayals of the doom-hounded, and made him a thrilling tragedian.

CHAPTER THREE

THE SIXTIES AND THE SEVENTIES

GUSTAVUS VAUGHAN BROOKE walked off the Australian stage for ever in 1860. His voice had awed even the fire-eating gold-rush audiences to mute participation in the anguishes of the planet-struck heroes of the Shakespearian tragedies. Other tragedians, lots of other Shakespearians, were to stride from the wings on to the stages of Australia during the 1860s and 1870s.

The period was exuberant with them, each company with its own convictions as to interpretation, its own quirks of production, and its own animosities towards rival companies. Mr and Mrs Charles Kean turned up their noses at Barry Sullivan's less "gentlemanly" methods of advertising. George Rignold's staging was *grandezza*; Mrs Scott Siddons's was *maigre*. Alfred Dampier was a meticulous and intelligent performer; James Anderson was an uninspired one. Another Shakespearian, Walter Montgomery, denigrated Anderson's offerings as "a gorge of beef and mutton". Montgomery himself was accused of "overweening vanity", and some of his critics publicly stated "an irrepressible desire to kick him off the stage".

Walter Montgomery was a wayward Shakespearian with inspired patches, particularly in *Hamlet,* when he reached heights of genius. His egotistic manner offstage, and his

45

exhibitionist behaviour, laid him open to a charge of insanity by the more discreet Anderson and the more uppity journalists, one of whom dubbed him the "Cantering Cad of Collins Street" after, at four o'clock one afternoon, Montgomery had progressed up Collins Street, standing on the back of a horse. When Prince Alfred, Duke of Edinburgh, after whom so many back-street pubs in Australia are named, was visiting Melbourne in 1868, Montgomery was able to hob-nob with him, and flourished this fleeting relationship— as so many others have flourished a pleasant encounter or two with royalty—to the irritation of his enemies, who mocked him as The Right Honourable Barren Montflummery, and maliciously suggested that "His Royal Highness the Duke of Edinburgh will appear as William, in *Black-eyed Susan*, under the gracious and distinguished patronage of the Right Hon. Barren Montflummery!"

Montgomery was, however, an exciting actor who thrilled the general public as Hamlet, and as Antony in *Antony and Cleopatra*.

Shakespearians less uneven in quality also graced the lively theatrical scene.

(Thomas) Barry Sullivan was born on July 5, 1821, at Howard's Place, Birmingham. At fourteen he began work in a lawyer's office. In 1837 he saw Macready in *Macbeth*, and, in the same manner as Gustavus Vaughan Brooke had done five years earlier, became obsessed with the idea of following in the great actor's footsteps.

Sullivan joined a touring company and later a stock company in Cork at a wage of fifteen shillings weekly. By 1840 he was playing important parts, and so improved himself that he was able to transfer to a better position in an Edinburgh stock company at thirty shillings a week. He was five feet nine inches tall, had a ringing voice of wide range, dark curly hair, and the well-muscled legs that are always such an advantage in Shakespeare.

46

In 1844 he played with Helen Faucit—with whom Brooke had played—an excellent Antonio in *The Merchant of Venice* to her Portia. His competence as Antonio led to the lead as Petruchio opposite Helen Faucit's Katharina in *The Taming of the Shrew*. He was established, and in the front rank. He played with Brooke in Glasgow, and toured the provinces of Scotland and England. His career was not a heady and sky-rocket one, but it was a solid one; it was not a coruscating one, but his well-conceived characterizations were often illuminated by passion.

On February 7, 1852, he did what all ambitious actors then wished—and, perhaps, even now wish—to do. He played Hamlet in London, at the Haymarket Theatre. He next toured America, constantly improving his technique, and extending his repertoire.

In August 1860 he had a season at St James's Theatre, London, playing on alternate nights one or other of the title rôles in *Hamlet, Richelieu, Macbeth,* and *Richard the Third,* with three performances of each play.

In 1862 he sailed to Australia, making his début in Melbourne on August 9. During his four years in the colonies, even though his seasons overlapped those of Charles Kean and Ellen Tree, he played to full houses. In Shakespeare he played Hamlet, Othello, Iago, Richard the Third, Macbeth, Shylock, Lear, Falstaff, Faulconbridge; other great parts being Charles Surface, Claude Melnotte, and Richelieu. He was always popular. Something engaging in his personality, which was austere and, at the same time, restless and impassioned, made itself felt publicly, as it did privately, where it earned the deep affection of many friends.

In 1866 he returned to England and was chosen to play Benedick to the Beatrice of Helen Faucit, who came out of retirement for the occasion, in *Much Ado About Nothing,* for the opening of the Shakespeare Memorial Theatre at Stratford-on-Avon.

His last appearance was at Liverpool in *Richard the*

Third, in 1887. He suffered a stroke of paralysis, and lingered on, to die on May 3, 1891.

Alfred Dampier was born in London on February 28, 1847. He was educated at Charterhouse, where he showed early an interest in literary composition, and in Shakespeare. After leaving school he was associated with, and a conspicuously good actor in, a flourishing amateur club called the Ellestonians. After touring professionally in England, Scotland, and Ireland, his inborn abilities were sufficiently fortified by experience for him to play in Manchester with Henry Irving. Dampier was of fine character, poised, certain of himself, but earnestly anxious to improve and polish.

In 1872, at twenty-five, he was engaged by the Theatre Royal, Melbourne, as actor-producer. His first Melbourne appearance was as Mephistopheles in his own version of *Faust*. He followed it with appearances as Hamlet, Othello, Iago, and Richard the Third, but had less than the fire necessary to capture audiences entirely on Shakespeare. With many new theatres open, competition was stiffer. Dampier produced melodramas, and plays of his own such as *Valjean*, based on Victor Hugo's *Les Misérables*. Managers of that era knew the public was composed of two main sorts of audience, and made an accommodating repertoire their stock-in-trade. Attacks on the Australian commercial theatre, since the 1920s, as being degenerate are less attacks on what they present than attacks on what they do not present.

Dampier had an intelligent interest in Australian subjects for drama, and he searched for material. Much of this material was poured into the mould of the melodrama, that most moral of plays, with evil put to shame, and good rewarded by a happy-ever-after ending. This was only to be expected —it was the fashionable mould. Today, the results are unfairly mocked, unfairly because they were, at least, expressions of a vigour now lacking.

48

Hindley Street (north side), Adelaide, in about 1867

The same building, 1874, converted to the Theatre Royal and a hotel

Theatre Royal, Hindley Street, Adelaide, after rebuilding, in the late 1870s

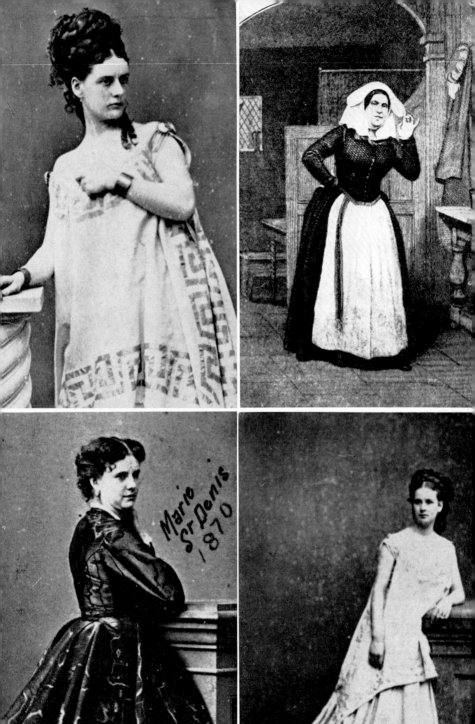

Mario
St Denis
1870

Dampier's interest became an enthusiasm. After his *Hamlet* in Sydney, in February 1877, he made a tour of Australia, New Zealand, America, and so to England, taking with him F. R. C. Hopkins's Australian play *All for Gold.* This he presented at the Surrey Theatre, London, in February 1881.

When he returned to Australia he leased the City and the Standard Theatres in Sydney, and the Alexandra Theatre, Melbourne, and diligently attempted to write, or to find playwrights who would write, Australian plays. He presented *Robbery Under Arms, For the Term of His Natural Life*, and similarly wild Australian dramas written by himself, or in collaboration with others.

A story is told of his opportune presence of mind. One night, as he was playing Captain Starlight in *Robbery Under Arms*, the scenery toppled, and came crashing towards the stage. "A landslip!" he shouted, "A landslip! Save yourselves! Run for your lives!" He and the cast ran.

He played this part, his final appearance, in Sydney, in 1905. He had never quite recovered from a heavy fall through a stage trap-door in New Zealand, and felt it necessary to retire. He spent forty years on the stage, nearly thirty of them in Australia, and had performed a solidly valuable service for it.

He died in Sydney on May 23, 1908.

George Sutton Titheradge was born in Portsmouth, England, on December 9, 1848.

After experience, of the comprehensive sort then usual, in Bristol and Portsmouth, and after a number of appearances with the tragedian Dillon, Titheradge appeared as Hamlet, in Calcutta, in 1876.

This led to his playing a minor but important part in the history of the British Empire. On January 1, 1877, he was the Herald at the Calcutta Durbar, and it was his cultured voice that announced Queen Victoria Empress of India.

49

Hattie Shepparde	*Eliza Winstanley as Mistress Quickly in "The Merry Wives of Windsor"*
Marie St Denis	*Eleanor Carey*

D

His first appearance in London was in October 1877. On April 8, 1878, he played Iago to Henry Forrester's Othello.

He returned for a while to India, and thence came to Australia, where he joined Arthur Garner's London Comedy Company in Sydney, his first part there, in May 1879, being that of Lord Arthur Chilton in *False Shame*.

In 1883 he was engaged by Williamson and Garner to play William Denver in *The Silver King*. His success in this part assured him of a continuity of leading rôles, and led to his inclusion in the Brough-Boucicault Company in 1887. Titheradge's forte was the cultured and distinguished Englishman. Among his century of parts there were many of these models of manliness; the type that can be summed up in the character of Aubrey Tanqueray in Sir Arthur Pinero's *The Second Mrs Tanqueray*, which he played to perfection. For the ten years he remained with the Brough-Boucicault Company he played such parts—well-bred, decent, masculine Englishman—with faultless aplomb. The one time this company broke its pattern, to present *Much Ado About Nothing*, Titheradge played Benedick to Mrs Brough's Beatrice.

In 1898 he went to London to join Mrs Patrick Campbell, who had created the part of Paula Tanqueray, and was to be the first Eliza Doolittle. After London, he toured America with this witty and devastating woman, and audacious actress. Until 1908, when he returned to Australia, he appeared with various companies in England and America.

During 1908 and 1909 his parts included the leads in *The Thief, The Taming of the Shrew, The Silver King,* and *The Village Priest,* one of his best expositions of the natural manner of acting he was master of.

After 1909 he went into semi-retirement, and from then on made only occasional appearances. In 1912 he played in *The Village Priest* with Mrs Brough. In 1914 he made his final appearance as Shylock in *The Merchant of Venice* in Sydney.

Titheradge died in Sydney on January 22, 1916. At the time of his death, this cultured, charming, and respected man was president of the Actors' Association, the forerunner of Actors' Equity.

George Rignold was born at Leicester, England, in 1839. His father, William Rignold, was an actor and a small-time theatrical manager.

As a child, Rignold was taught the violin, and played in the theatre orchestra. His stage début was as the messenger in *Macbeth*. He then joined the Bath and Bristol Circuit, gaining more experience with the Terrys, the Robertsons, and Maude Wilton. This led to engagements in London, where he appeared as William in *Black-eyed Susan*, Caliban in *The Tempest*, and Romeo in *Romeo and Juliet*. By 1875 he made a resounding success of the leading rôle in *Henry the Fifth* at Booth's Theatre, New York—a success he was to repeat often in Australia, to which he came in 1878. Apart from a season in Drury Lane, which an Australian syndicate sponsored, and a short tour of England and America, he spent the rest of his life from 1880 in Australia. He was a sound actor, a shrewd actor-manager, and somewhat a show-man in private life—his private life, in fact, was usually effectively public. He had imperious mannerisms, which were condoned because of his charm and good looks. He carried these good looks with such dignity that he was known, with affectionate mockery, as Handsome George. His Shakespearian heroes and character parts alternated with the melodrama heroes of *Youth, In the Ranks, The Lights o' London*, and so on; and less usual parts such as Paolo Macari in *Called Back*.

In his last production of *Othello*, at the Criterion Theatre, Sydney, in 1899, he surpassed his former work, both as actor and producer. From then on he rarely came out of retire-ment, and then usually in Benefit performances. In 1902 he went to London to appear in a Benefit for his brother. In

1907 Bland Holt persuaded him to appear as Jason in *The Bondman*. His last appearance was at a Benefit for George Sutton Titheradge, in December 1910.

He died, after an operation in Sydney, on December 16, 1912.

James Cassius Williamson and Maggie Moore also came to Australia in the 1870s. Williamson's career is the subject of a later chapter in this book; Maggie Moore's can be outlined in this chapter, which attempts to group together those more prominent players who first set foot in Australia during the sixties and seventies of the nineteenth century.

Maggie Moore was born in San Francisco on July 10, 1851. When she arrived in Melbourne in 1874 she was already famous as Lizzie Stofel in *Struck Oil!* After an eighty-night run in Melbourne, and an Australian tour, she and Williamson went on a triumphal world tour. *Struck Oil!* played the Adelphi Theatre, London, for one hundred nights in 1876, as also did Dion Boucicault's play *Arrah-na-Pogue*, in which Maggie Moore was Arrah, and Williamson played Shaun.

When they returned to Australia in 1879 Maggie Moore continued to endear herself to the public, which had fallen in love with her in *Struck Oil!* Her endearing qualities were her warmth, ebullience, and naturalness; and the ability to glide from moments of irresistible humour to moments of pathos. So deep was the affection she aroused in the general public that she was awarded the greatest honour Australians can award its goddesses. A racehorse was named after her.

Maggie Moore was a delightful comedienne, a superb step-dancer, a mimic without malice, and had the light touch and sweet voice so suitable to comic opera. Her earlier successes were, like Nellie Stewart's, in comic opera: as Josephine and Buttercup in *H.M.S. Pinafore*; Mabel and Ruth in *The Pirates of Penzance*; Lady Jane in *Patience*; and Bettina in *La Mascotte*.

During the 1890s it was only her vivacity that kept alive inferior productions such as *The Shadows of a Great City*, in which she was Biddy Roonan; and *Meg the Castaway*, in which she was Meg. After Williamson gave up acting for organization in 1890, his part of Jan (later John) Stofel was played by John F. Forde. Maggie Moore, who was perennially Lizzie Stofel, played the part, in 1918, in the Pugliese Enterprises film with Harry Roberts. Boyd Irwin was producer. In 1918 she also played Annie, the negress, in *The Easiest Way*; and Mrs Potash in *Business Before Pleasure*; both with Tal Ordell, the versatile comedian from Gippsland, Victoria.

She was divorced from J. C. Williamson in 1899. She toured England and America from 1903 to 1908, when she returned to Australia, and played innumerable parts. Occasionally there were *Struck Oil!* revivals, in which Jan Stofel was played by H. R. Roberts, Maggie Moore's second husband.

As she passed the age of sixty, she played fewer parts, but ever successfully, and invariably with her inimitable touch. She was always at the back of the public consciousness. Off-stage she was charitable, tender-hearted, and as warmly humorous as on the stage.

Of her performance as Mrs Karl Pfeiffer in *Friendly Enemies*, in 1918, it was written: "She imbued the character with a dignity and gentle pathos which crowned her long career with fresh laurels." Her career had been long. In 1924 she celebrated the fiftieth anniversary of her arrival in Australia.

In 1925, at the age of seventy-four, she retired from the stage to live with her sister in America, where she died in 1926 after being struck down by a San Francisco cable tram.

Others who stepped from the wings on to the lamp-lit and gas-lit stages in the sixties and seventies included Joseph Jefferson, the American (*Rip Van Winkle*); James Stark

(*Richelieu*); Coppin in a "round of his popular characters" and *Coppin in California* (he had just returned from America); Madame Celeste (*The Woman in Red*); George Darrell, an actor-manager who wrote a number of melo-dramas; Charles Mathews, the ageing English comedian; Shiel Barry, the Sydney actor; Hattie Shepparde, the Launceston actress; and Mrs Scott Siddons, descendant of Sarah Siddons, with her Shakespearian Company.

The year 1875 was a most exhilarating one for colonial audiences. The revered Italian tragedienne Madame Ristori arrived. Born in 1821, she had been Italy's leading actress since she was fifteen, and was one of the female deities of the European theatrical pantheon. Adelaide Ristori, Marchesa Capranica del Grillo, appeared at the Victoria Theatre, Sydney, on July 16, in the first play of a season of tragedies she was to present: *Mary Stuart, Marie Antoinette, Medea, Phèdre Lucrezia Borgia, Pia de Tolomei*, and *Judith*. She played her anguished heroines in Italian, the language the members of her adroit company also used. "If", raved the drama critic of the *Australasian Sketcher* on October 2, 1875, "all actors and actresses were as great as she is, the world would soon be regenerated. Poetry would assert itself, and become part of our life." This acclamation was no less fervent than that of a number of great men: Lamartine, Dumas, De Vigny, Cavour, and Janin. Paderewski had been tremendously impressed by her "air of grandeur".

Her characterizations, which were overwhelming, had the haunting, passionate, and poetic quality that marks her off as an actress of genius. On her first triumphant night in Sydney, a horde of citizens preceded, surrounded, and followed her carriage, which was drawn by exalted theatre-goers in a torch-light procession back to the Exchange Hotel in Macquarie Place.

At the close of the season, the fifty-four-year-old actress, one of the greatest ever to visit Australia, gave a further forty-one performances during a tour of Melbourne, Ballarat, Bendigo, and Geelong.

In the same year, and during the same months, Madame Janauschek, a German actress, was either reckless or ill-timedly unfortunate enough also to present a repertoire of doomed women . . . Mary Stuart, Deborah, Lady Dedlock, and Leah (*Leah the Forsaken*). Madame Janauschek was a tragedienne of quality but, however competent and striking a performer she was, paled to nothing beside Ristori. Her robust build and her Teutonic noises seemed lumpish and unseemly when displayed in the same colonial city, and during the same months, as the Italian's queenly appearance, intensity, perfect control at moments of scarifying emotion, and "noble voice".

In 1876 Bland Holt's Australian career began, in the burlesque *Ixion*, at the Victoria Theatre, Sydney.

Joseph Bland Holt, born in Norwich, England, on March 24, 1853, first came to Australia at the age of four with his father, Clarence Holt, a mediocre tragedian, who was joint lessee of the Theatre Royal, Melbourne.

Bland Holt made his stage début when six. He was educated at the Church of England Grammar School, Brighton, during his father's Australian seasons. During New Zealand tours he went to the Otago Boys' High School, where Fergus Hume, author of the mystery best-seller *The Mystery of a Hansom Cab*, was also educated.

When the Holts returned to England, the young Bland Holt became a professional actor, at fourteen. For the next nine years he toured England, America, and New Zealand, playing a full range of parts, and getting his most stringent and valuable experience with the tragedian Charles Dillon. This training was to make Holt a skilled and versatile actor, and an indefatigable producer. In spite of the genre in which he was to thrill and astonish a generation of playgoers—melodrama—he was aware of subtleties of style, and insisted that his cast employ them. The flavour of the Holt manner lingered on for years in the work of many of the actors and actresses, later notable, who worked with him.

Bland Holt's first production in Australia was Merritt's *New Babylon*, at the Victoria Theatre, Sydney, in 1877. The leading lady was Myra Kemble, a beautiful woman with an exquisite voice, magnificent red hair, and, on or off the stage, an exciting presence. *New Babylon* was the beginning of Holt's actor-manager career, which was to last for thirty years.

He became Australia's Monarch of Melodrama. His first repertoire of "twenty-four new and original dramas" was a repertoire of blood-and-thunder *à la* Drury Lane, of innocent maidens in sunbonnets, honest-to-God yokels, evil earls, and gentlemanly heroes, of Virtue inevitably triumphant over routed Wickedness. Not only did he woo the less intelligent public with these easily digested meals; he lavishly embellished his fare. In a hunting scene, for example, there appeared horses, hounds, and a stag. Another play included a horse race. No effect seemed beyond him: a balloon ascent in *The Great Ruby*; a bridge of human beings from one cliff-top to another in *The Span of Life*; a bicycle race in *Riding to Win*; the railway station at Brighton (England), and Dartmoor itself in *With Flying Colours*. He was the first producer to introduce a motor-car on the stage; and once included authentic circus acts in a circus play. Holt had himself, during his training, once worked as a circus clown, and was a fine comedian.

From the point of view of the audience, Bland Holt's legacy to the art of theatre was titillating rather than elevating. Much more valuable were the high standards he set in stagecraft, and the brand of finely shaded acting he required from his cast even within the frame of his shockers and tear-jerkers. Bland Holt's companies moved between his base theatres, the Lyceum Theatre, in Sydney, and the Theatre Royal, Melbourne, and toured widely.

He was hard-working; and personally supervised to the last detail the settings and machinery of his wonderfully mounted productions. Flaccid or old-fashioned play-scripts he altered ruthlessly to make them dramatically tenser and more up to date. His kindliness and generosity gained the respect and affection of stage people. Being a prudent and successful manager, he was able to retire in 1909, at the age of fifty-six. From then on, until he died in 1942, he lived between his house in Kew, and his seaside house at Sorrento which was a sort of theatrical *salon*.

Among the scores of players who benefited from contact with Bland Holt were John Cosgrove, Myra Kemble, Dorothy Brunton, Madge Titheradge, Vera Pearce, and Marie Löhr, who all, at some time or another, appeared in his numerous melodramas, such as *The White Heather, Hearts are Trumps, In London Town, In Sight of St Paul's*, and *A Million of Money*.

On August 31, 1901, a Bland Holt production of *Riding to Win*, a melodrama by Frank Herbert and Walter Howard, opened at the Theatre Royal, Melbourne. Its advertised highlight was the bicycle race on the stage in which Australia's most famous cyclists took part. Today it is fascinating to examine the working-script, and to find, for example, that it is not the one-set play brow-beaten audiences of these times must bear with.

RIDING TO WIN

SYNOPSIS OF SCENERY

ACT ONE

The Garden of Rivers's House, Seaview, Queenscliff. (Noontide)

57

Act Two

SCENE i.   Banks of the Yarra, Studley Park. (Day Time)
SCENE ii.   Alexandra Avenue, Melbourne. (Day Time)
SCENE iii.   Bedroom and Corridor in Rivers's City Residence. (Night Time)

Act Three

SCENE i.   Phillip's House in the City. (Night Time)
SCENE ii.   Botanical Gardens, Melbourne. (Evening)
SCENE iii.   Frank's House in Richmond—Door Apartments.

Act Four

SCENE i.   Cyclists' Dressing Room, Exhibition Grounds.
SCENE ii.   Bicycling Track, Exhibition Grounds.
SCENE iii.   Outside Exhibition Grounds, Nicholson Street.
SCENE iv.   Interior of Redburn's Boathouse.

(All scenes in Act Four—Night Time)

These eleven scenes, one of which contained a hidden tank of water on which a boat was rowed, were rich with detail, and alive with supernumeraries (extras) whom Holt saw were dressed in the recognizable costumes Melbournites wore in 1900 to fit the activities they took part in.

SUPERNUMERARY PARTICULARS

Act One: 12 Girls in Tennis Costume.
11 Men in Tennis Costume.
2 Men on Bicycles.
1 Servant (Girl).

Act Two:

SCENE i.   3 Girls in Light Dresses.
1 Man in Boat (Boating Costume).
1 Man in Boating Costume.
Doubles for Evers and Nell Redburn.

58

SCENE ii.	3	Girls in Rough's Dress.
	2	Girls in Good Walking Dresses.
	1	Man in a Frock Suit.
	2	Men on Bicycles.
SCENE iii.	1	Railway Porter.
Act Three:		
SCENE i.	8	Men in Evening Dress.
	1	Servant (Man).
SCENE ii.	2	Girls in Good Walking Dresses.
	1	Man in a Frock Suit.
Act Four:	5	Trainers.
	1	Inspector (Speaking).
	2	Policemen.
	2	Supers in Bicycling Costume.
		Double Dresses for 2 Cyclists.
		All Famous Cyclists wear Own Colours.
		All Girls wear Varied Dresses.
	10	Men at 1/- a Night.

There is a compulsion to scour the script to discover why, for example, one Railway Porter appears at Night Time in the Bedroom and Corridor of Rivers's City Residence, or why doubles are used for Evers and Nell Redburn. A newspaper review shows why doubles were needed:

"The real climax of Act Two, Scene One, occurs where Phillip Evers throws the blind girl's sister Nellie into the Yarra in order to murder the girl, who loves him, and is in his way. At this point immense enthusiasm was caused by a large black and white dog which jumped in the water, and dragged the drowning woman to the bank. Afterwards the boatman throws in the villain with another fine splash— straw hat, patent leather boots, two-and-a-quarter inch collar and all. The dog, expressing his canine satisfaction thereat in joyous barks, became quite the lion of the evening."

The following extract from the script is, although crude in texture, a clear indication that the hard-doer Digger type was already, fifteen years before Gallipoli, a well-developed one. Sam Flutter, played by Holt himself, is talking to Frank, the hero who, having fallen on evil days, is employed as a boatman.

> FRANK: Are you going up to Mr Rivers's house now, Flutter?
> FLUTTER: Yass, that's about the dart! I'm er-goin' ter tap him for me old billet.
> FRANK: Didn't the government promise to give you soldiers' billets?
> FLUTTER: Der yer tike me fer er bloomin' mug? When them parliament coves promises er thing fer sure, it's good enough fer me ter know I don't get it. How's Miss Doris, sir?
> FRANK: I haven't spoken to her since the day Mr Rivers parted us.
> FLUTTER: Straight dinkum, sir, how did yer come ter tike on this sort er yacker?
> FRANK: The story of my disgrace got about. Wherever I went it cropped up against me. Then I fell ill, and put in a few bad months at the hospital and—well, Sam, I can stand it. But about yourself—they kept you busy in Africa?
> FLUTTER: Oh, I did me little bit. One day on ther veldt on sentry-go I spots three bloomin' Boers, so I ups with me rifle, and drops one of ther cows, and ther other twelve makes er sprint fer me. I lays out five more, but ther thirty coves keeps on er-runnin' towards me. "Strike me fat!" I says as I gives 'em ther whole magazine. Then ther sixty of 'em fell atop o' me, an' though I ventilated er dozen with me bayon*ette*, I thinks ter meself, er hundred bloomin' Boers are er bit too much fer er cove, and I holds up ther white rag. "Shoot him like er dorg!" shouts the two hundred blanky Boers as they stand round er-holdin' o' me. "No," says ther Captain, "spare his days, me men, fer he's only done his duty like er brave Australian soldier boy."
> FRANK: You must have found that sort of thing rather sultry.
> FLUTTER: Oh, that was nuffin'! We's had ther likes o' that every day afore breakfast. When I was captured they sneaked me uniform, they sneaked me hat an' boots, an' left me nuffin' ter wear back ter camp except er quid o' terbacker, an' er old kerosene tin.

A little later Flutter's Gawd-he's-a-dag Australianism is even more recognizable.

FLUTTER: Tombstone biscuits fer breakfast, sole leather fer dinner, an' ther water ther officers' eggs was boiled in was ther soup fer tea. One dark night as ther Boers was all round us firing like Billy-o, ther shells goin' bang-bang-bang, and ther bullets ping-ping-ping like er lot o' hailstones, er parson cove starts his chin music. Says he, "Oh, me dear sinful brothers, what is it yer thinkin' on now in this most awful moment?" "Old son," I says, "me thoughts is in er hash-foundry in George Street, Sydney, where all meals is sixpence, with three cups o' tea and er round o' toast thrown in."

Bland Holt's minute attention to detail is shown also in the neatly recorded curtain times.

CURTAIN TIME SHEET . . . Theatre Royal, Melbourne, Aug. 31, 1901

	UP	DOWN
Act One	8.2	8.46
Act Two	8.57	9.48
Act Three	9.55	10.32
Act Four	10.40	11.1

CURTAIN TIME SHEET . . . Lyceum Theatre, Sydney, Sept. 6, 1902

	UP	DOWN
Act One	8.2	8.45
Act Two	8.57	9.42
Act Three	9.50	10.22
Act Four	10.30	10.52

It is "sophisticated" to denigrate melodrama or, rather, the uninformed idea of what melodrama is: twee Drama Societies egged on by homosexuals are given to send-ups imagined to be satirical. The foregoing extracts from work-sheets of a run-of-the-mill melodrama indicate the theatrical validity of the genus. The eleven sets, of which some exquisite models still exist, were the work of craftsmen, and reproduced places familiar to audiences who were, therefore, immediately and doubly involved in the play. Bland Holt always gave customers more than their money's worth. *Riding to Win* ranged socially from Queenscliff to Richmond, from Alexandra Avenue roughs to toffs in evening dress; it had an attempted drowning, an engaging dog, a popular song, comely girls, a feverish bicycle race by topnotchers, a blind girl, a wronged hero, wickedness brought low, and patient goodness rewarded by that most popular of arrangements, marriage. Nor did it bypass the topical—a Boer War soldier was the latest invention. Sam Flutter was hilariously and unbitterly irreverent of institutions in a self-identifying Australian way. How much more appeased Holt's audiences must have been with this rich soup, than today's audiences fed on a thin and acrid gruel.

It was during the Bland Holt era that Australasian-born players began to shine forth among those necessarily imported. Although J. C. Williamson's flat statement: "Australians will not have Australians!" was largely true, and is still largely true of the mob's attitude to those eminent in the civilized arts, there were enough players appreciated in their native land to take the edge off the shrewd little American's remark. While a stream of overseas artists, genius or merely gifted, tragedian or comedian, famous or infamous, were coming and going across the stages of the wildly burgeoning colonies, Australia was training (as it cannot now train) and displaying (as it cannot now locally display) its own breed of first-rate producers and actor-managers, comedians subtle or low, peaches-and-cream leading ladies, matinée idols, character actors and actresses, and those competent all-rounders who, if they never reach the dangerous heights, never sink into the depths of lost-for-ever, but remain as inconspicuously but importantly on the theatrical scene as bread does on a meal table.

Of these many all-rounders, Meta Pelham, who, in 1934, at the age of eighty-four, was the oldest living actress in the British Empire, will serve as the outstanding example, as

62

well as the worthy representative of a worthy theatrical multitude.

Meta Pelham, born in 1850, twenty miles from Dublin, was a niece of Sir George Vanston. She was brought to Australia when she was three, in the same year that the first Australian play of any consequence was printed—Charles Harpur's *The Bushranger*, 1853, an early attempt to trap the Australian *ethos* by pinning down butterfly bushrangers and larrikins. Attempts are still being made in the same branch of lepidopterology. At sixteen she married a Mr Poole. Her stage name was taken from the title of the Bulwer Lytton novel.

Her professional début was made on December 12, 1877, at the Academy of Music, Bourke Street, Melbourne, which was later renamed, in the confusing and surely unnecessary way theatres and cinemas are renamed, the Bijou Theatre. She played Beatrice in *Much Ado About Nothing* with Mrs Scott Siddons's Shakespearian Company. Her career was to last as long as that of Mrs Charles Kean, the enchanting, high-minded, and famous Ellen Tree. During nearly sixty years on the stage, Meta Pelham appeared in every kind of rôle: Shakespeare, Ibsen, Pinero, out-in-the-cold-cold-snow melodramas, "sparkling three-act comedies", farces such as *Charley's Aunt*, backblocks comedy-dramas, and pantomimes such as *Sinbad the Sailor*.

Her value as a reliable supporting actress was recognized by successive actor-managers and producers in search of the best. Consequently, throughout the decades, her name appeared on the handbills of important companies: J. C. Williamson, the George Rignold–Kate Bishop Company, the Brough–Boucicault Company, the Allan Wilkie Shakespearian Company, the Gregan McMahon companies, and the Frank Thornton Company.

Launched in 1877, she was still giving impeccable performances half a century later as, for example, when in

1928 she appeared as Jane O'Hara in *Paddy the Next Best Thing*; as Mrs Coade in Barrie's *Dear Brutus*, at the King's Theatre, Melbourne, produced by Gregan McMahon, with Beatrice Day, Leal Douglas, and Zillah Carter in the cast; and, in the same year, at the Princess Theatre, Melbourne, as the charwoman Midget, in Sutton Vane's *Outward Bound*.

Her training had been in the unsparing school of her times; in touring companies that travelled through blinding midsummer in slow trains that dallied to shunt at every whistle-stop station; by Cobb and Company's crammed coaches; by rough-riding steamers to New Zealand, Tasmania, and Perth. She played Maria in *The School for Scandal*; bedded-and-boarded in shanty pubs of almost Cro-Magnon primitiveness; played Queen Gertrude in *Hamlet*. She acted through the decades in which gold-miners still tossed nuggets on the stage for their favourites: this gesture was once made to her at Sandhurst, where a small bag of gold landed at her feet.

In January 1898 she appeared with Frank Thornton at the Criterion Theatre, Sydney, as Ruth Holt in *Sweet Lavender*. After touring Australia with the Thornton company, she went to London with them. Here, in April 1899, she was a great hit in *The Younger Generation*, and also as the Countess in *Our Miss Hebblewhite*. Returning to Australia, she continued to give scrupulous performances of hundreds of characters, from the Nurse in *Romeo and Juliet* to the Grandmother in *Tilly of Bloomsbury*; from Mrs Malaprop in *The Rivals* to *Old Lady 31*.

Although Meta Pelham could not ever be said to be an electrifying actress, she was always competent, and infinitely adaptable: one of an army of performers whose painstaking craftsmanship provides the solid support and muted background to those more volcanic and flashy stars whose careers burnt down, often, as quickly as they flared up. Let this fine actress, then, stand as representative of others too numerous to be given more than passing reference in this limited work. Her kind was fortunately legion; our space is unfortunately meagre.

She was, incidentally, one of the players of Irish heredity of whom so many have made an impression on the Australian theatre: Gustavus Vaughan Brooke, Nellie Stewart, George Musgrove, Gregan McMahon, Maggie Moore, Arthur Shirley, Dion Boucicault, Francis Nesbitt, Mignon O'Doherty, Thomas Barry Sullivan, and James Cassius Williamson are only some of them.

Meta Pelham was the twenty-year-old Mrs Poole when Marcus Clarke was writing the pantomimes *Goody Two Shoes* and *Little Boy Blue* for the Christmas season of 1870. Mrs Marcus Clarke, whom he had married the year before, 1869, was Marion Dunn, one of the most delightful actresses of the day.

Before Marion Dunn, who had been born in New Zealand, married and retired, she was "The Pet of the Public", and also, it seemed, of the critics. The following extract from a review of her performance as May Edwards, the heroine of Tom Taylor's *Ticket-of-Leave Man*, was written no less fervently than most of her reviews: "We must confess that we feel unequal to do justice to the exquisite manner in which she rendered that diverse and difficult character. Miss Dunn has for the last two months ravished the play-going public by her talent."

She was "petite, piquante and pretty", and began her career as a child-actress during the brief Charles Kean régime in Melbourne, and was as multi-faceted as any actress of the era. With the gaudy but brilliant Walter Montgomery, she played Ophelia, Nerissa, Desdemona, and Lady Anne in *Richard the Third*; and toured New Zealand with his company, which included Hattie Shepparde as leading lady. An advertisement for the Prince of Wales Theatre, Auckland, reveals something of Montgomery's eccentric wit, and his veneration of a sound English title.

E

GRAND LEGITIMATE DRAMATIC SEASON
MACBETH and OTHELLO

This Grand Series of Intellectual Representations will be
under the Special Patronage of His Excellency, Sir George
Bowen, K.C.M.G., Governor of New Zealand, who, with Lady
Bowen, will graciously attend the Theatre.

Complaints of the discomforts of the Circle having
reached the management, paper-hangers will rectify
the one, & plumbers & glaziers the other.

Notwithstanding the immense expense attending this engagement,
there will be no advance in the prices.

Dress Circle, 5s; Stalls, 2s 6d; Pit 1s.

Children in arms, one guinea.

No smoking permitted on any account.

GOD SAVE THE QUEEN AND THE GOVERNOR!

Marion Dunn's retirement from the stage after her
marriage was not a permanent one. She appeared as Marie
Louise in *Louis the Eleventh*, Lady Helen in *The Iron
Chest*, and Mrs Mildmay in *Still Waters Run Deep*. In
October 1883 she appeared as Susy in *The Silver King*, with
George Titheradge, who had been imported by Williamson
and Garner in 1880 to create the part of Wilfred Denver.
Arthur Garner played the gentlemanly villain, Captain
Skinner *alias* The Spider. In 1883, the Williamson-Garner-
Musgrove Triumvirate, precursor of The Firm, had been in
existence a year.

Before her marriage Marion Dunn had appeared also in a
number of musical pieces: *The Child of the Regiment,
Cinderella*, and *Aladdin*, playing side by side with her
friend Julia Mathews.

Julia Mathews was born in England, but came to Australia
as a child. Her history is brief enough, but has something of

the ballad in it. She began acting as a child in Melbourne, and as she grew older was discovered to have a fine singing voice. While this was being trained, and she was acting and singing on the stage, she went on tour to Beechworth. Here, Robert O'Hara Burke, later to die on the disastrous Burke and Wills expedition, was stationed as a trooper. He became infatuated with her, so much so that, when the expedition set off from Royal Park, Melbourne, he could not resist riding back from Essendon in an unsuccessful attempt to see her. His statue now stands opposite the Princess Theatre, Melbourne, where in September 1863 a Farewell Benefit was held for Julia Mathews, whose eyes were set, as Burke's had been, on far horizons. She was the first Australian-trained singer to appear—in Offenbach's *La Grande Duchesse de Gérolstein*—at Covent Garden Opera House. Her career was as ill-fated as that of the explorer who loved her. She died of yellow fever, in America, on May 1, 1876.

May Robson's name meant much to film audiences of the 1930s and 1940s when, as an old but vigorous woman, she played leads and supporting rôles in many talking pictures.

Daughter of Captain Henry Robeson—she dropped the *e* as an actress—she was born in Australia on April 9, 1865, and was educated at schools in Paris, London, and Brussels. Her first stage appearance, in 1884, was at the Brooklyn Theatre, New York, as Tilly in *The Hoop of Gold*. She was an immediate success as an *ingénue*, and thereafter played a series of young heroines at such New York theatres as Madison Square Theatre, the Lyceum, Palmer's, and Miner's Fifth Avenue Theatre.

Her success, particularly as a vivacious comedienne, led to a contract with Charles Frohman, for whom she appeared in a gallimaufry of plays: *The Importance of Being Earnest, A Woman's Reason, Sowing the Wind, The Luck of Roaring Camp, Raspberry Shrub, The Fatal Cord,* and *Are You a Mason?* She also played Audrey in *As You Like It.*

67

Although she toured extensively throughout America, it was not until she was forty-five that she made her début in London, in the leading rôle in *The Rejuvenation of Aunt Mary*, at Terry's Theatre, on August 22, 1910.

It was not until the age of the talking picture that her fame became world-wide, when the skill gained during her long stage career was displayed in her convincing portrayal of a gallery of elderly female characters: slum hags, society dames, worldly grandmothers, little-old-ladies-passing-by, and sharp-tongued and witty eccentrics.

Pattie Browne, another Australian actress born in the 1860s, made her début as a human being in Sydney, on May 10, 1869, and her stage début, as a child-actress, in 1882. Possessed of a charming appearance, and an equally charming voice, she played many small parts for George Musgrove and J. C. Williamson. Ultimately, she was engaged by the Brough-Boucicault Company, appearing in their productions at the Bijou Theatre, Melbourne, and on tour. She became one of the popular postcard actresses. Her more notable parts included those of Honor in *Sophia*, Poly Eccles in *Caste*, Avonia Browne in *Trelawney of "The Wells"*, and Eily O'Connor in *The Shaughraun* of Dion Boucicault *père*.

Her London début was as Lady Thomasin Belturbet in *The Amazons*, at the Court Theatre, London, on March 7, 1893. This part, and her treatment of it, took the public's fancy. Pattie Browne became a London favourite much in demand. She succeeded Ada Reeve as Lady Holyrood in *Floradora*, at the Lyric Theatre, London, in 1899.

In 1900 she returned to Australia and J. C. Williamson, on contract to play the leading rôles—pert and mischievous creatures were Pattie Browne's forte—in *The Little Minister, Sweet Nancy*, and *The Dovecot*.

In 1902 she was back in England again in *The Admirable Crichton*; from then on she continued to play leads in a series of such ephemeral comedies and comedy-dramas as *Madame President, The Girl from Ciro's, The Three of Us, The Price, The Silver Slipper,* and *The Toreador.*

Whereas, among the more theatrically famous Australians born during the 1850s and 1860s, actresses rather than actors predominate, the opposite is true of the 1870s. Indeed, among the actors born in the 1870s, three, at least, were to have a lasting impact on the world of three-sided rooms, trees of cut-out canvas and net, blue moonlight, and paper snow, on the high-pitched and highly strung stage world with its overlapping values and unreal reality. In 1871, Oscar Asche was born at Geelong; in 1872, Albert Edward Bailey was born at Auckland, New Zealand; the last of the trio, born in 1874, at Sydney, was Gregan McMahon. Since their contribution to the theatre goes far beyond mere performances, they will be dealt with at greater length in a later chapter. It is necessary, to complete the present chapter, to note several other players born in the same decade.

By 1888 Violet Varley, an exquisitely beautiful woman, born in 1871, was already attracting notice not only for her beauty, but for her promise as an actress. She died, in 1895, before that promise could be fulfilled.

William Stratford Percy, born in Melbourne on December 23, 1872, must also be briefly recorded for, although his career and fame were largely in the world of musical comedy, comic opera, and pantomime, he nevertheless played enough comedy parts in "straight" plays to warrant mention. His first appearance was in a children's production of *The Pirates of Penzance*, in which he was the Pirate King. In the same comic opera, he made his grown-up début, at the Princess Theatre, Dunedin, New Zealand, on July 23, 1896. His London début was made at the Oxford Theatre, when he was forty-three years old, on November 1, 1915.

Otto Peter Heggie, O. P. Heggie of the Hollywood films,

who was born at Angaston, South Australia, on September 17, 1879, demands more space. As in the case of May Robson, his main reputation with the middle-aged generation was his silver screen one as a cool performer in a variety of carefully delineated character parts.

To an earlier generation, however, it was his stage work that was outstanding. His work was, in fact, so outstanding that in 1914 he was chosen by a tribunal of the leading English stage critics as "one of the six actors to whom the public must look for the future of the English stage". In appearance "handsome and manly", it could be imagined that he would play only those parts that go no further than the happy endings of profiled hero after profiled hero, but his range was always disconcertingly and noticeably wide, even in the days when all actors and actresses, it seems, were able to switch, at a moment's notice, from Sheridan to slush, from light comedy to blackest villainy, from clean-cut hero to quavering octogenarian.

He was educated at Winham College, Adelaide, and the Adelaide Conservatoire of Music, and made his stage début in 1899 at the Theatre Royal, Adelaide, in *Stolen Kisses*. From that performance he did not look back, becoming a member of W. F. Hawtrey's Company of which Gregan McMahon was also a member. Between 1899 and 1905 he appeared in many plays, including *The Three Musketeers, Secret Service, A Message from Mars, Tom, Dick and Harry,* and *The Two Mr Wetherbys*.

On September 5, 1901, he appeared at Coppin's indubitably final stage appearance, a Benefit performance for the Old Colonists' Association and the Dramatic and Musical Association. This was a matinée at the Princess Theatre, Melbourne, composed of three comedies: Brandon Thomas's *A Highland Legacy; Why Smith Left Home*; and Byron's *Not Such a Fool As He Looks*, in which Coppin appeared as Mould the Process Server, with a cast composed of players

from the Princess Theatre, the Theatre Royal, and Her
Majesty's.

In *A Highland Legacy*, the cast was:

GORDON MACDONNEL	Thomas Holding
TAMMY TAMSON	W. F. Hawtrey
MR DOBSON	O. P. Heggie
CAVENDISH HOWLEY	Gregan McMahon
JOE FIXEM	St Clair Bayfield
MRS BUTLER	Hilda Wright
CLARA (Mr Dobson's Daughter)	Winifred Austin

On this occasion, O. P. Heggie, then twenty-two, as Mr
Dobson, played an elderly retired stockbroker. Even so early
in his career, Heggie was displaying the ability with which
he was to play an extraordinary variety of parts—aged stock-
brokers were as little trouble to him as degenerates, tramps,
and prize-fighters, all of them parts he was to play at one time
or another, as well as the socialistic youth in Shaw's *Misalliance*, Tee Pee in *The Chinese Lantern*, Quince in *A Midsummer Night's Dream*, Meravel in *Madame X*, Androcles
in *Androcles and the Lion*, Captain de Foenix in *Trelawney
of "The Wells"*, and Vaska Pepel in *The Lower Depths*.

Heggie's London début was as Pippy in *The Lemonade
Boy* at the Criterion Theatre, on October 13, 1906. In 1907
he was engaged by Ellen Terry to tour America with her in
the important rôle of Alexander Oldsworthy in *Nance
Oldfield*.

Other characterizations which earned him the applause of
audiences, and the praise of hard-bitten critics, were those
of Sir Ralph Bloomfield-Bonnington in *The Doctor's
Dilemma*, Barrato in *Footloose*, Peter Juhasz in *Fashions for
Men*, Oliver Blayds in *The Truth About Blayds*, Old Man
Minick in *Minick* (September 1925), and Sherlock Holmes
in *The Speckled Band*. Sir Arthur Conan Doyle was so impressed by Heggie's performance as Holmes that he wrote

to congratulate the actor on the closest personification of the famous detective its literary creator had ever seen.

After 1927 O. P. Heggie played an increasing number of parts on the films, the arrival of sound adding much to his value and to his popularity as a character actor. He had important parts in *Trelawney of "The Wells", Smilin' Thru, Zoo in Budapest, Anne of Green Gables, The Bride of Frankenstein, Chasing Yesterday,* and *Ginger.* He had just completed a supporting rôle in *Shark Island* when he died of pneumonia in Hollywood on February 7, 1936.

His recreations had been the non-cerebral ones of riding, shooting, cricket, and golf.

All in all, the 1870s were historically among the most interesting, fruitful, and bracing years in the Australian theatre.

Famous people—Madame Ristori, Madame Janauschek, Emily Soldene, Clara Vesey, Mrs Scott Siddons, Charles Mathews—came and went.

Famous people—J. C. Williamson, Maggie Moore, Bland Holt, Alfred Dampier, George Titheradge, George Rignold —came and remained, some for a few years, some for many years, some until the end of their lives.

In the same period there were born a number of Australians who were already, perhaps, earmarked by fate to make their various alterations and additions to the theatrical pattern of the twentieth century. Among these were the three baby boys who, as men, were to be particularly notable, either overseas or in their native land—Asche, Bailey, and McMahon.

There were also on the scene, more or less conspicuously, those Australians or adopted Australians who had established themselves—Eliza Winstanley, Mrs Herman Vezin, Eleanor Carey, Julia Mathews, Hattie Shepparde, Marion Dunn, George Darrell, Mrs Lewis, Shiel Barry—whose real name was Andrew Donohue—Norma Whalley, and others. As well, there were those, like Meta Pelham, who were taking the first steps, making the first appearances, beginning their careers.

Among these was a young woman who was to become Australia's most beloved actress; a woman who asked that, when she died, no mourning be worn; an actress whose memorial in Sydney is a fittingly delightful public garden of roses. To give an outline of the long career of Nellie Stewart it will be necessary to retrace our steps to the 1850s when she was born.

CHAPTER FOUR

NELLIE STEWART, AND THE GOLDEN AGE

NELLIE STEWART was born on November 28, 1858, at 41 Woolloomooloo Street, now Cathedral Street, Woolloomooloo, Sydney.

Her mother, who had been Theodosia Yates, was a great-granddaughter of Richard Yates and Mary Ann Yates, celebrated in the London of David Garrick's day. In 1842 Nellie Stewart's mother, then Mrs Stirling, was brought from Drury Lane by the "talented and indefatigable" Mrs Clarke, in a company with which Mrs Clarke perfervidly hoped to calm and elevate the uncouth audiences of Hobart Town, Van Dieman's Land. Despite the most killingly courageous efforts for three years in the brutish convict settlement, Mrs Clarke had to retire defeated. During this battle, Mrs Stirling was called upon to display every one of her many gifts, in classic tragedy and comedy, in opera, burlesque, farce, and promenade concerts. She sang in the comic opera *John of Paris*; was Amina in *La Sonnambula*; starred in *Middy Ashore*; and played Nell Gwyn—thus foreshadowing her daughter's later fame as the same character—in *Charles the Second; or The Merry Monarch*; and once sang through the whole of *Lucia di Lammermoor* so that the company, which did not have a score, could learn the opera. This amazing woman, who became Mrs Guerin while in Hobart, went to Sydney when

Mrs Clarke's company broke up in 1845. By Guerin, member of a theatre orchestra, she had two daughters, Maggie and Docie, who took the name Stewart when their mother married Richard Stewart. This third husband was an actor in a Coppin company in which Mrs Guerin also played, and later was actor-manager of his own small company, which was enlivened and enriched by the gifts of his wife, his stepdaughters, and at a very early age by his own daughter Nellie.

Nellie Stewart's début was made at Coppin's Haymarket Theatre, Melbourne, as a child in Kotzebue's *The Stranger; or, Misanthropy and Repentance,* an oft-repeated five-act drama of the heavily romantic Teutonic sort then modish. She was five years old. She later remembered the Haymarket Theatre as smelling of gas, cigars, and an unidentifiable and metallic sub-odour rather like a railway station's.

Whatever gifts Nellie Stewart inherited from theatrical ancestors were nurtured by her parents. Richard Stewart taught his daughter to fence; Henry Leopold was her dancing-master; and Lalla Miranda's father, David Miranda, gave her singing lessons. She was more conventionally educated at the Model School, Nicholson Street, Melbourne.

In 1877 Nellie Stewart and her half-sister Docie played leading parts in George Darrell's *Transported for Life.* Darrell was an actor-manager with a talent for writing hearty melodrama. *The Sunny South* was his best and most profitable work, a "Wonderful Anglo-Australian Drama" in "Five Huge Sensations!"—The Diggings Scene; The Bank Smash; The Battle in the Bush; The Bushrangers' Lair; and The Zig-Zag Railway. Its first production, in 1881, had the beautiful Australian Essie Jenyns creating the part of Babs Berkeley. Later in the 1880s it was successfully staged in London.

Nellie Stewart played Ralph Rackstraw in *H.M.S. Pinafore,* in 1878, and a year later sang and danced her way through seven parts in *Rainbow Revels.* This early revue, the work of Garnet Walch, who was secretary of the Melbourne Athenaeum and wrote many pantomimes and light pieces, was specially written to give full scope to the varying talents of the Stewarts. Young Dick Stewart was business manager; Richard Stewart and the three young women, Nellie, Maggie, and Docie, dominated the stage. This potpourri, which entranced Melbourne, was successful enough to finance a tour of India and, after that, of America. It was while Nellie Stewart was in America, in 1880, that Coppin cabled offering her the part of Principal Boy in that year's Christmas pantomime, *Sinbad the Sailor,* which ran for fourteen weeks.

Nineteen years later, in 1899, at the age of forty-one, Nellie Stewart could still be a ravishing Principal Boy, when, for £50 a week she played in the Drury Lane Christmas pantomime *The Forty Thieves* . . . she always appeared miraculously young on the stage. In 1909, at fifty-one, she played the youthful *Sweet Kitty Bellairs*; in 1910 she was a perfectly convincing and girlish maiden, the Princess Mary, in *When Knighthood was in Flower.*

Although by 1880, when Coppin cabled her, she had already been on the stage for seventeen years, and was well known to the Melbourne public, it was Coppin who made her a star. The part of Principal Boy in lush productions with gorgeous towering sets, transformation scenes, rippling tunes, and "magical" lighting effects, was usually a pretty sure path to public popularity. In Nellie Stewart's case, it was a decidedly sure one. At twenty-two she was alluring in the ostrich plumes and jewel-encrusted tights of a Principal Boy; her dimple, her grace of movement, her vitality, and her delightful voice enchanted men and women alike.

Certain sign of fame for that period, her photograph was to be seen in every barber's shop and postcard album. In the late nineteenth and early twentieth century, there was a craze for sending and collecting postcards. The more expensive of these were moulded or padded to reproduce in voluptuous relief the corseted curves of the actresses who were among the favourite subjects. The postcards were tinted, spangled, embossed, stuck with minute bows and rosettes of silk, and were sometimes even scented. Nellie Stewart became one of the postcard favourites with other beauties of the time: Marie Studholme, Zena and Phyllis Dare, Billie Burke, Ada Reeve, Tittell Brune, Gabrielle Ray, Blanche Stammers, Florence Trevelyan, Grace Palotta, Lily Langtry, and Mrs Brown-Potter.

In 1881 she played her most important part up to that date as Griolet in Australia's first Musical Extravaganza, *La Fille du Tambour-Major*, at the Opera House, Melbourne. The producer was George Musgrove, soon to be a power in Australian theatre and intimately connected with Nellie Stewart's professional and personal life—he was to be her "great and good man".

Nellie Stewart's earlier fame came largely through her dynamic stage presence and her singing voice which, though not of La Scala quality, was nevertheless a true one of much sweetness. In thirteen years she sang leading rôles in thirty-five different comic operas. Her physical radiance and exuberant health were bywords. Despite almost continual appearances, overseas as well as in her native country, this exuberance remained undiminished; her stamina was so cast-iron that understudies never had the chance to replace her. In December 1883 there occurred a telling instance of her mettle. Immediately after a solid season as Patience, in *Patience*, she was playing Principal Boy in the pantomime *Jack and the Beanstalk*, when she fell heavily from halfway up the beanstalk. Offstage, her arm was discovered to be broken. It was put in splints and, doubtless to the chagrin and disappointment of her understudy, Nellie Stewart returned to her task of enchantment, and to fulfilling the convention of "the show must go on". It is interesting to speculate whether the cups of cold beef tea she drank in her dressing-room during intervals, and even between exit and

77

entrance, had much to do with her evergreen and unscathable vigour.

Nellie Stewart was never an actress in the tradition of Ristori, Rachel, or Bernhardt; she lacked their grandeur or fury or inspired intensity. She was trained, however, to the finest point in the lore of the stage, and used every artifice to make her natural abilities appear at the best advantage. Adhering to her rule—"Always be picturesque, even in tatters"—she was ever lovely to look at. She worked hard and honestly to burnish and perfect. In earlier parts, her immense vitality had led her into mannerisms. These she learnt to prune until, particularly in scenes of tender emotion and delicate gaiety, her work was a model. Her diction was faultless, her sense of movement and timing never in error, her femininity expressed without cloying sweetness.

Well educated, considerate, and kindly, she was, as a woman, free of the venoms that wormholed the natures of many of her sex and profession. She had a sense of humour, and her opinions were of a firm, uncomplicated sort. She found Americans spoiled and feminine in quality—an astute assessment at a time when less perceptive minds found them merely brash and vulgar; she deplored the over-use of electric lighting on the stage as being destructive of illusion; she was repulsed by the gamblers of Monte Carlo, and the non-human plane on which they existed.

On January 26, 1884, she married Richard Goldsbrough Row. "A girl's mad act" she later called it. Her direct and simple approach to all her problems was the approach she took when she discovered she had made an error in judgment. She parted unflinchingly from Row. Several years later she began her thirty years' relationship with George Musgrove. In 1882, with the ubiquitous Coppin as sleeping partner, Musgrove, J. C. Williamson, and Arthur Garner had formed a Triumvirate, a partnership ultimately to become monopolist in theatre management. It started with the ownership of the Princess Theatre and the Theatre Royal in Melbourne, the Theatre Royal in Sydney, and the right to use the Theatre Royal in Adelaide.

In 1885 Nellie Stewart, in the Triumvirate's *Cinderella*, played the heroine in bare feet, the first time this almost improper display had been made on the Australian stage, perhaps on any stage. It was not until ten years later that the production of Du Maurier's *Trilby* in London gave rise to the slang use of "trilbies" for feet, an implication of the shock of a barefooted heroine.

Throughout her sixty-seven public years, Nellie Stewart appeared from time to time on the London stage—for example, as *Blue-eyed Susan* in 1892. She did not set the Thames on fire, even in *The Forty Thieves* in 1899. For one thing, by then her singing voice was marred. Although she had toured with a comic opera company through Australia and New Zealand (1893-1895), it is pretty certain that the major damage had been done in March 1888, when she performed the foolhardy feat of singing Marguerite in Gounod's *Faust*, at the Princess Theatre, Melbourne, for twenty-four successive nights. The overstraining was aggravated by later appearances in Musgrove's 1889 production of *Paul Jones*, some London appearances, and the comic-opera tour. Even four years' break from stage work, from 1895 until 1899, helped little.

She was able, however, to sing the song "Australia" at the opening of Federal Parliament in 1901 by the Duke and Duchess of York—later King George the Fifth and Queen Mary—in the Exhibition Building, Melbourne.

During her *Faust* season of 1888 the Italian singer Federici, playing Mephistopheles, fell dead one night as he descended to hell through the stage trap-door. This disconcerting incident gave rise to the legend, still not scotched, of Federici's ghost. Older players and stage-hands still swear that the stage of the Princess Theatre is haunted by the Italian's wraith.

If by 1902 Nellie Stewart's singing voice had vanished, other gifts had not. Nor had her courage. She always confronted adversity realistically. At her darkest period, after the Great War, she accepted backstage work, "helping in production" with such shows as *Chu Chin Chow* and *The Lilac Domino* for Hugh D. McIntosh, and doing behind-the-scenes jobs for J. C. Williamson's.

In 1902, however, she still had a string to her bow. By 1900, the Triumvirate had been reduced to a one-man monopoly in the person of J. C. Williamson. It was at J.C.W.'s Princess Theatre, Melbourne, on February 15, 1902, that Nellie Stewart opened in Paul Kester's play *Sweet Nell of Old Drury*. The play was not an immediate success, but presently, as Nell Gwyn, she had captivated the public, and at the age of forty-four created the part which will be always associated with her, as other parts have been with other actresses: Sarah Siddons and Lady Macbeth, Sarah Bernhardt and Camille, Mrs Patrick Campbell and Paula Tanqueray, Vivien Leigh and Scarlett O'Hara, Dame Judith Anderson and Medea, Dame Sybil Thorndike and Joan of Arc, Lady Diana Duff Cooper and the Virgin in *The Miracle*.

In her new non-singing career, she was, until the earth-tremors of change unsettled the foundations, and fissured the walls of the whole theatrical structure, the darling of Australian audiences. She appeared in parts selected to portray best her genius for characters of an *insouciante* or femininely emotional type; Peggy in *Pretty Peggy,* Camille, Zaza the *cabotine* of the café concert, and a particularly haunting Trilby.

In 1906 she and George Musgrove were on tour in San Francisco when the earthquake happened. The loss they sustained was a calamity from which they were never fully to recover.

Disaster, of course, made no difference to her popularity. When, in 1909, *Sweet Nell of Old Drury* was revived at the Melbourne Princess, the queues were so long and, in that era of many theatres, so unusual, that the management served afternoon tea and scones to the playgoers who had been in

Marie Löhr in "Hans the Boatman"

Nellie Stewart in "Camille"

George Rignold and Kate Bishop in "Othello"

Mrs Scott Siddons as Rosalind in "As You Like It"

Marie Löhr

line since eleven in the morning. In 1910 she played Maggie in *What Every Woman Knows*, Barrie's play of an essentially uncharming woman. Her treatment was a triumph of experience and charm. Gregan McMahon, who had played Zou-Zou to her Trilby, played James Wylie, the "silly Scottish son", in *What Every Woman Knows*.

In 1911, Raymond Longford, greatest of the early Australian film-producers, an ex-seaman on sailing-ships, and an ex-actor, directed Nellie Stewart and George Musgrove in the film *Sweet Nell of Old Drury*.

By 1916, when George Musgrove died, most of their savings had gone. What the San Francisco earthquake had begun, unsuccessful investments, lavish but non-productive enterprises, and a degeneration in the theatrical body, all helped to finish. Nellie Stewart was in for a lean time. So was Australian theatre. The Great War, the weed-like development of the moving picture industry, and an advancing flabbiness of theatrical muscle, all contributed. Nellie Stewart retreated to the shadowy wings, making rare appearances. Once, for a charity, she played Romeo in the Balcony Scene of *Romeo and Juliet* to the Juliet of her daughter, Nancye Stewart.

She made her final appearances, in July 1930, at the Comedy Theatre, Melbourne. In the same year that Greta Garbo, in her second talking picture, was playing Cavallani in *Romance*, Nellie Stewart was playing the same part at the Comedy. She was seventy-two, but this was not apparent from the auditorium, as she moved with the litheness of a young woman, and, with the merest huskiness tingeing her voice, gave the touch of truth to the eternally trite words of the playwright. A month before her death Nellie Stewart played the saucy orange-girl who became a king's best-loved mistress. Just twelve years short of a century earlier, Nellie Stewart's mother, wearing no more make-up than a little violet powder, had as it were prophetically also played Nell

81

Gwyn, at a Benefit for herself, in Hobart, in *Charles the Second; or, The Merry Monarch.*

Asking that no one wear black to mourn her, Nellie Stewart, most lovable of actresses, and women, died in 1931.

Coppin's flair for springing star material gave impetus to Nellie Stewart's career, as to the careers of others. James Cassius Williamson was one of the others. Opinions as to the value of Williamson's impact on the Australian scene vary. It is hard to gauge whether his embracing hold on theatres was enervating stranglehold, or beneficent. Early in the twentieth century there were still many lusty companies; the scene was alive and lively. The success of one would spur others to outdo the successful one in choice of material, in presentation, and in efforts to "improve public taste" rather than merely to go along with it or, worse, to debase it.

Wars, moving pictures, the Depression, amusement taxes, and, latterly, television, having had their effect, it is more difficult to gauge the proportion of effect in theatrical totalitarianism. It is certainly true in Australia that the theatre lost vigour, integrity, and taste as company after company was sponged up or off.

James Cassius Williamson, born on August 26, 1845, in Mercer, Pennsylvania, was the son of a doctor of Irish descent, and had no theatrical heritage. At sixteen, nevertheless, he made a stage début in Milwaukee; at seventeen he was touring Canada in comedy parts. In 1863 he joined Wallach's Company as general utility man. His early career somewhat resembled Coppin's, for he was, at one time or another, call-boy, stage carpenter, scene painter, stage manager, and actor. He once learnt the part, and played it, of Sir Lucius O'Trigger of *The Rivals* in twenty-four hours.

By 1870 he was first comedian at the Broadway Theatre, New York. In 1871 he went to the Californian Theatre, San Francisco.

Here he met Margaret Virginia Sullivan, a rising young comedienne who step-danced, sang, and mimicked under the name of Maggie Moore. They were married in February 1873. Maggie Moore's parents were Irish immigrants to Australia, who had left Sydney to take part in the Californian gold rush. Daughter Margaret Virginia was born in San Francisco, on July 10, 1851.

Williamson, like Coppin, was not a tall man, and was driven by the need to have that sense of increased inches given by power and money. In the play *Struck Oil!*—the script of which he had bought from an ex-miner—and the volatile, twenty-two-year-old Maggie Moore, he found the means to begin fulfilling his need. With the shrewdness of one who had learnt by hard experience what tickles the cheaper fancies of the public, he interpolated in *Struck Oil!*, already an openly sentimental piece, numerous "warmly human" opportunities for Maggie Moore to do what she did so well: sing in dialect, dance, and mimic famous actresses. *Struck Oil!* ran for successful months in Salt Lake City.

Far off in Australia, Coppin heard. Coppin moved, and invited. Williamson accepted. The Williamsons sailed for Australia in the S.S. *Mikado*. Maggie Moore gave a vivid description of the arrival at Sandridge (now Port Melbourne) in the pouring rain, and the dreary trip by cab to the White Hart Hotel (now part of the Windsor Hotel) in Spring Street, Melbourne.

Struck Oil! opened an eighty-night season at the Theatre Royal, Melbourne, on August 1, 1874, with J. C. Williamson playing the folksy Pennsylvania Dutch part of Jan Stofel, and Maggie Moore the "mingled-laughter-and-tears" part of the wife, Lizzie Stofel. After the Melbourne season, the company toured Geelong, Ballarat, Sandhurst, and Castlemaine in Victoria, and proceeded thence to the Queen's Theatre, Sydney. Also in the company's repertoire were *Uncle Tom's Cabin*, in which Maggie Moore played Topsy, and J. C. Williamson played Uncle Tom; and *The Old Curiosity Shop*, in which Maggie Moore doubled the parts of Little Nell and the Marchioness.

With a profit of ten thousand pounds, *Struck Oil!* left Australia on a triumphal progress—India, Egypt, London (one hundred nights at the Adelphi Theatre), Holland, Germany, and, after three years, back to New York and San Francisco.

Coppin, however, called again. Ambition called to ambition. The ten thousand pounds that Williamson had taken out of Australia could have impressed him as being indicative of what a young go-getter could do on the fields the older Coppin had already cleared and ploughed. In 1879 the Williamsons returned to Australia with *H.M.S. Pinafore*, in which J.C.W. played Sir Joseph Porter, with Maggie Moore as Buttercup. Their Gilbert and Sullivan season in Sydney and Melbourne included *The Pirates of Penzance*, and *Patience*.

Williamson, like Coppin, was a gifted comedian, with Irish characters, as in Boucicault's *Arrah-na-Pogue* and *The Shaughraun*, his specialty. Other parts in which he excelled, apart from his Jan (or John) Stofel, were Sim in *Wild Oats*, Matthew Vanderkoopen in *La Cigale*, Dick Swiveller in *The Old Curiosity Shop*, and Rip Van Winkle.

In 1882 the Triumvirate was formed. In 1890 Williamson gave up acting for organization which, as his powers increased, necessarily needed all his time and ability. He died in Paris on July 6, 1913.

George Musgrove, another member of the Triumvirate, was born at Surbiton-on-Thames, England, on January 21, 1854. He was brought to Australia when he was twelve, and was educated at Flinders School, Geelong.

Although the blood of the Kembles and Sarah Siddons ran in his veins from his mother's side of the family, and she herself had played in Drury Lane, Musgrove was not a performer. He was an entrepreneur, often a canny one, as when he produced *The Belle of New York* in London, making sixty thousand pounds from a show which was, it was thought, too American for English tastes. His inclinations as producer lay in the direction of musical extragavanza, musical comedy, lilting melody, and pretty-pretty scenery. He was almost the first entrepreneur to present to the stage-door Johnnies and Champagne Charlies, the mashers and swells, with their lofty starched collars, and German-silver-knobbed canes, those groups of stately mutes, larger than life and undulant as houris, called show-girls.

He was, however, willing to tackle anything, sometimes with unprofitable recklessness, sometimes with resounding success. His ventures included Gilbert and Sullivan, with Nellie Stewart as a delicious Yum-Yum in *The Mikado*, in 1886. In 1880-1881 one of his earliest successes, *La Fille du Tambour-Major*, with Nellie Stewart in one of her earliest successes, ran for one hundred and one nights. In 1900-1901 he ran a season of Grand Opera—most parts being played by the Carl Rosa Opera Company—which included *Tannhäuser*, and *The Flying Dutchman*. In 1903 he produced *Twelfth Night, As You Like It*, and *A Midsummer Night's Dream*. From the 1880s his career was allied with Nellie Stewart's, even though Musgrove was married and a father. This brusque but kind-hearted man, who had a great love of the theatre, died on his sixty-second birthday in 1916 after having, like others of his era, made and lost fortunes.

Arthur Garner, the other member of the Triumvirate, had come to Melbourne from England in 1873. He and his wife were light-weight players, his forte being comedy, and his ambitions lying in entrepreneurship. In 1880 he was with the London Comedy Company, which toured perpetually and widely, and had an interest in the Bijou Theatre, Adelaide. When J. C. Williamson, needing accomplices in the first machinations for power, lured Garner away from this small-time actor-managership, their strongest rival in the more glittering and saccharine aspects of entertainment was George Musgrove, whose *La Fille du Tambour-Major* was playing to crammed houses. They talked him into joining.

The last to join, Musgrove was first to break away from the Triumvirate, in 1890. In 1893 Williamson bought Garner out—or off. Coppin, Williamson's earlier Frankenstein, had retired from his behind-the-fan complicity several years before, during one of his own recurring financial eclipses. By 1900 Williamson was in unalloyed control. He formed a new theatrical company. The Firm, as it was to become known, began its reign. In its first decade or so, much that was encouraging was done—the fostering of native talent, the importation of great performers, the production of works of value. What was done later, and is being done today—with monopoly foolproof, rivals bulldozed out of existence, or absorbed and brainwashed—is a topic for analysis beyond the précis of events and trends, and the unshaded sketches of personages, which are all this book pretends to offer. Suffice it to say that J. C. Williamson's dictatorship began at a time when the theatre was lusty and only just coming out of the period in which there was some justification for those who regarded playhouses as "Synagogues of Sin".

As late as the 1870s the epithets of the morally outraged were still loud in the land. Certain aspects of the theatre were "a disgraceful, flagrant, heinous scandal", "an infamy hardly equalled in any civilized city in the world", and "an outrageous insult to our wives and daughters".

Carpets, plush, chandeliers, and elaborately chased spittoons might abound. Circumspectly swaddled goddesses of Graeco-late-Victorian contours, all in gilded plaster, might sprawl in a tangle of lyres and bare-bottomed *amoretti* along the tops of proscenia. Intellectuals might be offered Shakespeare, Sheridan, and the divine Sarah and her *voix d'or* in Sardou. Christmas pantomimes might find the playhouses stacked from pit to gods with family parties dressed

86

to kill, with their gloves, their fans, their mother-of-pearl opera glasses. There might be all the intentions in the world to be artistically vigorous, ornamentally frivolous, hilariously farcical—even delicately salacious—but the theatre management did not always stop there. The playhouse had become fashionable, more respectable, rather more sophisticated, and very much more comfortable, but aspects of it were still— it was fair to admit—arraignable.

The vestibule of the Theatre Royal, Melbourne, for example, was known as The Paddock. There should be no need to translate this into a clearer and coarser term. Not only were the vestibules flourishing bars, they were promenades for the ladies of the town, and hangouts for those elements of the population who, permanently or temporarily, occupied no niche in respectability: card-sharps, pickpockets, junior officers of merchant vessels on the ran-tan, new chum immigrants who had sold their luggage, betting men, stock-riders in town for sin, larrikins in slouch hats and paget coats, with crushed glass sprinkled on the shoulders, begging street Arabs from the Ragged School in O'Brien Lane, off Little Bourke Street.

Each theatre was hemmed in by grog-houses (in 1879 there were more than 800 in Sydney), and seedy establishments selling saveloys, oysters, fish and chips, mutton pies, obscene "notions and novelties", cheroots, postcards, shag, oranges, mussels, shrimps, and walking-sticks. Above or behind many of these near-by places were the rooms in which the Messalinas of the vestibules sold their services to their acquired acquaintances.

Perhaps, in the final count, these hanger-on activities should be regarded as no more than a careless overflow from the brimming theatrical vat, or as a cheaper form of escape, of which going to the theatre was merely another form. Anyway, by 1876, when it became a serious offence to serve alcohol in theatres, the more obvious "evils", and the more blatant "frail sisters", went elsewhere.

Other indications of the potency so apparent in the cities and larger provincial towns, with their permanent and often palatially appointed theatres, were to be seen in the range and number of the touring companies. It was not only The Firm, and the hard-working actor-managers, and the hard-bitten entrepreneurs, who pushed their companies of famous imports and popular locals out beyond the provinces to the sun-bitten remotenesses where there were more blowflies and bull-ants than people.

During the palmy years, an uncountable and unrecorded number of itinerant troupes brought entertainment to the most end-of-the-road and one-horse towns: *Othello* and bell-ringing; *Back from the Tomb* and *The Pirates of Penzance*; nigger minstrels and *Struck Oil!*

These enrichments to the lives of shearers, timber-cutters, cockatoo farmers, and others suffering the ennui of isolation, appeared FOR ONE NIGHT ONLY in the unlined hall of stringy bark and corrugated iron; in the patched marquee set up by the saleyards; in the Rechabite Hall or the Mechanics' Institute; in shearing-sheds; or the dining-room of the country pub. They appeared. They left. Teddy MacLean's Troubadours. The Cosgrove Comedy Company. The Quintrell Family. The Steele-Payne Family. There were dozens of them. John Lemmone's Company set up its worn scenery in three hundred and fifty towns in New South Wales alone.

They came. They went. Many left nothing but the faintest spoor. A poster peeling from a tree-trunk. An advertisement in the theatrical magazine, *Lorgnette*, with despair to be read between the lines. A two-line cut-throat notice in the stage-reviewer's column of the *Weekly Times*.

Many of these barnstormers, with their wrecks of panto-mimes in third-hand costumes, and their casts of gin-tippling derelicts in *Uncle Tom's Cabin*, deserve the silence that conceals them. Others strode and gesticulated and ranted on makeshift stages, in lonely settlements where train or coach came one day a week, and they are still remembered

88

by elderly people as dramatic geniuses far outshining the shadowy celebrities of cinema or television screen. Immortality enough! Some of these robust strolling players were case-hardened, outrageous, or eccentric enough to die wealthy. Of them all, Dan Barry was surely the most eccentric.

He was christened John Ringrose Adams, son of a Tasmanian lawyer. His eccentricity was early displayed when, as a young reporter in Melbourne, he was responsible for a vulgar hoax. He published the news of a reputed cave-in of all Ballarat, with gruesome fake detail. A repetition of this kind of hoax, in Adelaide and in Hobart, made John Ringrose Adams a name not worth having. Dan Barry, actor-manager, came into existence—"the worst actor and best showman in Australia", said J. C. Williamson whose play-scripts Barry plagiarized, for he stole plays which, by an alteration of title, and slight adjustments, he claimed as his own property. His playbills announced that he had commissioned such people as Gladstone, Parnell, and the Archbishop of Canterbury to write these plays for him. His eccentricities were many. He never removed his hat, outdoors, indoors, or for women. He was accompanied everywhere, even to bed, by his bulldog, Paddy.

The Alexandra Theatre, Melbourne, was the scene of his city productions—anything from Shakespeare and four-act dramas to minstrel shows and clog dances.

His advertising was successful from its very impertinence. Arriving at Ararat the night before his production of *East Lynne*, he went to reconnoitre the hall. Here he found a temperance meeting in progress. Assuming the character of a perfervid teetotaller, he harangued the gathering evangelistically, recommended *East Lynne* as an anti-drink play, and sold seats on the spot. Barry never missed an opportunity.

When murderer Frederick Bailey Deeming was hanged for repeated wife-slaughter, Barry was off the mark with *Deeming; or, The Rainhill Horrors and the Cemented*

Hearth. In this piece of inferior Grand Guignol, his familiar, Paddy the bulldog, was to enact a dog supposed to sniff out one of the annihilated Mrs Deemings bedded down under a hearthstone. Paddy was as indifferent an actor as his master. Despite a chunk of meat under the stage hearth of the Alexandra Theatre, Paddy refused to be tempted into sniffing, and squatted grinning at the audience.

Barry's crazy energy, and razzle-dazzle careering in and out of backblocks, general-store settlements all over Australia must have been killing for his badly paid troupe. One tour alone, up the Murray and Darling Rivers from Echuca to Walgett, was 1,130 miles long. Buck-and-wing dances, *Hamlet,* tambourine-playing, farces, bushranging melodramas —all were grist to the mill of this egocentric oddity, himself a farcical bushranger. The mill, however, ground out sovereigns. In 1908 Barry died a wealthy man.

It is pleasant to record that his eccentricity, with more than a touch of shrewd madness in it, went so far as to include giving a sovereign to a beggar while the donor, accompanied by his hat and Paddy, was chewing a penny saveloy bought at a street stall.

Just as the barnstormers came and went, criss-crossing the hinterland, so, on the less mobile and more exalted planes, the really great, the merely famous, and the temporarily conspicuous, also came and went. Throughout the 1880s and 1890s Australia saw, among scores of fleeting visitors, Louise Pomeroy, Wybert Reeve, W. E. Sheridan, W. H. Vernon, Genevieve Ward, Mrs Chippendale, and Miss de Grey. The fascinating Mrs Brown-Potter, and her handsome lady-killing offsider Kyrle Bellew, appeared. Janet Achurch, a poised and brilliant actress, appeared as Norah in *The Doll's House,* the continent's first experience of Ibsen. John L. Sullivan, the vain, burly, beer-swilling, pugilistic Champion of the World, performed—in full evening dress!—as a blacksmith's striker in *Honest Hands and Willing Hearts,* which was specially written for him. Madame Majeroni, niece of the magnificent Ristori, came in *East Lynne, Jealousy, Fedora,* and *Friendship.*

In 1891 Sarah Bernhardt came, with her magic and her tantrums, her extraordinary wardrobe, her Jewish floridities, her pet kangaroo and her tortoises, to give flame-like and top-speed performances of the smouldering women of Victorien Sardou.

In 1885 the Triumvirate imported Dion Boucicault in his own comedies. J. C. Williamson had always been a Boucicault fan.

Dion Boucicault was born in Dublin in 1822 and, at sixty-three, was the most urbane of men—a witty and charming *bon viveur.* In Australia he played a season of *The Shaughraun, The Colleen Bawn,* and *Arrah-na-Pogue.* He had written three hundred plays, his first, *London Assurance,* being produced when he was twenty-one. At the end of the season he left for America, but his daughter Nina, Dion *fils,* and another member of the company, George Sutton Titheradge, remained in Australia. Nina Boucicault became famous as the first of the famous Peter Pans, as her father became famous as the first producer of *Peter Pan.*

Titheradge, Nina and Dion Boucicault, joined with Robert Brough and Mrs Brough (Florence Trevelyan) to form the Brough-Boucicault Company. The Broughs, like the Boucicaults, were members of a clever family with a solid theatrical ancestry of performers and playwrights. The Brough-Boucicault Company was therefore a highly accomplished team, polished, and painstaking. It took over the Bijou Theatre, Melbourne, and the Criterion Theatre, Sydney, presenting for years its technically flawless productions, notable among which were *The School for Scandal, She Stoops to Conquer, Much Ado About Nothing, Fedora, Madame Sans-gêne, Caste, Diplomacy, Lady Windermere's Fan,* and Pinero's *Iris,* and *The Second Mrs Tanqueray.* After 1893, the company supplemented its stay-at-home Melbourne and Sydney productions with regular tours. The Broughs and Boucicaults, and their meticulously schooled casts, had the technique of the costume play well in hand; no one was better than they at making a leg, snapping a fan pointedly shut, nonchalantly flicking nothing from a Valenciennes lace ruffle at precisely the right moment. Their combined poise was formidable. In retrospect, their total contribution to the theatre in Australia appears greater than that of any other company, or, indeed, of any other individual, even assessing it against the background of this Golden Age.

George Rignold was another actor-manager of the Golden Age. With his trilby, fur-lined and fur-collared coat, waxed moustache, and showily dramatic use of the word that Mrs Patrick Campbell, as Eliza Doolittle, had not yet startled the general public with, he was, flowing hair included, the very pattern of his type. He came to Australia in 1878, aged thirty-nine, and was in the Triumvirate's company when they ousted Bland Holt from the Theatre Royal, Sydney—their first take-over—in 1882. Between 1887 and 1900 Rignold was lessee of His Majesty's Theatre, Melbourne. He was a fine tragedian; his Hamlet, Macbeth, and Othello, and his Mark Antony in *Antony and Cleopatra*, being more convincing than his Caliban, Falstaff, and Bottom. As most level-headed actor-managers did, he layered so-so comedies and melodrama between the Shakespearian plays.

Rignold employed a London-born pantryman named William Morris Hughes as a supernumerary, at two shillings nightly, during a run of *Henry the Fifth*. In 1886 this Englishman was, for a while, business manager to J. C. Williamson. He later became a politician. The political arena is dotted with the actor *manqué* and the writer *manqué*.

Sometimes players invade the literary field. William Shakespeare is the outstanding example. Oscar Asche, Elissa Landi, Ruth Chatterton, Eliza Winstanley, and Orson Welles are among those who were more skilled as players than writers, whereas the stage-struck Charles Dickens was a more skilful writer than player. Hugh McCrae, the poet, was among Australian writers and artists who have invaded the stage. In November 1917 he appeared in a two-part programme at the Playhouse Theatre, Sydney, in a playlet *Over the Hills*. The opening play on the same evening was Galsworthy's *The Pigeon*. As Rory Megan in this play, the world-famous cartoonist, David Low, "remorselessly presented every imaginable trait that made the character despicable". In January 1918 Hugh McCrae played Charles the Wrestler in the Bert Bailey–Julius Grant production of *As You Like It*. In 1917 he played in Bert Ives's film *The Life of Adam Lindsay Gordon*.

Rignold amalgamated with Marie Löhr's mother, Kate Bishop, to form the George Rignold–Kate Bishop Company, which introduced Ada Farrar and Julius Knight to Australia.

Julius Knight was the matinée idol of his day, the beloved of the Gallery Girls. This race of queue-formers and gods-haunters was a force to be reckoned with. Wise managers saw that they were pandered to; boxes of chocolates were distributed to them; they were entertained at afternoon tea with the worshipped star on hand to radiate charm, and to sign autograph albums. Fanatically faithful, they were to be kept so, for their hostility could mangle the reputation of a show, siphon off to a lower level receipts at the box office, and throw a shadow across the bright path of a player. Stars have had cause to be grateful for the hysterical loyalty of this powerful and dangerous tribe. Nellie Bramley, an extremely popular "woman's woman" in her heyday, never needed to buy handkerchiefs, stockings, underclothes, gloves, or supper-cloths, for her fans showered these upon her. Max Oldaker, most handsome and suave of matinée idols, also received numerous offerings, and had one persistent fan who sent expensive handkerchiefs, scarves, gloves, slippers, and shoes, each accompanied by a card from "Upstairs Left". Needless to say, Max Oldaker smiled and bowed upstairs left after each night's performance.

Julius Knight was the most popular actor of swashbuckling and romantic parts. He was one of The Firm's men, playing in such costume dramas as *Monsieur Beaucaire, The Scarlet Pimpernel, The Sign of the Cross, Resurrection, The Three Musketeers,* and *A Royal Divorce.* His reign was long enough for most of the well-known actresses to have played with him: Nellie Bramley, Lizette Parkes, Judith Anderson (when she was Francee Anderson), Katherine Grey, and Olive Wilton, who played the Empress Josephine opposite him in *A Royal Divorce,* and, one of her favourite parts, Milady, in *The Three Musketeers.*

One foible of Knight's was that he enjoyed knitting, and was to be seen sitting in the drawing-room of Menzies Hotel, Melbourne, using his needles with some of the dexterity, and all of the aplomb of a Madame Defarge.

As the nineteenth century ended, the theatrical weather was radiantly sunny. Before a playhouse had been empty long enough for dust to settle after one Closing Night, the next Opening Night had begun. Companies swarmed in and out of provincial towns and the backblocks.

In this buoyant *milieu* it was obvious, and logical enough, that many of the prominent and dominant entrepreneurs, actor-managers, leading ladies, and matinée idols had come from overseas. Some, certainly, were already Australian by adoption. Some were settled in, for ever it seemed.

Australia was, however, growing up, and so were Australians, among them the three infants, noted *en passant* some pages back, who had come into being in the 1870s—Oscar Asche, Bert Bailey, and Gregan McMahon.

CHAPTER FIVE

ASCHE, BAILEY, McMAHON, AND OTHER INFLUENCES

JOHN STANGER HEISS OSCAR ASCHE was born on January 26, 1871, at Geelong, Victoria. His Norwegian father, a barrister, graduate of the Christiania (Oslo) University, did not practise his profession in Australia, but was successively a gold-digger, a mounted policeman, a store-keeper, and finally a prosperous publican at Mack's Hotel in Geelong, which he left in 1878 for Dandenong where Oscar Asche went to school for a time before going to Melbourne Grammar School.

At the age of sixteen, and already a tall and handsome fellow, Oscar Asche left Melbourne Grammar. After a holiday in China he was articled to an architect, a profession he cared little about. He wanted to be a farmer. This idea his parents did not approve. When the architect died, Asche left home, and spent some time as a jackeroo, during which period he became impassioned with the idea of being an actor. Perhaps somehow to help scotch this notion, his father sent him on a holiday to Fiji. It scotched nothing. His father gave in. At the age of nineteen, Oscar Asche sailed to Norway to study drama under Jogens Hansen Björn-stjerne at Björnson's Dramatic School in Bergen.

Within a year, Asche was playing Ibsen with the students. At Oslo, he met Henrik Ibsen himself, and was advised by the playwright to continue study in England, and to make particular effort to iron out his Australian accent.

In England, where he was able to live comfortably on an allowance of ten pounds a week from his father, Oscar Asche improved his accent, tried unsuccessfully for parts, and became an ardent Shakespeare fan. He went six nights in succession to see Henry Irving and Ellen Terry in *Henry the Eighth*. In December 1892 he returned to Norway to give a Shakespeare recital.

On March 25, 1893, he made his London début as Roberts in *Man and Woman*, with Arthur Dacre and Amy Roselle, at the Opéra Comique Theatre. He was twenty-two, nordically blue-eyed, six feet tall, and of magnificent physique. F. R. Benson, sensing possibilities, made him a member of the Benson Shakespearian Company. Asche stayed with the company for eight years. At first he played small parts, such as Charles the Wrestler in *As You Like It*, a part fitting his physique.

The early days with Benson were hard ones for Asche. In 1893 his father, because of his own financial problems, withdrew the allowance, and Asche had to exist on a wage of two pounds ten weekly, which he received only while acting. Between plays he often slept on Victoria Embankment, earning minute tips during the day by calling cabs. Ultimately, he progressed from small parts to bigger ones— Brutus in *Julius Caesar*, King Claudius in *Hamlet*—and his weekly wage was increased to four pounds. In 1900 he played Pistol in *Henry the Fifth* at the Lyceum Theatre, London. His experience with Benson was a superb training in traditional Shakespeare. Later in life he was to flout some of these time-honoured interpretations, and to flout them brilliantly. It was only by knowing the traditional that he was able to diverge from it intelligently and successfully.

In 1901 he made his first impact on London audiences and critics as Freddy Maldonado, in Sir Arthur Pinero's *Iris*. His success in this part took him to New York. "It is", wrote *The*

96

Essie Jenyns in "The Merchant of Venice"

Tittell Brune in "L'Aiglon"

Ristori in "Medea"

Sarah Bernhardt in "Hamlet"

Times critic, "not every actor who can play a wild beast, and yet seem human, but Oscar Asche contrives to do it."

When he returned, he, and his beautiful and talented wife, Lily Brayton, worked with the Beerbohm Tree Company. She had been with Benson, and had married Asche in 1899. In 1903, Oscar Asche played Benedick opposite Ellen Terry's Beatrice in *Much Ado About Nothing*. Other rôles with Tree were Bolingbroke in *Richard the Second*; Christopher Sly and Petruchio in *The Taming of the Shrew*; Angelo in *Measure for Measure*; and Bottom in *A Midsummer Night's Dream*.

In 1907 he set up his own company, becoming a member of that breed of actor-managers whose numbers, once so great, were already diminishing.

The Oscar Asche–Lily Brayton Company established itself with an explosive performance of *The Taming of the Shrew*. Asche's dynamic Othello, and his unconventional Jaques in *As You Like It*, were among parts that enhanced his reputation, ensured a public, and made the company prosper.

In 1909-1910, he returned to Australia, overjoyed to be famous. "What a homecoming it was!" he wrote. "Nothing, nothing can deprive me of that. I had made good, and had come home to show them. Whatever the future years held, or shall hold for me, nothing can eliminate that."

Asche's performance of the whirlwind Petruchio was very popular in Australia. His volatile manner in *The Taming of the Shrew* was a carbon copy of his offstage manner.

There were many tales of his temperamental typhoons. During a Melbourne performance of *Othello* he was lying on the sofa in his dressing-room, after the exhausting third act, and refuelling himself with whisky. Excited by the takings of a Full House, Arthur Levy, business manager of the Theatre Royal at that time, came chattering with the news into the dressing-room.

Asche sprang to his feet, stopping Levy in his tracks as

Lola Montez:

Spider Dance   *In the Green Room*

        Spanish Dance

G

he towered massively above him, and thundered, every organ-stop of his voice full out, "How dare you speak of filthy lucre to Othello! How dare you! Out! Out, before Othello strangles you!"

Ron Testro, a minor player, stated bluntly in the Press—but after Asche's death—that Asche was the vilest-tempered star ever to play in Melbourne. Dozens of other stories convey the impression of a man given to exuberant storms of ferocity. It was the same Testro who gave one of those glamour-dispersing glimpses of stage life. In the days of the Bland Holt melodramas, one of the hair-raising climaxes in the 1902 presentation of *Span of Life* was the scene where Mr and Mrs Bland Holt, as hero and heroine, could only escape the villain by walking across a human chain of three bodies linking one cliff-top with another. Ron Testro was one of the three links. Testro commended Mrs Bland Holt for removing her shoes each night: about Bland Holt, who did not remove his boots, he was far less gracious.

When Oscar Asche returned to London after his Australian visit, he acquired Edward Knoblock's play *Kismet* and, after shortening and rewriting much of it, put it into production, himself playing Haaj.

He returned for a 1911-1912 Australian season during which he did an opulent *A Midsummer Night's Dream* and an equally opulent *Antony and Cleopatra*, he as a swaggering Antony being outshone by the sinuous Lily Brayton as a quicksilver Cleopatra. He also presented *Kismet*.

Was *Kismet* the first of his answers to the film industry, and a falling-in with a cheapening public taste? Was it the result of a desire to write, which he could not resist? Was it merely a need to go further with exotic trappings than he had already gone in *Antony and Cleopatra*? Was it a money-spinning throw? Asche was improvident. He made much money, but spent it with imperial stupidity. He had a farm in Gloucestershire, an absurd show-place that swallowed money. He had kennels of expensive greyhounds, on which he disastrously gambled.

Private life and outrageous temper aside, Oscar Asche had given something to the theatre that must not be under-rated. It was the gift of braggadocio and spectacle and reson-ance and virility. His Shakespearian innovations were valid ones. Asche himself was not a superlative Shakespearian, but he was a full-blooded one with superlative moments. His preference for the more blatant and ornamental of the works —a turbulent *The Taming of the Shrew*, an almost Oriental-ized *Antony and Cleopatra*—did not let him exempt himself from careful and intelligent efforts to fit his virility into less florid, less popular, and more rarely played works, for example, *Measure for Measure*, in which Lily Brayton's Isabella was a masterpiece.

His switch from the essentially Anglo-Saxon Greeks, Romans, and Italians of Shakespeare to the beads-and-bracelets-and-turbans of *Kismet, Chu Chin Chow*, and *Cairo*, to a factitious Orientalism, is interesting, both in reference to the man himself and sociologically. Oscar Asche somehow links himself, sociologically, with a litter of phenomena: the persistence, on drawing-room tables, of *The Rubáiyát* of Omar Khayyám bound in flaccid moss-green suède; Amy Woodforde Finden's *Indian Love Lyrics*; Edmund Dulac's water-colours inspired by the Persian; Diaghilev and Nijinsky and *Scheherazade*; James Elroy Flecker's *Hassan*; Poiret's dress designs, and, at the end of the scale, Theda Bara and Louise Glaum, and the craze for aigrettes, scarab brooches, oscillating ear-rings, chunks of ersatz jade looped on silken cord about female necks, tasselled pouffes of tanger-ine satin, and harem trousers.

In October 1914 he presented in London his own play *Mameena*, based on Rider Haggard's *The Child of the Storm*, in which he played Saduka. It began well. It faltered. It failed. The Great War was on.

Oscar Asche now wrote *Chu Chin Chow*. It ran for almost

99

five years, from August 31, 1916, to July 22, 1921, breaking all records of long-running. It was lapped up as a sensuous spectacle by war-tired England, and by the soldiers returning from the shambles of Europe.

Even if robes, turbans, and grandiose settings did come to seem an expression of Asche's personality, it would be unfair not to let him say what he said of his part as Abu Hassan in *Chu Chin Chow*: "You cannot imagine how terribly boring it was going down those stairs, night after night after night, to say the same old lines." There is no record of his similarly denigrating his countless appearances in Shakespeare. Did he realize that the come-down from Ibsen and Shakespeare to pretentious Ali Baba-ism was a slackening of his own and the theatre's standards? His pre-Reinhardt splendourizing of *A Midsummer Night's Dream* in a diluted Reinhardt mode is perhaps defensible—the core shines through the glittering husk. His involvement in bejewelled muck is less defensible. The silliest farce and the most absurd melodrama are, in intention, nearer the heart of the matter. Life is nearer to farce than to *Chu Chin Chow*; melodrama is merely life without life's anticlimaxes and unhappy ending.

It must—surely—have been a relief, "night after night", for this massive man in his fifties to escape from the gargantuan hollowness of *Chu Chin Chow*, to a supper of five pounds of steak, and a nightly bottle of whisky.

Asche brought his celebrated monster to Australia in 1921. In 1922 he played Hornblower in Galsworthy's *The Skin Game*; Freddy Maldonado in Pinero's *Iris*; and a Shakespearian season, with himself as Casca in *Julius Caesar*. The public, however, was not what it had been for Shakespeare, Pinero, and Galsworthy. The 1920s and 1930s were largely witnessed, theatrically, beyond the rouged knee-caps of chorus-girls, above the tinkle of tea cups in french-window comedies, and the firing of blank bullets by stage crooks.

In England again, Asche found he was becoming un-fashionable, and was unable to over-top himself. He appeared in a few films. He had earlier written *Count Hannibal* with F. Norreys Connell, and *Eastward Ho!* with Dornford Yates. He now wrote and produced two failures: *The Good Old Days*, and *The Spanish Main* (written under the name of Varco Marenes), in the latter of which he played Captain Patrick O'Gorman.

In 1929, he wrote his autobiography; in 1930, a frightful novel *The Saga of Hans Hansen*; in 1931, another equally dreary one called *The Joss-sticks of Chung*. He died in England on March 23, 1936.

As a young man he was a fervent cricket fan, and the kind of player the M.C.C. could use in matches against minor counties. He was always a steady supporter of Australia and, therefore, an eager and conspicuous spectator at Lord's during Test matches. Maybe his affection for his own country was part and parcel of his affection for himself.

His interest, as he grew older, in spectacle, and the artistically and emotionally shallow aspects of theatre, is an interest not easy to analyse. If it were an attempt to make a counter-attack on the forces hacking at the fabric of the theatre as he had known it, he was not alone in attempting to make a counter-attack.

Oscar Asche's efforts kept thousands of the treacherous public glued to theatre seats rather than to the seats of cinemas. Bert Bailey and Gregan McMahon, his contemporaries to the very decade, also attempted counter-attacks, both of them defensible as means to an end. That one or other of the counter-attacks has to be more defensible than either of the rest, depends, of course, on what one thinks of as theatre.

An attempt to make an outside decision here leads only to circular argument, endless analyses, and unsolvable problems.

Born one year later than Asche, in 1872, in Auckland, New Zealand, Albert Edward Bailey was brought up in Australia. Matily transmogrified into Bert Bailey, he was to have an entirely different effect on the atmosphere of Australian theatre. Neither rose-coloured East of Suez, nor Shakespeare with a flourish, was for Bert Bailey.

His essential attitude to the theatre, when he had reached the stage of exposing it, was summed up by the forthright critics of the early 1900s who stated time and again, and in a variety of ways, that his chief attribute as a man of the theatre was "a deep sense of the importance of money". Ultimately he was called, by one of the astute writers of the *Lone Hand*, "one of the few frank capitalists" of his profession. "Frank" implies "Walk up, sucker!" and a strong-minded avoidance of all aspects of theatre except a sentimentally false one.

His progress towards wealth via trite entertainment began modestly. He was a probationer at the Ashfield Telegraph Office, Sydney. He advanced from being floor-manager of the Crystal Palace Skating Rink, York Street, Sydney, to being a Descriptive Vocalist, at the Canterbury Music Hall, George Street, Sydney.

As a youth he was as stage-struck as Oscar Asche, but without Asche's more civilized and civilizing intention. Asche, for example, new to London, goggled at Henry Irving, night after night. Bailey, between August 1919 and August 1920, when *On Our Selection* was staged at the Lyric Theatre, Shaftesbury Avenue, goggled at forty pantomimes. This was the immature half of Bailey. The other half was undiluted cynicism, a quality rare in players, rare even in actor-managers. Egoism and egotism, arrogance and vanity and "temperament" and self-delusion and monotonous dedication can be expected, and found, among their qualities. Cynicism is rare.

At seventeen, Bailey joined a touring company run by Edmund Duggan, an Irishman. Randolph Bedford was also in the company. Bedford was one of the race of frustrated writers and failed actors who later descended to politics.

Bailey played his first part at Wollongong, outside Sydney. After a year of backblocks perambulation, he joined William Anderson's Dramatic Organization. He fancied himself in his "favourite brand of eccentric humour"—low comedy to others—but played everything: an aborigine in Randolph Bedford's *White Australia*, Hans in *Hans the Boatman*, Armand in *Camille*, Remendade in *Carmen*, Florenstein in *The Bohemian Girl*, and the Marquis in *Maritana*. Anderson produced as many Australian plays as he was able. Alfred Dampier, the meticulous Shakespearian, was also intensely interested in the development of Australian playwriting. Innumerable plays were written with an Australian background. Most of these were no more than rattle-trap melodramas, almost invariably set in the Woop-Woop Never-Never, and inhabited by a heterogeneous mustering of Australian fauna: bushrangers, troopers, sheep, mortgaged settlers' virgin daughters, and comic Irish handymen of the begorrah sort.

A few of the better plays—and none was outstanding—were Charles Harpur's *The Bushrangers* (1853); the plays of a Sydney barrister, Walter Cooper—*Foiled; or, Australia Twenty Years Ago* was one—produced by Dampier in 1871; *All for Gold*, by Francis Hopkins, a Murray River pastoralist, also produced by Dampier, in 1877. In 1878 George Darrell produced two of his own plays at the Melbourne Royal: *Back from the Grave*, and *Transported for Life*. This was in July. In June, at the same theatre, Bunster's *Class* had opened, a play of social contrasts, set in Melbourne. Dampier also produced, between his Shakespearian productions in which his daughters Lilian and Rose played leads, *Robbery Under Arms*; Marcus Clarke's *For the Term of His Natural Life* (1886, Royal Standard Theatre, Sydney); *The Wreck of the "Dunbar"* (1887); and, in celebration of Australia's first centenary in 1888, John Perry's *The Life and Death of*

Captain Cook. In 1889, Charles Warner presented C. Haddon Chambers's *Captain Swift* at the Royal, Sydney, with Ada Ward (who later, in retirement, inveighed against the sins of the theatre), Herbert Flemming, Alfred Phillips, and Grace Warner. It was criticized as "upholstery and dramatic ashes" and "an expensive failure".

The former criticism could well have been applied to the many Australian plays attempted by William Anderson, for he was as enthusiastic as Alfred Dampier, who died in 1908, and he picked up the torch Dampier had carried for so many years.

Whatever Anderson's influence may have been on Bert Bailey, there is no doubt that he was early interested in finding a vehicle to carry Australia, profitably if not authentically, on to the stage. In collusion with Edmund Duggan he wrote *The Squatter's Daughter*, and *The Man from Outback*. It was not until 1912 that he hit on the one idea of his life. If from that moment Bert Bailey never looked back, it can also be said that he never looked forward.

A Queenslander, Arthur Hoey Davis, under the pen-name Steele Rudd, had written for a nationalistic Sydney weekly, *The Bulletin*, a series of sketches of life among outback selectors. These had been collected in one volume called *On Our Selection*, and were immensely popular with the non-reading section of the reading public. With Rudd's help, Bailey contorted the personages of the book into characters in a play. Bailey then entered a partnership with Julius Grant: the Bert Bailey Company.

On September 16, 1912, at the King's Theatre, Melbourne, *On Our Selection* was presented to a generation which, in common with succeeding generations, was not to be long out of vision or earshot of this creation which, like an amoeba, kept on splitting into amoebae.

On Our Selection, as a play, was as popular as the book had been. It went to the Lyric Theatre, London, correcting any image the English might have been forming of Australia as part-civilized.

The play was produced when the Australian film industry, which had begun in 1899, was also occupying itself with "Australian life". In 1905, O. G. Perry shot the world's first full-length feature film in Studley Park, Melbourne, for J. and N. Tait—*The Story of the Kelly Gang*. In 1907 *For the Term of His Natural Life* (Osborne and Jerden), *Robbery Under Arms* (Jim McMahon and E. J. Carroll), *Living Melbourne* (T. J. West), and *Thunderbolt* (John F. Gavin) were filmed. Bailey's *The Squatter's Daughter*, with Olive Wilton in the title rôle, was made in 1913, by which year a number of Australian films had been made: *John Vane, Bushranger* (Spencer, 1909), directed by S. Fitzgerald, with Jim Gerald, Lance Vane, and Max Clifton. Other 1909-1910 films for Cozens Spencer's unit were *Captain Midnight, The Bush King*, with Alfred Rolfe directing Lilian Dampier, *Rufus Dawes (For the Term of His Natural Life)*, *Captain Starlight (Robbery Under Arms)* and, in collaboration with Hugh D. McIntosh, *The Burns-Johnson Fight*, a four-thousand-foot record of the championship match on Boxing Day 1908, shot by Ernest Higgins. The Johnson and Gibson Company filmed *Mystery of a Hansom Cab* (Walter Dalgleish), *Never Too Late To Mend*, and *The Luck of Roaring Camp* (Ethel Buckley). In 1911, Cozens Spencer financed *Fatal Wedding* (Raymond H. Longford, Lottie Lyall, Walter Vincent) and *Dan Morgan, the Terror of the Australian Bush*, while Australian Life Biograph Company produced *Colleen Bawn*, and *The Wreck of the "Dunbar"*. Films of 1912 included Spencer's *The Midnight Wedding* and *The Tide of Death* (Lottie Lyall, Gus Neville); *Swagman's Story* (Co-op Films), with Clara Stevenson, George Corti, James Martin; *All for Gold* (Billy Percy Productions); Australian Photoplay's *The Octoroon* and *The Crime and the Criminal*; John F. Gavin's *The Assigned Servant, Keane of Kalgoorlie, Frank Gardiner, King of the Road*, and *Ben*

Hall and His Gang. Other 1912 films were *A Woman of the People*, with Ethel Buckley; Franklyn Barrett's *Called Back*, featuring Charles Hawtrey; and *Tales of the Bush.* Bailey's 1913 effort was flanked by other 1913 efforts: *A Blue Gum Romance,* and *The Life of a Jackeroo,* by Fraser Films; *Sea Dogs of Australia,* and *An Australian Hero and the Red Spider,* by J. S. McCullagh; *The Road to Ruin*; and six productions by the Lincoln-Cass Films group—*Moondyne, The Crisis, The Sick Stockrider, Transported,* and Roy Redgrave and George Bryant in both *The Crisis,* and *The Reprieve.*

By 1920 the film industry was firmly established. *On Our Selection* (Southern Cross) was filmed at Baulkham Hills, outside Parramatta, and at Millbank Station, near Leeton. Lottie Lyall and Raymond H. Longford wrote the scenario. The cast included Percy Walshe (Dad), Beatrice Esmond (Mum), Tal Ordell (Dave), Evelyn Johnson, Lottie Beaumont, and Arthur Greenaway.

The Bailey and Grant partnership, founded to launch *On Our Selection* as a play, continued to sponsor Bert Bailey as Dad in endless variations of the one theme. On March 31, 1928, with Bailey as Dad, and Fred Macdonald as Dave, it could still be seen at King's Theatre, Melbourne.

There was to be no abatement. When talking pictures were introduced, Bailey and Grant allied themselves with Cinesound, and Bailey was starred in talkie versions of *On Our Selection* in 1931, *Granddad Rudd* in 1935, *Dad and Dave Come to Town* in 1938, and *Dad Rudd, M.P.* in 1939.

Ultimately, Bert Bailey did retire from Dad-ship to live at Lake Macquarie, and later in Sydney. He is recorded as being a cricket fan, an unquenchable raconteur, and helpful, at no cost, with all sorts of advice to young actresses and actors. He died in 1953.

It is more than sixty years since Steele Rudd wrote his *Bulletin* sketches, and more than half a century since Bert Bailey was responsible for making them walk and talk. That these garrulous left-overs from the shanties of the 1890 out-back have undergone successive modernizations over sixty years can hardly be blamed on Rudd. He died in 1935. Much of the filleting and dressing up is the aftermath of Bailey, whose one-track devotion to the task of keeping Dad and Mum, Dave and Mabel, talking is his contribution to the theatre.

The value of this contribution is a tricky and touchy sub-ject. Granted that it is useful for a nation to have, for example, Dave as a goofy Aunt Sally at which to hurl sardonic self-criticism, and as a personification of male Woop-Woopism in a saga of dirty yarns—but there the matter does not end. Gods do not make men; men make gods. Bailey's influence has either been good, or bad; merely harmless and valueless, or dangerously harmful. One can admire him for providing the world of entertainment with the first group of characters presumably to illustrate essential Australianism, or vilify him for setting up a collection of crudely carved folk-idols with a sinister command of the techniques of mass-hypnosis which make the sentimental and the false appear in the satisfying and self-flattering colours of the normal and the true.

Gregan McMahon was born in Sydney, the eldest son of Irish parents, on March 2, 1874. He was educated at Sydney Grammar School, and St Ignatius' College, Riverview, Syd-ney. At matriculation, he got First Class Honours in Classics. In 1896 he graduated as Bachelor of Arts at Sydney Uni-versity, and was articled to a Sydney solicitor's firm. His hobby was the theatre. By May 1900 he was so good an amateur actor that Robert Brough invited him to join his company. McMahon unhesitatingly abandoned law. In June Gregan McMahon made his professional début at Brisbane, as the waiter in *Liars*. By 1902 he was playing Horace Parker in *A Message from Mars*.

Robert Brough ran one of the best companies ever to work in Australia, and it was strongly braced by members of the

Brough family, all of them talented, including Mrs Robert Brough, *née* Florence Trevelyan. Her sisters, Bessie Major and Emma Temple, spent some time with the company, as did Robert Brough's mother, Mrs Gibson, and her daughter, Brenda Gibson. The company was the strongest and most sturdily all-round, in repertoire and cast, of the companies not yet crushed by the J. C. Williamson juggernaut, the weight of whose purpose was beginning to be felt by the actor-manager companies, and the direction of whose danger to the individual actor was being noticed by far-seeing players. Many bosses, they perceived, were preferable to one; many choices to one take-it-or-leave-it.

With Brough and, later, with W. F. Hawtrey, McMahon played in the headquarter theatres in Sydney and Melbourne, and went on extensive tours of Australia, New Zealand, and the Orient. Robert Brough died in 1906, and Gregan McMahon joined J. C. Williamson as a producer. This was a fate many were compelled to accept, as theatre after theatre was absorbed into the kingdom of The Firm.

Although never a breath-taking actor, McMahon was an intelligent and educated one, and, because of his comprehensive experiences with Hawtrey and Brough, a finished one. Brough's standards were to become McMahon's. His devotion to the cause of fine theatre was selfless and unstinted. Many now-famous players admit their indebtedness to him.

It was certainly Gregan McMahon's pleading with The Firm that resulted in the formation of the Melbourne Repertory Company. It may be too gracious to state that in 1911 The Firm was still in possession of enough conscience to applaud his scheme. They did, nevertheless, put it into action, with McMahon as producer. This was Australia's first repertory company. Repertory, in Australia, has come to mean amateur or semi-professional, but the original company was professional. Its first performance, in June 1911, was of St John Hankin's *The Two Mr Wetherbys*, the second act of Sheridan's *The Critic*, and Henrik Ibsen's *John Gabriel Borkman*.

The company had a repertoire of plays that intelligent playgoers and players alike could get the teeth of their minds into. McMahon was fortunate in having the admiration of George Bernard Shaw, who could be irritatingly autocratic in the matter of play production. To McMahon, of whom he said, "I know of only two worthwhile products of Australia—sheep and Gregan McMahon!", Shaw gave virtual *carte blanche*, so that McMahon was able to give the first productions in Australia of Shaw's works. His earliest Shaw production was in 1911, when Julius Knight and Katherine Grey played the leading rôles in *Arms and the Man*.

Between 1911 and 1916 the Shaw plays presented were *Candida, Getting Married, Major Barbara, Man and Superman, Fanny's First Play, You Never Can Tell*, and *Pygmalion*. During the same period, McMahon included in the selection *Rosmersholm* and *An Enemy of the People*, by Ibsen; *The Voysey Inheritance* and *The Madras House*, by Granville Barker; John Galsworthy's *The Pigeon, Strife*, and *Loyalties; The Seagull*, by Chekhov; and *The Mate*, by Arthur Schnitzler.

During the Great War, the Melbourne Repertory Company had to disband, and Gregan McMahon returned to the production of less thoughtful works for J. C. Williamson and Company. J. C. Williamson himself died in Paris on July 6, 1913.

Although the war halted McMahon's good work, this did not daunt him. He turned to Sydney, and J. and N. Tait, almost the last of The Firm's rivals of any stature: all others had been soaked into the vaster organization. He persuaded them that a Sydney Repertory Company was possible. Half a dozen plays a year were presented: Shaw, of course; Bridie, Galsworthy, Pirandello (*Right you are, if you think so*), Casella, Daviot, A. A. Milne's *The Dover Road*, John Drinkwater's *Abraham Lincoln*, Ferenc Molnar's *Liliom*, Anatole

France, Barrie, Ibsen, Maugham, and O'Neill. The audience was a subscription one. McMahon's own characterizations were models of craftsmanship. The best were John Tanner (*Man and Superman*), Lob (*Dear Brutus*), King Magnus (*The Apple Cart*), Ulric Brendel (*Rosmersholm*), and the Father (*Six Characters in Search of an Author*).

The Sydney enterprise lasted for seven years. J. and N. Tait then dropped their more or less highbrow venture to move in on, and to take an active part in the control of, The Firm they had once been in competition with.

McMahon, whose sincerity and idealism were not to be tampered with, though it led him often into debt, now formed his own company in Melbourne, in 1929. This company, the Gregan McMahon Players, was semi-professional. Well-known actors and actresses were only too happy, although poorly paid, to appear in a McMahon production. They worked side by side with hand-selected amateurs, McMahon-trained, many of whose names were later to be seen in lights above London theatres, or on the posters advertising Hollywood talkies.

McMahon's casts played to a subscription audience, the "discerning and cultured" minority for whom The Firm rarely provided fare. The later 1920s, and the 1930s, were theatrical rock-bottom. Despite this, the era seems, now, thirty-odd years later, to have been rich and refreshing. For those who cared, the mind-stirring works of McMahon and Allan Wilkie towered above the saccharine shallows of the commercial theatres with their empty "comedies" and trite "dramas" freshly tepid from London and America. Programmes from the commercial theatres of the period are a revealing funeral register of the names of nine-day-wonder stars, of shingled cuties, vapid juvenile leads with Ronald Colman moustaches, one-play players, the pathetic morning glories of a debased theatrical system.

McMahon's first headquarters were in the Bijou, Melbourne. Later, the Garrick, across Prince's Bridge, was used;

later still, the Comedy, in Exhibition Street. In eleven years, nearly a hundred plays were presented. On occasion, in lighter vein, McMahon offered revivals of old-time melo-dramas such as *The Lights o' London,* which had been a favourite of George Rignold's in the 1870s, and *A Message from Mars,* surely the first science-fiction drama.

McMahon still occasionally played, his most popular rôle being that of Sylvanus Heythorp in *Old English.* It is in this part that playgoers of his time most fondly remember him, particularly the death-scene of the badgered old stoic, which McMahon made a classic of timing and of moving finesse.

In 1938 he was given a C.B.E., a recognition no greater than the gratitude of those playgoers for whom, year after debt-haunted year, he provided what no other professional producer would provide. As great was the gratitude of the hundreds of players who were given worthwhile work, or launched in the direction of fame, or saved from dry-rot, or licked into shape by this patient, intelligent, kindly master. A complete roll-call would be too long, but here is a selection of names: Coral Browne, Doris Fitton, Lloyd Lamble, Ruby May, Beatrice Day, Norman Wister, Thomas Skewes, David Reid, Norma Gunn, Phyllis Best, Maurice Moscovich, Meta Pelham, Leon Gordon, Hal Percy, Frank Neil, Leal Douglas, Zillah Carter, Ken Tuckfield, Jos Ambler, Frank Allenby, Emilie Polini, Maggie Moore, Olive Wilton, Marie Ney, Irene Mitchell, and Janet Johnson. Otto Peter Heggie who, as O. P. Heggie, was much in demand in Hollywood before he died in 1936, did character work with McMahon. Clyde Cook, a double-jointed comedy actor, also of Hollywood, worked with McMahon.

McMahon, Bailey, and Asche, all Australians, all born in the 1870s, all chose—without equivocation—to expose their abilities, convictions, and intellectual attitudes, to congrega-tions of others. It proves nothing to count the rows of heads. Much depends on him who counts. He may be counting minds, half-minds, or what are no more than hat-pegs. The total may indicate public taste.

Allan Wilkie was born in Liverpool, England, in 1878.

Intelligent, well-educated, and dedicated, Wilkie's dedication was on another plane than McMahon's. McMahon was devoted to the more cerebral playwrights of the late nineteenth and the twentieth centuries: Wilkie was an authority on Shakespeare, his range being wider by far than that of the many Shakespearians Australia had seen: Brooke, Dampier, Rignold, Sullivan, Montgomery, Anderson, Charles Kean, Conrad Knowles, Edwin Booth, and those who—even at the level of Dan Barry—tossed off *Othello* on Saturday night, after a matinée of *Deadwood Dick's Revenge.*

Wilkie's early experience with Beerbohm Tree, Julia Neilson, and Fred Terry, supplemented by his study of Shakespeare, gave him confidence to form his own company. He toured England for years, later South Africa, India, China, and Japan, before coming to Australia in 1915. For years he battled to draw audiences from a public which had lost not only the relish their parents and grandparents had had for the world's greatest playwright, but also their forbearance of him.

It took him five years to train enough players to form a solid and permanent company, which opened at the Princess, Melbourne, in 1920. This company was to perform the feat, astounding when one considers the theatrically frivolous era he was playing in, of presenting twenty-five Shakespearian plays in twelve hundred consecutive performances. These plays were not presented in the lavish manner of Kean or Asche, with colossal settings, stairs running from stage level to stage level, and an abundance of decorative supernumeraries. Simple backcloths, dark curtains, and the necessary minimum of stage-fittings . . . a throne, a table, a divan . . . meant that there was no need for long intervals during

112

which elaborate scene changes were made. Wilkie was able, therefore, in much the same way as the Elizabethan producers had been, to let scene rapidly pursue scene. There was no break in the dramatic current, no cooling off of the audience between scenes. There was, moreover, no need to lop acts and prune characters, as producers inclined to scenic extravagance had to do on behalf of tons of canvas. Wilkie let Shakespeare speak for himself; the plays, after all, had their scenery built-in in passages of poetry. This treatment, of course, required from the players interpretations of power and subtlety. Wilkie saw that the casts were historically costumed, and that when magnificence was required, as it so often is in Shakespeare, the magnificence was suitably eye-filling.

As McMahon did, Wilkie laboured courageously against the great odds of the period and, in 1925, was likewise honoured by a C.B.E.

Frediswyde Hunter-Watts, his wife and his supporting lead, was an actress in the chilly classic mode, competent in the rôles of the tragic heroines; sound in portraying the less doom-ridden ones; and perhaps at her best in the more mannered and stylish rôles of Sheridan and Goldsmith, whose works were also part of the company's repertoire.

Among his players were Lorna Forbes, Marie Ney, Frank D. Clewlow, Laurier Lange, Mona Barlee, Arthur Keane, Alexander Marsh, John Cairns, Milton Sands, Mollie Ick, Nellie Ferguson, J. Beresford Fowler, Ellis Irving, Mary Charles, and Hector Bolitho who for a period edited Wilkie's *Shakespearean Quarterly* which was published from January 1922 to October 1924.

In June 1926 his fittings, furnishings, and wardrobe of irreplaceable costumes were destroyed by a fire at Geelong. Horrified intellectuals subscribed £3,000, which enabled Wilkie to carry on in an amputated way, and to give a long season at the Majestic Theatre, Newtown, Sydney, in 1928. In 1930 he left Australia to tour New Zealand, from where,

H

in 1932, he and his wife went to Canada. After a visit to England they returned to British Columbia in 1938, and gave occasional recitals. Frediswyde Hunter-Watts died in England in 1951. Allan Wilkie, hale and hearty, lives in Scotland.

Since McMahon and Wilkie, major works have had to be presented by amateur or semi-professional groups, some with sturdy reputations, and an existence of decades. They are not for treatment here. Nevertheless, attention must be given to the outstanding work of Olive Wilton.

She admired McMahon's and Wilkie's work, and was long and intimately enough involved with the theatre to accept McMahon's view that, "in counting heads, the increasingly many more at *High Jinks* or *Lightnin'*, and the far fewer at *Six Characters in Search of an Author* or *Cymbeline*, showed that the public taste was diminishing to the other side of nothing". Ultimately, she found herself slaving to provide for the informed minority, while at the same time hoping to tempt and inform the lackadaisical majority. It is not this book's intention directly to commend or denigrate those intent on Cultural Uplift for the Clottish Masses. Evangelists get their own mysterious inner satisfaction from this sort of engagement with the forces of ignorance and indifference. Melba's trenchant "Sing 'em muck!" is advice that cultural do-gooders like McMahon, Wilkie, J. Beresford Fowler, Olive Wilton, Doris Fitton, and John Alden rarely put into practice.

Olive Dorothea Graeme Wilton, born in Bath, England, in 1883 had her earliest training in Ben Greet's Dramatic School. At seventeen she played the lead opposite the famous Ibsen actor, Courtenay Thorpe, in F. Marion Crawford's *A Cigarette-maker's Romance*, on tour of England. This was followed by an engagement with Mark Blow as Princess Flavia in Anthony Hope's *The Prisoner of Zenda*. Olive Wilton says that her long, red-gold hair had much to do with her being chosen to play Princess Flavia, Viera in *A Cigarette-maker's Romance*, and Glory in Hall Caine's *The Christian*. "At this time", she says, "parts were being written where this asset of 'a woman's crowning glory' of my colour was a 'must'."

Thus launched, she was taken up as an *ingénue* by the light comedian, Edward Terry, and played the British Isles, New York, and Canada in a number of pieces such as *The Passport, Love in Idleness*, and Sir Arthur Pinero's *Sweet Lavender*.

She first came to Australia in 1906, in which year, on March 6, at the age of twenty-three, she married Benjamin A. Cornell.

Olive Wilton came to Australia with the Grace Palotta and Willoughby Ward Company, and played supporting rôles in *The Man from Mexico, The Talk of the Town, Mr Hopkinson*, and *The New Clown*. Her contract specified that she live in the best hotels; and that publicity appearances, dressed to the nines, were to be made at race meetings and "social gatherings" alive with the abominable breed which gushingly lionizes the imported actor and actresses. When the company's Sydney and Melbourne seasons were over, she returned to England.

In 1909, William Anderson visited England on a talent-seeking trip, and saw Olive Wilton, at the King's Theatre, Hammersmith, as Cigarette in *Under Two Flags*. She was doing the famous and perilous horseback ride up the zig-zag platform into the flies because the stand-in jockey was too drunk to do the doubling. Olive Wilton had, however, more than red-gold hair and horsemanship to commend her. She was "tall, commandingly beautiful, and polished in manner and speech"; and had "spirit and verve . . . touches of intimate skill . . . was always sincere in every detail of her work . . . an earnest and thoughtful artist". Anderson engaged her. On the ship to Australia she shared a cabin with Michael Redgrave. He was a ten-month-old baby, travelling with his mother, who was to split leads with Olive Wilton. The father, Roy Redgrave, was already in Melbourne, at the King's Theatre, with Anderson. Anderson was enthusiastically producing Australian plays, six yearly. In *My Mate*, "a bush love story", which opened at the King's Theatre on February 11, 1911, with Nellie Bramley in the cast, Olive Wilton played Jessie Morland. This sort of outdoor, outback, horse-riding part alternated with the parts of "bad women" in such heart-wringers as *Sailor's Sweetheart, The Girl Who Took the Wrong Turning,* and *The Worst Woman in London.*

Audiences did not always take kindly to the home product. Olive Wilton recalls being upstage—on horseback!—mustering thirty actual sheep, in a play by Temple Harrison, the Australian actor. The galleryites were antagonistic. As the cast tried to make itself heard above brawling and catcalls, Harrison, who was on stage, shouted across the footlights, "Give us a chance, you b————s!" It is always unwise to attack an audience. This one became violent. The curtain was rung down. The play was killed.

When Anderson's Dramatic Organization closed down, Olive Wilton joined The Firm and supported Emilie Polini in *De Luxe Annie*. Olive played Mrs Archer, and John Fernside appeared in two small parts. The producer was Gregan McMahon. Fernside also played Hugh Pryde, at the Palace Theatre, Sydney, in September 1918, in *The Invisible Foe*, Olive Wilton playing Mrs Hilary, "a humorous social butterfly". She played many parts for McMahon, including Mrs Dubedat, in *The Doctor's Dilemma*, and Mrs Borkman, in *John Gabriel Borkman*.

She starred with Julius Knight, as the Empress Josephine in *A Royal Divorce*, and as Milady in *The Three Musketeers*. In Eugène Brieux's *Damaged Goods* she played the leading rôle of Mrs Dupont. This play, a sound drama, drew packed houses because it dealt with venereal disease. Before the curtain rose, a doctor nightly warned the audience that any who had come "with the intention of enjoying entertainment" were in the wrong theatre, and that money would be refunded to anyone wishing to leave. No one ever did leave. Even clean dirt fascinates.

She toured endlessly with The Firm's teams or with visiting companies—dirty, deadly, and dreary trips by train to the extremities of Australia, or by ship to Perth, New Zealand, and Tasmania. Tours sometimes lasted nine months. One tour, as Mrs Pendleton in *Daddy Longlegs,* was with the Americans, Kathleen McDonald and Charles Waldron, who had been laughed off the stage of the Criterion Theatre, Sydney, in *The Willow Tree,* in which Roy Redgrave was playing the priest.

Olive Wilton was among the players early to foresee victimization by theatrical monopolists. In 1910 the first meeting for the protection of Australian actors was held in a small hall in Exhibition Street, Melbourne. Olive was appointed to the first Federal Committee, of which a forceful member was Barry Lupino of the famous family. This Actors' Association became Actors' Federation, and is now Actors' Equity.

In 1920 she left The Firm, and settled in Hobart. She formed a company and invested her own money in it, opening at Hobart's Theatre Royal, which is now Australia's oldest theatre, with Pinero's *His House in Order.* For five years she put on four major productions yearly, and was able to make a small profit. She realized that the drama-starved public needed training and, moreover, that expensive seats were beyond the pockets of many. She instituted drama classes, a drama club, and a series of performances at the Hobart Town Hall at which all seats were two shillings. This one-woman effort led directly to the foundation of the Hobart Repertory, which presented its first play, an old Nellie Stewart favourite, *Mice and Men,* in 1927. By 1937 the company had its own playhouse, for which Olive

Wilton produced until she retired. She is a member of the Arts Council of Australia, and the British Drama League.

Another indefatigable idealist is Doris Fitton. She was born in 1897 in Santa Anna, the then fashionable section of Manila. In 1902 she came to Australia to be educated in the Loreto Convent at Ballarat. Her education completed, she began to study drama under Gregan McMahon, her first appearance with his Melbourne Repertory Company being in an English comedy, *The Price of Thomas Scott*. McMahon's company, backed by The Firm, was regarded by The Firm as a training ground for young talent, and was watched by other J.C.W. producers in need of new faces. One of these producers, George Barnum, admired her McMahon performance enough to offer her a part in *Under Fire*, which was to go on tour. Young Doris Fitton's mother would not give her permission to accept this touring part. A little later, in a stationary production, by The Firm, of *Romance*, she was allowed to make her professional début.

In 1920 she married N. K. Mason, and lived in Sydney. By this time, Gregan McMahon was also in Sydney as producer for the Sydney Repertory Company. Its headquarters were in the Playhouse Theatre, now the Sydney Telephone Exchange. Here, Doris Fitton played the leading rôle for McMahon in his production of *The Dark Lady of the Sonnets*. She played Mary Fitton, her own ancestress, whom some authorities regard as Shakespeare's actual mistress, identifiable with the "literary" mistress so eulogized and agonized over in his sonnets. From then on, her acting career embraced many rôles—from a native girl in Maugham's *Rain*, Christine in *Mourning Becomes Electra*, to important parts in Chekhov's *The Cherry Orchard*, *The Seagull*, and *The Three Sisters*.

From 1931, she has dominated the Independent Theatre, Sydney, which she founded, and makes only rare appearances as an actress. One was in *The Stowaway* (1958), a film made in Tahiti by Chips Rafferty's Southern International Films, and a French company, Discifilm. The cast included Arletty, Martine Carol, Serge Reggiane, and Roger Livesey. She also appeared, in April 1963, at the Independent Theatre as the revengeful millionairess, Claire Zachanassian, in the German-Swiss Friedrich Dürrenmatt's play *The Visit*. She is somewhat a devotee of Sergeivich Alexeev Stanislavski's ideas of acting and production.

Doris Fitton is eclectic, with an inclination to the *avant-garde* writers such as Pinter, Ionesco, Brecht, and Beckett. As founder and directrix of the Independent, she feels she has responsibilities towards Australian dramatists, and produces their work, when it reaches her standard, as well as the works of Thornton Wilder, Arthur Miller, Tennessee Williams, and Claire Booth Luce.

Her devotion to things theatrical is single-minded and unswerving, but is not hermitic: she is on the Boards of the Sydney Opera House, the Australian Elizabethan Theatre Trust, the Australian Broadcasting Commission, and the Northside Festival of Arts Committee. In 1956, in recognition of her unflagging labours on behalf of the theatre, she was honoured by an O.B.E.

In what little time she can spare from her multiple theatrical activities, she works for the welfare of animals, and is a diligent and forthright president of the North Sydney Branch of the R.S.P.C.A. She believes in capital punishment; travels everywhere by taxi-cab; and can do South American dances taught her by a Cuban.

Oscar Asche, Bert Bailey, Gregan McMahon, Allan Wilkie, Olive Wilton, Doris Fitton—all were born in the final decades of the nineteenth century. All had experience of the Australian theatrical climate. At the beginning of the twentieth century, this was bracing to the point of headiness. It deteriorated gradually but inexorably until 1930, and with unpleasing speed after 1930.

What effect this thinning sunshine and thickening gloom had on the careers of these variously gifted half-dozen is not weighable to the last gramme. It is safe enough, nevertheless, to write that, however directly, however obliquely, to whatever extent, the careers of at least four of the six *were* affected. There can be no doubt anywhere that Gregan McMahon, C.B.E., Allan Wilkie, C.B.E., Olive Wilton, O.B.E., and Doris Fitton, O.B.E., came by their honours the hard way. The need to endure years of fiscal discomfort, to fight and inaugurate and connive and proselytize, stiffened their sinews, and honed their attitudes. In a sunnier and blander time there would have been less need to carry such heavy torches.

It will be as well to reconsider the agents that brought about the dismal change in climate. There are many, and they include such difficult-to-trap ones as the anti-cultural Australian ethos, but the main ones are as blatant as bulldozers.

The first and most murderous was the film industry, which could have been a stimulus to the theatre, and a dazzling ally. Unfortunately the industry fell into the hands of the one nation which had hurtled from pioneer barbarity to materialistic power without developing a culture worth comparing to the culture of the smallest and time-shabbiest nations of the older world. With its bottomless economic resources, this most infantile and uncivilized of communities set about de-civilization. America was financially powerful enough to decimate the living theatre, and so to twist public taste that the fewer theatres remaining found it necessary to twist their policies. Theatres were taken over by film distributors and converted to cinemas. It is because of this, no doubt, that Australians are still likely to say, "We're going to the theatre", rather than, "We're going to the cinema". This habit persisted even when Babylonian, de luxe cinemas were going up everywhere during the 1920s, with their deep carpets, enormous chandeliers, vast lounges,

Ernst Lubitsch lavatories, acres of looking-glass, marble stair-cases, and gilded Wurlitzers descending in whirlpools of sugary melody. It indicates further retrogression that these luxurious cinemas, which ousted theatres, are now themselves some-what redundant, and that the perverted public prefers the relative discomfort of its own two-by-four house to watch tinier versions of the poorer films they would not have crossed the road to see ten or twenty years ago.

War and economic depression had their obvious, regret-table but understandable, and direct effect. Less direct was the effect on the tone of entertainment. Grimmer times impel audiences to seek shallower and gaudier forms of entertainment.

In Australia the 1930 Entertainments Tax was a racking turn of the screw. Of all the forms of entertainment the flesh-and-blood theatre was most brutally taxed.

Even monopolists were affected. The Firm, from time to time, with shrewd magnanimity, had imported famous marvels in reputable works. Usually these marvels were some-what beyond the first flush. Their appearance, however, created the impression that The Firm was doing something worth while. The 1930 taxes made them less magnanimous on behalf of even this imitation of good theatre. Increased taxation meant increased seat prices, decreased audiences, and increased theatrical unemployment. Cutting costs meant dismissing actors and actresses, musicians, stage-hands, elec-tricians, front-of-house and clerical staff, writers, dressers, scene-painters, cleaners . . . all departments were cut down. Although it would seem scarcely possible, the standard of offerings was also cut.

It is difficult to know how many potential Bernhardts and Keans were discouraged into remaining in oases of security and oblivion rather than walking the theatrical desert. Probably there are fewer than one might be inclined to think. The egotism of the breed is scarcely as strong as its egoism; adversity might serve to muffle the former, it often drives the latter to more defiant effort. Anyway, McMahon and Wilkie, and, later, Olive Wilton, Doris Fitton, and John Alden were alert to talent informed by intelligence, and willing to give it the chance to display itself. Generally, however, what did happen, and what continues to this day to happen and, despite the Australian Elizabethan Theatre Trust (or because of the same maladroit organization), will continue to happen, is that those who have the gifts, and the courage, to walk the desert, walk out of it as quickly as possible, over the horizon to famous expatriatism.

CHAPTER SIX

THE EXPATRIATES AND THE STAY-AT-HOMES

THROUGHOUT the years, the tally of expatriate Australian players steadily increased as it became difficult to get more than a pinch-gut minimum of work in their native land. Sometimes, however, the case seemed not hopeless.

Just before the Great War opportunities occurred in a developing film industry. The war itself created almost as many opportunities as it blocked: English and European film-making being at a standstill, Australian film-making flourished. Midway through the war, J.C.W.'s, unfalteringly opportunist, bestirred itself to compete with film producers who had been successfully busy for years. Among the more energetic pioneer producers were E. J. Carroll, John F. Gavin, Franklyn Barrett, Beaumont Smith, and Raymond H. Longford.

Raymond Longford began work as a sailing-ship apprentice, and finished up as night watchman on a Sydney wharf. In the years between deck and wharf he made a contribution of thirty films to the infant industry. Longford left the sea to become an actor with the Edwin Geach Touring Company. Lottie Lyall was its young leading lady. Most of Longford's films starred her, establishing her thus as the first Australian film personality.

His earliest films were financially sustained by Cozens Spencer, a go-ahead but neurasthenic English backer. Among Longford's films were *A Maori Maid's Love* (1910), Lottie Lyall, George Chalmers, Rawdon Blandford; *Sweet Nell of Old Drury* (1911), Nellie Stewart, Gus Melville, George Musgrove; *Ma Hogan's Boarder* (1912), Billie Gilbert, Queenie Cross, Ern Vockler; *Trooper Campbell* (1912), Lottie Lyall, Robert Inman, Frank Phillips; *Taking His Chance* (1912), Lottie Lyall, Vivian Edwards; *The Romance of Margaret Catchpole* (1912), Raymond Longford, Lottie Lyall—the 1912 films being made at the Rushcutters' Bay Film Studios, Sydney. Other Longford productions were *Australia Calls* (1913), which starred Australia's first licensed aviator, W. E. Hart; *Pommy Arrives in Australia* (1913), Tien Hogue, Lottie Lyall, Helen Fergus; *'Neath Australian Skies* (1914), Raymond Longford, Lottie Lyall; *The Mutiny of the "Bounty"* (1915), George Cross, Ada Guildford, Lottie Lyall; *The Church and the Woman* (1917), Lottie Lyall, Harry Roberts, Percy Walshe; *The Woman Suffers* (1918), Lottie Lyall, Boyd Irwin, Connie Martin; *The Dinkum Bloke* (1923), Raymond Longford, Arthur Tauchert; *A Gentleman in Mufti* (1924), Lottie Lyall, Arthur Tauchert; *Peter Vernon's Silence* (1925), Rawdon Blandford, George Chalmers; and *Fisher's Ghost* (1926).

Longford wrote, directed, and played parts in his productions of which the greatest was *The Sentimental Bloke* for E. J. Carroll. One of Australia's pioneer photographers, Tasman Higgins, shot part of the film in the Eastern Market, Melbourne, the setting of C. J. Dennis's poem. Dennis chose Arthur Tauchert, a vaudeville comedian, to play the title rôle hero. Alex Kerr, an authentic picture-framer in the Market, played Steeny Isaacs; Lottie Lyall was Doreen; Gilbert Emery, a seasoned Australian actor, later successful in Hollywood, played Ginger Mick. In 1920, Longford produced *Ginger Mick*.

Between 1910 and 1930 nearly two hundred silent feature

films were made, most of them almost frantically Aussie in character: *Sydney by Day and Night, The Sunny South, The Pioneers, The Bondage of the Bush, The Laugh on Dad, The Waybacks, The Squatter's Wife's Secret, The Girl from the Outback, Possum Paddock, The Swaggie's Story, Around the Boree Log,* and *Down Under* with Nancy Mills.

Film companies proliferated. J. C. Williamson Films presented in 1916: *Within Our Gates, For Australia* (Charles Villiers, Boyd Irwin, Gwen Day Burroughs); *Officer 666* and *Get-Rich-Quick Wallingford,* with Fred Niblo; *Seven Keys to Baldpate* (Monte Luke, Dorothy Brunton); *Within the Law* (Monte Luke, Muriel Starr). In 1917 J.C.W. Films produced *The Grey Glove* and *The Jungle Woman.*

Between 1914 and 1918 patriotic films were the thing: *Australia at War, Hero of the Dardanelles, Anzac V.C.s, Murphy of Anzac, Australia Prepared, Australia's Peril* (Franklyn Barrett, 1917) with John de Lacey, Ronald Conway, Charles Beetham, and *How We Beat the "Emden",* with Charles Villiers, Gwen Day Burroughs, and Alma Phillips.

Among the more conspicuous stars of the silents were Yvonne Pavis (*Circumstance,* with Carlton Max and Cane Arthur; *A Daughter of Australia,* with Gilbert Emery and Charles Villiers; *Sunshine Sally,* with John Cosgrove and Dinks Patterson); Annette Kellerman (*Venus of the South Seas,* with Robert Puride); Thelma Newling (*The Reverend Dell's Secret,* with Rex Simpson, Bill Shepherd; *Should a Doctor Tell?,* with Fred Oppey and Anne Parsons); Dorothy Hawtree (*Lust For Gold,* with Gilbert Emery, Charles Villiers; *Boy of the Dardanelles,* with Catherine Tearle, Charles Villiers); Claude Dampier (*The Adventures of Algy, Hello Marmaduke*); Phyllis du Barry (*Sunrise*); Billie Sim (*Tall Timbers*); Arthur Tauchert (*Joe; The Adorable Outcast,* with Edmund Burns, Edith Roberts, Walter Long; *The Digger Earl,* with Gordon Collingridge; *Odds On,* with Phyllis Gibbs and Check Hayes); John F. Gavin (*For the*

Term of Her Natural Life, with Ethel Bashford; *The Murder of Captain Fryatt*, with Harrington Reynolds, Kenneth Farrell, Olive Proctor; *The Key of Fate*); Tal Ordell (*The Man from Snowy River*, with Cyril McKay, John Cosgrove; *Silks and Saddles*, with Brownie Vernon, "Kennaquhar", Charles Lawrence; *Rudd's New Selection*, with Lottie Lyall, J. P. O'Neil; *The Kid Stakes*, with Charles Roberts, Ray Salmon; *The Gentleman Bushranger*, with Dot McConville, John Cosgrove); Charles Villiers (*A Cooee from Home*, with Gertrude Darley, Bryce Rowe; *A Daughter of the East*, with Paul Eden, Dorothy Hawtree; *The Loyal Rebel*, with Reynolds Dennison, Leslie Victor); Godfrey Cass (*The Kelly Gang*, 1919, with Claude Turton; *The Hordern Mystery*, with Claude Turton, Thomas Sinclair, Beatrice George, Beatrice Hamilton, Floris St George, Flo Little; *The Rushing Tide*, with Betty D'Arvall, Norman Lee, Eardley Turner); Nellie Bramley (*The Bells*, with Arthur Styan); Guy Hastings (*Will They Never Come?*); Sara Allgood (*Just Peggy*); Tien Hogue (*Robbery Under Arms*, 1920, with Kenneth Brampton, Hilda Dorrington); Ivy Schilling (*The Blue Mountains Mystery*, with Marjorie Osborne, Billy Williams); Marie Lorraine (*Those Who Love*, with Kath Trefle, Charles Beetham); Zillah Bateman (*Caught in the Net*, with John Mayer, Charles Brown); Vera James (*A Girl of the Bush; Know Thy Child*, with Lotus Thompson, Ronald Conway, Nada Conrade); Rawdon Blandford (*Painted Daughters*, with Nina Devitt, Martin Walker; *The Bush Whackers*, 1925, with Lottie Lyall, George Chalmers); and Percy Marmont and Maud Fane in *The Monk and the Woman*, by Franklyn Barrett and Monte Luke.

Beaumont Smith concentrated on the Hayseeds series: *Our Friends the Hayseeds* (Roy Redgrave, Margaret Gordon, Walter Cornock); *The Hayseeds Come to Sydney; The Hayseeds' Backblocks Show; The Hayseeds' Melbourne Cup; Prehistoric Hayseeds* (Hector St Clair, Gordon Collingridge), and *Townies and Hayseeds* (Harold Parkes, Lotus Thompson).

Other silent Australian films were *Whaling in Jervis Bay, Percy's First Holiday, The Rebel (Allen Doone), My Partner, The Bishop's Silence, The Angel of His Dreams* (Ada Guildford, H. Twitcham, J. Stanford), *The Woman in the Case, The Life Story of John Lee, The Cornstalks, Satan in Sydney, Coming Home, Women and Gold, The Shirker's Son, Dad Becomes a Granddad, East Lynne* (Charles Hardy), *Riding to Win, Gambler's Gold, The Diamond Cross, High Heels, Mated in the Wilds* (Elsa Grainger), *The Golden Flame, Retribution, Should Girls Kiss Soldiers, The Fortunes of Christina McNab, Sweet and Twenty, A Newcastle Nut* (William Faith), *The Triumph of Love* (Jack Chalmers), *A Rough Passage* (Stella Southern, Elsa Grainger, Harryford Hobbs), *When the Kellys Were Out, Dope* (Gordon Collingridge), *The Pioneers* (1925, Gus Neville, George Chalmers), *Those Terrible Twins* (Ray Griffin as Ginger Meggs), *My Partner, Should a Girl Propose?, The Hills of Hate* (Dorothy Gordon, Gordon Collingridge, Bill Wilson), *The Unsleeping Eye, The Sealed Room* (George Bryant, Nellie Ferguson, Grace Savieri), *Environment, The Price* (Mary Mallon), *The Man Who Forgot, The Men Tamers, The Menace* (Perle Osborne, William G. Carter, C. Lamara), *The Miner's Daughter, The Northbound Limited* (George Palmer, Thelma Nelson, Robert Williams), *Hounds of the Deep* (Jamieson Thomas, E. B. Williams, George Hastings), *The Exploits of the "Emden", Trooper O'Brien,* and *Trobriana* (Elza Stenning, Albert Potter, Stanley Murdoch).

Silent films stuck closely to several well-fingered recipes —convicts, bushrangers, sinful priests, the outback, good-versus-evil—but the crudities, artlessnesses, and vulgarities had a home-grown sincerity. Films after World War II, despite overseas backing and meretricious direction, were no more sophisticated in subject or treatment. They did lack the clumsy local *élan.*

The merry-go-round of film production before the Great War was lively. The mainspring ran down when the American industry grew mammoth overnight. The merry-go-round faltered almost to a stop, and with it some of the hopes of Australian players. Emigration of talent revived. Although the loss of so many players cannot be wholly blamed on to Australian conditions, the list of gifted *émigrés* is nevertheless longer than an arm. If not an indictment it is, at least, an indication that Australia's "progress" is lopsided.

Dame Judith Anderson, of the numerous players who deserted a land of diminishing opportunities, is an outstanding expatriate.

Judith Anderson was born Frances Margaret Anderson-Anderson, in Adelaide, on February 10, 1898. Her early career was the usual one of stage-struck young women. She took lessons in voice production and dramatic art from Lawrence Campbell and, as Francee Anderson, played *ingénues* in Sydney amateur productions. Her work caught the eye of Julius Knight, and she made her professional début with him, in 1915, at seventeen, as Stephanie in *A Royal Divorce*, at the Theatre Royal, Sydney. On June 10, 1916, she appeared at the same theatre with Julius Knight and Lizette Parkes in *The Silver King*, and was favourably received. Thus fortified, and with several more parts behind her, she then most cold-bloodedly broke the pattern usual to even exquisitely beautiful, intelligent, and gifted young actresses.

Zora Cross, a perceptive drama critic, in the *Lone Hand* of February 1, 1918, wrote:

"It is not so long ago since Francee Anderson, the pretty *ingénue* with J. and N. Tait's, was a promising Sydney amateur. Then she played bits here and there, until her charm and ability made Julius Knight single her out for special instruction. Graceful, dainty, and pink with youth, she made much progress, and now the Taits have secured her for permanent use. Under the watchful eye of Gaston

Mervale she is still improving, and though lengthy parts do not often come her way, a keen observer can see that she is ready and competent enough for them."

The next sentence reveals the confidence of the twenty-year-old Francee Anderson. "She was", continued Miss Cross, "to appear in *Turn to the Right* but has left for U.S.A."

With the world still being macerated by the Great War, and women, particularly in an essentially puritanical Australia, still subject to social condemnation for behaviour of a too independent and forceful sort before the age of twenty-one, Judith Anderson had packed her suitcases and dress-baskets, and sailed for America. She could hardly have foreseen that she would live from those suitcases for years.

Her intentions were clear-cut, and fearless. They were, indeed, almost callous because, although gifted and shrewd, she was not beautiful, especially in that era when stages were crowded with really radiantly beautiful women. Her nose was long and not straight, her eyes were small. Aware of these imperfections, she nevertheless attempted to interest the American producer, David Belasco. Her attempt, and succeeding attempts, failed.

Judith Anderson had very little money. Of the ensuing fight for survival, she says, "I paid a big price in those months of poverty and despair."

When she returned to Australia in January 1927, as leading lady in *Cobra, Tea for Three*, and *The Green Hat*, hard-boiled and famous, she was not thirty. She had made her American début in 1918, at the old Fourteenth Street Theatre, New York. Once again, this highly charged and indomitable young woman had taken a first step in considered expatriatism: David Belasco's flat rejection of her abilities, and her hopes of an overseas career, had not sent her running for cover back to Australia. She had assessed fairly accurately that in her native land her particular talents would have only the most limited field, if any at all. Refusal did not turn her thoughts in the direction of the Mecca of

129

more conventionally ambitious actresses of the British Empire—London. New York was her choice. America's initial rejection did nothing to change that choice. Once the first step was made, she was willing to toil on in minor theatres, and undergo the fatigues of widely scattered tours —in 1920 she was touring with *Dear Brutus*—until given the opportunity to take a second step upward.

It was not until 1924 that, after thousands of miles of touring, and a succession of parts which did not reveal her gifts, she was cast in the important rôle of Elise van Zile in *Cobra*. She was an instant success. The critics were unanimous in praise. Of the producers who now sued for her services the most important and powerful was David Belasco, whose passion for realism was so great that he once used a huge linotype machine as part of a stage setting. Judith Anderson accepted the lead in Belasco's production of *The Dove*.

In a newspaper interview in 1924, Judith Anderson said what only the most intellectually brazen of women can front up to: "I wish I had a beautiful face. An ugly woman has to work doubly hard." One sees behind these words the complete acceptance of a brutal fact, that in the world of theatre the shape of a woman's nose, and a prominent mole on her chin, can make the sale of even the most overwhelming ability "doubly hard". Olive Wilton, in discussing her own earlier career, said the obverse of this, and proved the same thing. "I had long red-gold hair, masses of it. I only mention this as I rather fear that it was this feature that accounted for so much of my good luck in the early stages of my career."

Judith Anderson went on to say: "There are so many strange, alluring, hateful, lovable, weird, tender women of history, and of life, every one of them ugly. I want to delineate them all. I want to portray the unfolding of one woman's entire life, with the whole gamut of emotions run through. I love emotional rôles. Lady Macbeth is my favourite part, and I should like to play it."

Thus, at the age of twenty-six, Judith Anderson revealed the trend of her ambitions. She was prophetic to an extraordinary degree. As her prophecies—or, rather, prophetic wishes—came true, audiences were subject to the mesmeric one of the many Anderson gifts. She played a number of larger-than-life women: she herself is slight and small, five feet four inches tall, with blue eyes, and walnut brown hair. She admits "a great talent for gaiety", yet she was able to create the impression of creatures volted with doom, the she-monsters of legend and classic literature. She had expressed a wish to play Lady Macbeth. In 1941 she played Lady Macbeth to Maurice Evans's Macbeth in his Broadway production. She had expressed her love of emotional rôles, and her hope of delineating unusual women. She was ultimately to play Medea, Hamlet's mother, Queen Gertrude, Christine in *Mourning Becomes Electra*, Herodias, and Big Mamma.

After Belasco's production of *The Dove*, Judith Anderson was sought after to star in a number of productions, including *The Green Hat, Strange Interlude, As You Desire Me, The Mask and the Face, The Female of the Species*, and *The Old Maid.*

In 1937 she played Queen Gertrude to John Gielgud's Hamlet, and Lilian Gish's Ophelia, in Guthrie McClintic's production of *Hamlet*. It was in this same year she married Benjamin Harrison Lehman, a professor of the University of California. The marriage lasted two years only. In 1939 she and Professor Lehman were divorced.

In 1940, almost a quarter of a century after being turned down by Belasco, she played the sinister housekeeper, Mrs Danvers, in United Artists' film of Daphne du Maurier's *Rebecca*. This led to a seven-year contract with Metro-Goldwyn-Mayer. At long last, Judith Anderson was able, as she put it, "to stop living out of suitcases, and to buy a ranch-house in California". By this she meant that the nomadic life of even an actress of her quality had reached a point where she could afford to have a *pied-à-terre*, and to play parts, or go on tours, to work in Hollywood or on Broadway, only when she had an inclination to.

Some of her parts, which were interlarded with television appearances, were: the Schoolteacher in *Forty Little Mothers*, with Eddie Cantor (Metro-Goldwyn-Mayer, 1940); the cruel aunt in *The Strange Love of Martha Ivers* (Paramount, 1946); Herodias in *Salome* (Columbia, 1953) and Big Mamma in Tennessee Williams's *Cat on a Hot Tin Roof*, with Elizabeth Taylor and Burl Ives (Metro-Goldwyn-Mayer, 1958). In 1948 she received the Donaldson Award for "the most distinguished actress in the American theatre", and in July 1960 became Dame Commander of the Most Excellent Order of the British Empire, an honour bestowed by Queen Elizabeth II.

The part which will always be associated with Dame Judith's name is that of the tortured but implacably ruthless Medea, in which she reached the height of her special powers. She toured with this play, an American translation of Euripides by Robinson Jeffers far inferior to, and "easier" to the public than, the translation by Gilbert Murray, another long-time expatriate of Australia.

On July 11, 1946, Judith Anderson married again. Her second husband was Luther Greene, a theatrical producer. Her hobbies are simpler than might be expected from a bloodstained Medea, but are perfectly suitable to a "dainty" woman with a "talent for gaiety". Dame Judith says she likes poetry, music, antiques and dachshunds, and, on the outdoor side, gardening, horse-riding and tennis.

This skeleton account of Dame Judith's career is included because she was born in Australia. The question could arise: should she have been included? The Great War was still on when she left Australia to strive and attain, and to settle, in America. Her professional trips to Australia have been fleeting, the earliest as the star-crossed heroine of *The Green Hat* in 1927, a part that morally outraged the critics; the latest, nearly forty years later, with her world-acclaimed rendition of Medea which drew only those educated in reputable theatre, those wishing to be educated, and the culture vultures keeping up with the highbrow Joneses. It made no ripple on the consciousness of a general public to whom even disreputable theatre now takes second place to the sordid convenience of drive-ins, and the nightly non-experience of television.

Judith Anderson's appearances outside America, in London, in Canada, with the Old Vic Company in *The Sea-gull*, have been no more than stop-overs. She has always boomeranged back to America, where she has lived for two-thirds of her life. Is Australia, then, really justified in proudly claiming her? The question is posed to indicate one of the problems of this work.

There are those who were born in Australia, and went away, and stayed away to earn a greater or lesser fame, and of whom Australia is nationally proud. Oscar Asche, Dame Judith Anderson, and Coral Browne are but three examples.

There are those who were born overseas, left for Australia, and remained to earn what clipped and bitter-sweet fame can be earned there, and to whom Australia should be grateful. Coppin, Maggie Moore, and Olive Wilton are among those who seemed content with the relative deep peace of a colonial fame rather than the hurly-burly of a larger one.

There are those born outside Australia—Peter Finch, for example—who spent some years in Australia, but left it to make reputations they could only experiment with making in Australia.

To make a total of facts indicative of how "Australian" an actor or actress is, required a rough-and-ready account-ancy, and the composition of a pretty all-embracing jigsaw. Through the cracks in this, many players, alas, have slipped out of sight. Their accomplishments were too momentary to leave on record any more than a name and a shopsoiled adjective, spoor too faint to follow.

There are, however, a number of players born in Dame Judith's century, during the 1880s and 1890s, whose careers can, at least, be outlined.

Leon Errol was, like O. P. Heggie, May Robson, Errol Flynn, Louise Lovely, Clyde Cook, Enid Bennett, and Mae Busch (who was born in Melbourne on January 20, 1897), an Australian whose major fame was as a film star in American films.

During the later silent-film era, and the early talkie one, Leon Errol was a film comedian. He did not gain the reputation of his contemporary and brother Australian, Clyde Cook, but did have a laconic and inimitable style of his own. His career, ante-Hollywood, was in musical comedies and revues and extravaganzas; his film career was restricted to small but hilarious portrayals.

Leon Errol, born in Sydney on July 3, 1881, was educated at St Joseph's College. After matriculating, he began to study medicine at the Sydney University. A first stage appearance, at fifteen, at the Standard Theatre, Sydney, was, however, the truer indication of the direction of his yearnings. Abandoning the study of medicine, he played with various stock companies and for J. C. Williamson's in drama, comic opera, and musical comedy.

His first American appearance was at the Jardin de Paris, on June 20, 1910, in *The Ziegfeld Follies of 1910.* He appeared in successive Follies during the years 1911 to 1915.

He made his first London appearance on March 25, 1919, in the musical comedy *Joy Bells*.

Alice Crawford was born in Australia on January 5, 1882, and had early training under Wilson Barrett, in 1901 and 1902. After touring Australia, she went with the Wilson

Barrett Company to England, making her London début at the Adelphi Theatre, on December 18, 1902, as Marget in *The Christian King*. She toured extensively with Barrett's company in a variety of supporting rôles. Her first outstanding triumph, in May 1905, was at the Haymarket Theatre, London, as Josephine in *The Creole*. She created the rôle of Glory Quayle in *The Christian*.

Her notably pure diction, and the ability to depict womanly tenderness without distorting that quality to something dubiously weak and over-emotional, inclined her to give her best performances as Shakespearian heroines of the less alarming kind. On her return to Australia in 1907, for the Shakespeare Festival at Her Majesty's Theatre, Melbourne, she gave flawless portrayals of Miranda in *The Tempest*, Ursula in *Much Ado About Nothing*, Olivia in *Twelfth Night*, and Calpurnia in *Julius Caesar*.

Although thoroughly at home playing supporting rôles in here-today-and-gone-tomorrow dramas and comedies, she is most worthy of record as a tall and stately Shakespearian actress of great delicacy.

Australia produced a number of more versatile and spirited Shakespearian actresses, but Alice Crawford has her niche among them.

Later, she worked with Sir Herbert Tree, and toured England, the Continent, and America supporting him in such parts as Jessica in *The Merchant of Venice*, Emilia in *Othello*, and Mistress Ford in *The Merry Wives of Windsor*.

Claude Flemming had a public career of nearly fifty years.

He was born on a farm near Camden, New South Wales, on February 22, 1884, and was educated at St Mary's High School, Sydney. His first job was as a boundary rider, but he was early attracted to a stage career, not only as a means of self-expression but also as providing a way to see the world.

At nineteen he met George Rignold, the Shakespearian

actor-manager, at the Civic Club in Sydney, and expressed his ambitions. Handsome George was shrewdly persuasive—by putting up £200, Claude Flemming found himself a member of Rignold's company which, at the time, was on tour. Flemming made his début, at the Theatre Royal, Perth, in 1903 as the Dauphin in *Henry the Fifth*. For £3 10s. a week, he ran the gamut of supporting parts in Rignold's repertoire which, time and again, included *Henry the Fifth*, the play that Rignold was continually reviving because he fancied himself as Henry.

By 1906 Flemming was playing Rollins with Nellie Stewart in *Sweet Nell of Old Drury*, in America. This was the ill-fated tour of the San Francisco earthquake. On September 20, 1906, he appeared as Major Blatherwaite in *My Lady's Maid*, at the Casino Theatre, New York.

His first appearances in England were made on tour with the Beerbohm Tree Company. He also appeared as Taffy in an English film of *Trilby* in 1907; and as Mr Crisparkle in *The Mystery of Edwin Drood*, which was launched at His Majesty's Theatre, London, on January 4, 1908.

At this point in his career Claude Flemming switched to opera and musical comedy, playing at Covent Garden and the Savoy Theatre, *Die Meistersinger, The Angelus*, and *The Mountaineers*. During 1911 and 1912 he toured England; and played in New York, with Michael Faraday's Opera Company, as Massakroff in *The Chocolate Soldier*, the comic opera derived from George Bernard Shaw's *Arms and the Man*—and, according to Shaw, plagiarized. Since Shaw was viper-eyed, and hard as nails in business, this statement was certainly a gimmick. Theatrical advertising was gimmick-riddled.

Flemming, for example, was advertised on the American playbills of *Sweet Nell of Old Drury* in 1906 as an "imported English actor". The public is not only gullible, it is perverse, and prefers its players to be some sort of foreign. When Coppin gave his Benefit in London for

Crimean soldiers, he billed himself as "the celebrated Australasian comedian". Minnie Tittell Brune, the dashing American actress, after several seasons in Sydney, Melbourne, and Adelaide, had herself announced in London as an Australian. This beautiful creature's most applauded performance in Australia, in 1905, was in *L'Aiglon*.

Claude Flemming played the Grand Duke Boris in *Love and Laughter*, at the Lyric Theatre, London, in 1913. He returned to America, in 1914, as Frank Smith in *Pretty Mrs Smith*, at the Casino Theatre, New York. He had played in one English film, *Trilby*, but now spent several years playing Galahadian heroes, clean-shaven, forthright, downright and upright, in Hollywood. His first important part was opposite Alice Brady in her last film, *The Lure of Woman*, in 1914.

In 1917 he returned to England as Baldasarre in *The Maid of the Mountains*. For the next several years he moved between England and Australia, appearing in his home country, in 1919, in *My Lady Frayle, The Officers' Mess*, and *As You Were*. In 1920 he was at Daly's Theatre, London, as Sir Willoughby Rawdon in *A Southern Maid*, but in 1921 was back in Australia where, until 1924, he played in *A Southern Maid, The Firefly, The Cousin from Nowhere*, and as the Grand Duke Constant in *Sybil*, with Gladys Moncrieff.

Side by side with his stage work, Claude Flemming was also producing films. His longest film was £500 *Reward*, with snow scenes filmed at Mount Kosciusko, and starring Renée Adorée, who was later to become world-famous as Mélisande, the French village girl, opposite John Gilbert, in *The Big Parade*.

He continued to appear with Gladys Moncrieff—as Baron von Schober in *Lilac Time*, and the artist, Armand, in *The Street Singer*.

Claude Flemming was almost the first man to realize the educational-cum-entertainment possibilities of the

travelogue, and especially the travelogue in colour. He was a
pioneer in the medium that Fitzpatrick, years later, and in
thickly syruped sound, was to exploit so slickly.

Flemming's travelogues led him into curious adventures in
Honolulu, Bavaria and the Bavarian Alps, Morocco, and
Algeria. The most disturbing adventure was when he had to
arrange for an escort from the Foreign Legion to protect
him from the Berbers as he travelled through the Atlas
Mountains.

He retained his fine figure, good looks, and pleasant voice,
and continued to make stage appearances almost to the last;
he played Buffalo Bill throughout the three-year season of
Annie Get Your Gun, with Evie Hayes.

In the same year as Flemming, 1884, Reginald Leslie
Baker was born on February 8, in Sydney. Ultimately, as
Snowy Baker, he was to make as satisfactory a he-man film
hero as other athletes—Johnny Mack Brown, Maxie Bauer,
Babe Ruth, Johnny Weissmuller, Louis Wolheim, and Jack
Dempsey—made in their day.

Baker was educated at Crown Street School and, later, in
engineering, at the Sydney University, where he was awarded
Blues for cricket, football, athletics, and rowing. This
abundance was not remarkable for Snowy Baker, who had
been athletically exceptional from boyhood, All-Schools
Athletic Champion in 1898, and was to excel in nineteen
different sports.

At thirteen he was open swimming champion of New
South Wales; at fifteen played half-back in Rugby Union
football for New South Wales; at sixteen represented Australia against England in Rugby Union; at seventeen became
middleweight boxing champion of New South Wales; at
eighteen, in one night, won both the middle and heavy-
weight boxing championships of Australia. He rowed in
four championship eights in two years; was a member of the
undefeated Australian polo team (1903-1906), and was still

active enough in 1943 to lead a Californian polo team to victory. Tent-pegging, tilting, jumping, fencing, steeplechasing, swimming, diving, wrestling were among his endowments. He bought out Hugh D. McIntosh, who had built the Sydney Stadium for the Burns-Squires fight (1908), and opened stadiums in four other States. These he sold to John Wren, who formed Stadiums Limited in 1914.

Baker ran a physical culture school, published a sports magazine, and wrote a book on athletics. In 1918, the idol of the public, he was at the height of his huskiness. E. J. Carroll invested in the thirty-four-year-old athletic marvel, and featured him in two 1918 films, *The Enemy Within*, with Lilly Molloy, and *The Lure of the Bush*, with Rita Tress. Francis Birtles's *Through Australian Wilds* was an outstanding travel film in the same year. In 1919 Baker again appeared as simple hero of a simple film for simple people in *Man From Kangaroo*, with Brownie Vernon and Malcolm McKellar. *Does the Jazz Lead to Destruction?* starring Ethel Bennett and George Irving was another 1919 film of some provocativeness. In 1920 he made two more films: *The Jackeroo of Coolabong*, with Kathleen Key, Bernice Vere, and Arthur Tauchert; and *The Shadow of Lightning Ridge*, with Brownie Vernon and Veronice Vaire. Beaumont Smith's *The Betrayer* (Bernice Vere, Stella Southern, Marie D'Alton) and Captain Frank Hurley's *In the Grip of the Polar Ice* (the Shackleton Expedition) were two other 1920 films.

In 1923 Baker became manager of the Riviera Polo Club, Santa Monica, California. For the next thirty years, apart from one visit to Australia in 1952, a year before his death, he lived in America, although he never lost his head enough to become an American citizen.

At Santa Monica he taught the arts of horsemanship, polo, and boomerang-throwing to wealthy Americans and film stars. In the gold-plated film era he taught Rudolph Valentino the showier tricks of horse-riding for *The Sheikh*, and guided Douglas Fairbanks through the intricacies of whip-cracking for *Don Q., Son of Zorro*. Baker, who died in Los Angeles on December 2, 1953, was popular with film stars, one of his closest friends being Harold Lloyd.

Mayne Lynton, born in Bowness, Cumberland, England, on May 4, 1885, was sent to Glasgow to be educated. Returning to Bowness and his parents' farm, he found himself reluctant to take up rural life. He was repulsed by such chores as pulling frosty turnips in the winter fields. He therefore went back to Glasgow, where he took odd jobs, and badgered theatre managers. His persistence persuaded R. C. Buchanan (father of the musical comedy star Jack Buchanan) to give him a small part in *Rob Roy* with his touring company. Throughout 1905 and 1906 he played in such works as *The Manxman*, and a number of melodramas.

In 1906 he had a successful audition for the Benson Shakespearian Company. On tour with them he played anything and everything in the repertoire. By 1907 he was in London, from which headquarters he went on tours with this or that company. Walter Melville's Company was the type, presenting such gaudy works as *The Sign of the Cross* and *The Man in the Iron Mask*, and melodramas, including *The Route of Her Ruin*—a title mercifully changed to *Her Road to Ruin*.

Before 1912 Mayne Lynton was in America. Until 1914 and the beginning of the Great War he had experience in various fields of entertainment. This experience embraced parts with Douglas Fairbanks *père* in *Hawthorn of the U.S.A.*; with George Arliss in *Disraeli* and *Inside the Lines*; Shakespearian tours with the Ben Greet Company, and the Sothern-Marlow Company; film appearances with Mary Pickford and Marguerite Clark; and a tour of the entire United States of America as a lecturer, the subject being *Scott of the Antarctic*, illustrated by lantern slides.

The war began. Despite a foot injury—he had been

kicked by a farm horse in his youth—he became a lieutenant with the British Military Mission in Toronto, Canada. Later, he transferred to British Military Control (Security) in New York.

The war over, he worked for David Belasco in *Aphrodite*, a spectacular production in the Belasco manner, at the vast Century Theatre in New York. Dorothy Dalton, a silent film celebrity, was the star.

In 1920, while on tour with George M. Cohan's *Genius and the Crowd*, he met his future wife, Nancye Stewart, daughter of Nellie Stewart, and also a member of the cast. George M. Cohan, after triumphant years as the emperor of farces and musical comedies, had given way to a hankering to add an "artistic and serious work" to his more florid successes. *Genius and the Crowd* failed when it was presented in New York.

After touring America with Walker Whiteside in a dramatization of Robert Louis Stevenson's *The Master of Ballantrae*, Mayne Lynton came to Australia with a J.C.W.'s contract which, now hot, now cool, lasted for nearly thirty years. In the palmier theatrical days, a rôle in a successful play usually meant an engagement for a solid year because, after a play was launched in one city, it toured other cities and provincial centres.

From 1922 Mayne Lynton played leading rôles or starred in numberless productions of which the following are merely some: Mary Roberts Rinehart's *The Bat; The Cat and the Canary; Bluebeard's Eighth Wife*, with Lady Forbes Robertson; *Spring Cleaning*, with Pauline Frederick; *The Silver King*, in which he played the Spider; *Seventh Heaven; Monsieur Beaucaire*; a succession of parts with Muriel Starr and Emilie Polini. He appeared in two musical comedies, *Balalaika*, and a revival of *The Arcadians*. In 1926 he appeared in *For the Term of His Natural Life* (Australasian Films), a more ambitious version than Osborne and Jerden's 1907 production, Cozens Spencer's 1910 one (titled

141

Rufus Dawes), or John F. Gavin's one in 1917. In 1933 Mayne Lynton played in Charles Chauvel's talking picture *In the Wake of the "Bounty"*, which, distributed by Universal, launched Errol Flynn.

Mayne Lynton and Nancye Stewart were both pioneer broadcasters. They broadcast from the first Sydney studio, a padded room on the top floor of the *Smith's Weekly* building in Phillip Street. As broadcasting developed he became producer for the A.B.C., Melbourne, in 1936 and, after that, until 1942, for 3XY, Melbourne.

It was during the 1930s that Mayne Lynton recorded for Oswald Anderson *The Happy Prince*, and *The Ballad of Reading Gaol* by Oscar Wilde, and *The Widow in Bye Street* and *The Everlasting Mercy* by John Masefield. The latter three of these had a meticulously synchronized musical background (Rachmaninoff) played by Nancye Stewart.

From 1947 to 1949 Lynton presented Shakespearian matinées at the Theatre Royal, Sydney, of *Twelfth Night*, *The Tempest*, *As You Like It*, *Julius Caesar*, and *The Merchant of Venice*.

In 1949 he played in Tyrone Guthrie's production of *The Three Estates*, which opened the Edinburgh Festival of that year. He remained in England with such long-run plays as *Ring Around the Moon* (Globe Theatre, London), *Call Me Madam* (Coliseum, London), and *The Big Knife*. He played in TV plays for the B.B.C., and in several films, including Alfred Hitchcock's *The Man Who Knew Too Much*.

He returned to Australia in 1955, ill-health preventing him from making appearances.

Many Australian players—the finest as well as the shoddiest —have sought and found overseas fame. A rare few have found it in their own country. Most gifted of these home-keeping stars is Lorna Forbes.

Lorna (Ada) Forbes, who was born in Melbourne on

February 1, 1886, was educated at the Methodist Ladies' College. Her grandmother was an actress, Carrie George; her father, Wilson Forbes, was actor-producer for Meynell and Gunn, entrepreneurs in competition with J. C. Williamson's. Her mother, Ada Lawrence, was a delightful actress who is particularly remembered in Australian theatrical legends for unflinchingly playing out a show after having been thrown from horseback into the orchestra pit.

Lorna Forbes learnt Shakespeare at her father's knee, and her ambition from childhood was not only the understandable and foreseeable one of being an actress, but the more burning desire to act in Shakespeare. Her early training, she says, was gained from watching her parents rehearse, and was altogether orthodox. As did the other sons and daughters of hard-working theatrical families of the period, she played Little Willie in *East Lynne*. This, for Lorna Forbes, was at the age of five. Her first really professional part, at the age of fifteen, was in a Meynell and Gunn production of *Two Little Sailor Boys*. In the same cast were Maisie Maxwell, and a five-year-old girl, Louise Carbasse who, as Louise Lovely, was to become one of the beautiful film stars of the silent screen.

In 1903, Lorna Forbes went on the company's payroll as an understudy. Her first call came from Ballarat, where the company, on tour, was giving a season. Arthur Levy, the Theatre Royal manager, sent a telegram to Mrs Forbes (Ada Lawrence) asking that her seventeen-year-old daughter take the next train to Ballarat to replace the "heavy" (the villainess), Lilian Meyers, who had fallen sick. Mrs Forbes put Lorna on the train with a bag of sweets. The adventure of being a dyed-in-the-wool professional began. The train arrived at Ballarat a quarter of an hour before the curtain rose. Gilbert Emery met Lorna Forbes with a cab. They raced to the theatre.

Lorna Forbes vividly recalls that, being slender, she had to be enlarged with Turkish towels by the wardrobe mistress,

Mrs Robins (later famous and perennial as wardrobe mistress for J. C. Williamson's), to fit the villainess's costume: Lilian Meyers was "a big woman". Lorna Forbes's first scene was one in which she rifled a safe, at the same time speaking a long monologue. She had not studied the script at all, but had seen several performances during the Melbourne season. The possession of a photographic memory for lines and stage-moves was her surety. At the play's end, she remembers, she was carried in triumph to her dressing-room by Conway Wingfield, Jimmy Lyndsay, and Harcourt Beatty, actors thrilled by, and grateful for, her trouper-like perfection.

Lorna Forbes cannot recall the name of the play. This is less unusual than one might have thought. In interviewing, personally or by post, the players of an earlier generation, it has been surprising to find that they have, almost one and all, kept few or no records of past successes—no programmes, handbills, or newspaper cuttings. The reasons for this seeming indifference appear to be largely practical: the rootlessness of their lives; the endless journeying over Australia, Tasmania, and New Zealand; the limited space for hoarding when one lives out of dress-baskets, hat-boxes, and portmanteaux; the blurring of factual memory when one plays hundreds of parts throughout the years. Usually, the more intelligent and famous the player, the fewer printed records of a coruscating past were kept. Actors kept far more records than actresses. What all recalled, much more clearly than the when-and-where of their performances, were the amusing accidents, the alarming misfortunes, the human distresses and exhilarations.

Lorna Forbes married Frederick Chapman on October 14, 1906. Her own account of what led to the marriage is charmingly truthful: "Frederick Chapman, whose record in the musical world is as long as mine in the world of acting, was conducting the orchestra at the Criterion Theatre, Sydney, for a Matheson Lang season. I was playing Nancy, in a play like *The Manxman* . . . I forget the name for the

144

Lily Brayton   *Janet Achurch in "The Doll's House"*

Julius Knight in   *Robert Brough*
"Resurrection"

moment! . . . I looked across the footlights, and loved."
Other great actresses who looked across the footlights at the
gentleman in the orchestra, and loved, and married, were
Eliza Winstanley (and her Mr O'Flaherty), and Nellie
Stewart's mother (and her Mr Guerin).

After her début in 1901, Lorna Forbes played hundreds
of parts; toured wide and far; and underwent all the
trouper vicissitudes, and some additional ones: an earthquake in New Zealand; a near-shipwreck in the S.S.
Westralia; a fire next door to the Theatre Royal, Hobart,
with flames licking through the auditorium windows during
a performance of *The Tempest*. In the age of elaborate
productions of plays set in Australia, Lorna Forbes—as did
many a leading lady—was often required to ride a horse on
to a stage encumbered with "local colour", embowered in
nose-tickling eucalypts, and made perilous for an actress-
horsewoman by the explosions of bushranger pistols, or
the screams ("Hello! Cockie wants a drink!") of an ad-
libbing cockatoo introduced to give further verisimilitude to
a scene already containing dogs and sheep.

Lorna Forbes succinctly sums up this period: "After Ballarat, we did a season at the Palace Theatre, Sydney. The
company's last bill was *A Miner's Trust*, in which I played
the juvenile lead, a blind girl . . . and after that, I played
in hundreds—oh, *countless*—other melodramas in every
theatre in Australia."

She did not attain her most cherished ambition until, "I
was appearing with Frank Harvey and Ethel Warwick, at
the Theatre Royal, Melbourne, in *Joseph and his Brethren*,
when the magic I had always believed in came true. . . ." The
magic? She was invited to join the Allan Wilkie Company.
Her first part was Queen Elizabeth in *Richard the Third*.

There have been those, audience and critics, who, while
lauding the presence of a Shakespearian company in the
relative theatrical Sahara of the time, were irritated by the
mannerisms and spit-spraying rantings of Wilkie, and the

Grace Palotta in "Floradora"   *Florence Trevelyan*

Theatre Royal, Melbourne—last night, September 3, 1904
K

"fried-fish" attack of Frediswyde Hunter-Watts. Not once, by audience or critic, was Lorna Forbes traduced. Review after review contained nothing but enthusiasm. Hector Bolitho, who was then editor of the *Shakespearean Quarterly*, stated the view of all who found her work the best in the company:

> She has a womanliness about her work. It is art with the fine thread of human understanding woven into the fabric. Her Olivia in *Twelfth Night* is the richest thing in the production. I saw her nine or ten times as Mistress Page in *The Merry Wives of Windsor*— a performance of great delight.

Words recurring over the years in reference to her playing of almost all of Shakespeare's infinitely varied women are *intelligent, womanly, delightful, subtle, joyous,* and *flawless.* Frequently enough, the more acute critics have made remarks that echo the sentiments of the critic who wrote: "The natural appreciation which went to Wilkie, for his fortitude more than his acting, did not overshadow the faultless performances of Miss Forbes." More bluntly, "Miss Forbes, because she follows in the wake of an actor-manager, does not get half the limelight she deserves."

It is a matter for adjustment that Lorna Forbes, with more than sixty years of inspired acting to her credit, has not been honoured, as Wilkie was, or, further, as was Dame Sybil Thorndike, whom she understudied in *The Sleeping Prince* and *Separate Tables.*

No actress on the Australian stage has so impeccably and subtly portrayed the gallery of women as various as Portia and Cleopatra, Jessica and Mistress Page, Olivia and Volumnia, Celia and Katharina, Mariana and Goneril, Lady Macbeth and Juliet's Nurse, Emilia and Calpurnia, Hermia and Paulina.

She appeared also in Allan Wilkie's initial unsuccessful ventures, as, for example, *The Silver King* (May 24, 1919), in which she played Olive Skinner, the villain's wife, with

Tal Ordell as Geoffrey Ware. This recurring money-spinner, in October 1883, at the Theatre Royal, Melbourne, had introduced George Titheradge to Australia, with Arthur Garner of the Triumvirate, and the delicious Marion Dunn (Mrs Marcus Clarke), in the cast.

The break-up of Wilkie's company meant fewer Shakespearian parts for Lorna Forbes, but not fewer parts. She has been constantly in demand, in every possible field, and by people as notable as Sir Ralph Richardson, Fay Compton, and Dame Sybil Thorndike.

A mere selection of her parts indicates her range: Mrs Gladstone in *Victoria Regina*, Medea in *Medea*, Madame Arcati in *Blithe Spirit*, the Hag in *The Vagabond King*, the Maréchal of France in *The Du Barry*, the Duchess in *The Student Prince*, Eulalie McKeckie Shin in *Music Man*, and, in 1962, at the Princess Theatre, Melbourne, Frau Schmidt in *Sound of Music*.

Lorna Forbes, still a vital, immaculate, and adaptable actress, now lives with her husband in a house named *Illyria*, in a Melbourne suburb, and is a dedicated gardener.

She is the last of her theatrical line of five generations. Her only son, Russell Chapman, who was advancing his career on the London stage, joined the Royal Air Force during the Second World War, became a pilot, and failed to return from a raid over enemy territory in 1942.

Arthur Shirley was born on August 31, 1886, in Hobart, Tasmania, of an Irish father and an Australian mother of English parentage, and was educated at a Roman Catholic private school in his native city.

On leaving school he worked in the dispatch room of Tattersall's (Australia's famous sweepstake); then as junior clerk in a solicitor's office. At sixteen, stagestruck, he joined a semi-professional troupe of entertainers which toured Tasmania in a two-horse caravan.

In 1904 he sailed for Melbourne, hoping to break into

theatre of a more stationary sort. Biding his time, he was door-to-door salesman for a wholesale grocery firm, meantime nourishing his large frame—film posters later billed him as the Big Australian—on the sixpenny meals to be got in 1904 in the restaurants which lined Bourke Street from Swanston Street to Spring Street.

A devout youth, he next became a novice in a Sydney seminary. The lure of the stage proved, however, stronger than that of priesthood. In 1905 he left the seminary, and returned to Melbourne and stage-door-haunting.

His professional début was made in 1905, as a three-line Lord-in-Waiting, with Nellie Stewart in *Sweet Nell of Old Drury*, at the Princess Theatre, Melbourne. He admits himself lucky—the Lord-in-Waiting's Caroline costume and goffered wig perfectly fitted him. After touring with Nellie Stewart until she left for America in 1906, he joined William Anderson's Dramatic Organization in a minuscule part in *The Face at the Window*, at the Theatre Royal, Melbourne. He toured in this.

Throughout 1907 he played progressively larger parts in Bland Holt melodramas such as *The Breaking of the Drought*, *The Ladder of Life*, and *The Worst Woman in London*. In 1908 he was back with Anderson, appearing in *Camille* with Eugènie Duggan (Mrs William Anderson).

During the next two years he toured the backblocks of Victoria and New South Wales as leading man and all-parts-player with the John Cosgrove Company, and similar versatile groups. These companies took in their stride the presentation of, say, *Romeo and Juliet* with half a dozen players. Moreover, to satisfy the outback passion for "er bit er singin' 'n' dancin'" with their Shakespeare, Juliet and the Nurse were capable of singing "'Neath the Shade of the Old Apple Tree"; the Friar could render "Tomorrow will be Friday", and, as encore, "Little Brown Jug"; the entire cast—the men in tights of long underpants dyed—could dance a species of minuet.

In December 1910 Arthur Shirley was back at the Princess Theatre, Melbourne, as Lord Erskine in the George Marlow Company's presentation of *The Bad Girl of the Family*. After touring the provinces this opened on April 5, 1911, with its five acts and seventeen scenes, at "Sydney's Newest Theatre", the Adelphi, later the Grand Opera House, now the Tivoli. He also played, during Marlow's 1911 season, important rôles in works such as *The Girl Who Took the Wrong Turning*, and *Married to the Wrong Man*, with Nellie Ferguson, John O'Neil, George Cross, Frank Neil, and Ethel Buckley (Mrs George Marlow). To close the 1911 season Marlow presented *The Monk and the Woman*, with Nellie Bramley in the lead. Before the opening night, the mere title of this pseudo-historical play in a lavish French-medieval setting had inflamed letters-to-the-editor writers to hysteria. Once presented the play was well received.

In 1912, Arthur Shirley made his screen début, with silvered hair, in the title rôle of Cozens Spencer's sickly opus *The Shepherd of the Southern Cross*, Vera Pearce and Tien Hogue making their screen débuts with him. The film was first shown at the Lyceum Theatre, Sydney. During the same year he starred in another film, *Saved From the Sea*, and played the light comedy part of Plantagenet Fordham opposite Maggie Moore in the musical play, *Mrs McSweeney*, which opened at the Criterion, Sydney, toured Australian provinces, went to the Princess, Melbourne, and returned to the Palace Theatre, Sydney. In 1912-1913 he toured New Zealand with George Marlow's Company, also with George Musgrove and Nellie Stewart. As well, in 1913, he had his first experience of marriage (he was married twice), and his first experience of bankruptcy (he was twice bankrupt).

In 1914 he played in a mediocre film *The Straight and Narrow Path*. He then starred as the noble scapegoat, Dr Everard, in a better film, *The Silence of Dean Maitland*, with Harry Thomas (Dean Maitland), and Lottie Lyall as leading lady assisting Raymond Longford in direction. The film was financed by the Fraser Brothers, importers and distributors of films which were mainly Continental, with a few American. This was an era, soon to pass, in which no American film distributors operated in Australia.

Arthur Shirley joined the newly founded Beaumont Smith Productions playing leads in *The Glad Eye* (with Ethyl Dane), *Who's the Lady?*, and Rex Beach's *The Barrier*. Then, for George Marlow, who had acquired a co-manager, George Willoughby, he played a return season of *The Monk and the Woman*, at the Adelphi Theatre, Sydney, and a second lead in *Mr Wu*, with Cecil Mannering, the English juvenile. At the close of the Sydney run of *Mr Wu* he accepted a better-paid engagement with J.C.W.'s to play in support of Julius Knight at the Theatre Royal, Melbourne. He was engaged by E. J. Tait, The Firm's Sydney manager. Rehearsals began. So did the persecution of angry gods.

George Willoughby, enthroned manager, resentful that Arthur Shirley, mere actor, had not signed a contract to tour New Zealand in *Mr Wu*, served an injunction on The Firm restraining them from continuing to employ Shirley.

It is necessary to recall that no actor then dared be independent. Shirley had dared, and now dared further. He sued Willoughby for crippling his J.C.W. engagement. This defiance of the gods drove the gods together. In court, E. J. Tait, manager, sided with George Willoughby, manager. There was the clearest revelation that managements intended to keep actors suppliant. E. J. Tait denied that he had engaged Shirley. The judge castigated Tait for "deliberate and malicious perjury". Arthur Shirley got five hundred pounds damages, but his career as a stage actor in Australia was over. Even reckless entrepreneurs still outside The Firm's control would not defy The Firm's ukase. In June 1914, on the advice of Lalla Fisher, astute editor of *The Theatre*, Shirley sailed in the *Niagara* for America and Hollywood. He and his wife were living just off Broadway in an hotel behind the Astor Theatre when war broke out on August 4, 1914.

In the still primitive film industry podgy heroines of the Mary Pickford type were fashionable and, to support them, tall heroes with mobile faces. Shirley, over six feet tall, blue-eyed and handsome, filled the bill and played the hero in a series of two-reelers for Kalem Pictures. Ultimately, he appeared for most of the companies then powerful: Universal (as leading man for Mae Murray in *Modern Love* and its successors), Goldwyn (with Bessie Barriscale in a Blue Ridge Mountains series), Ince, Balboa, Triangle, Paramount, and Selig Productions.

He played in *The Valiants of Virginia* with Kathleen Williams; *Branding Broadway* with William S. Hart and Seena Owen; *The Triflers*—"the sparkling drama of a shop-girl with a *crêpe-de-Chine* soul"—with Edith Roberts; and appeared with Lon Chaney, Pauline Bush, Ruth Roland, Alice Joyce, Cleo Ridgeley, and Blanche Sweet. Other Australians were also breaking into films—Colin Tapley, Snub Pollard, Sylvia Breamer, Dorothy Cummings, Enid Bennett, and Louise Lovely who played her first Hollywood part opposite Shirley in Universal's *Stronger than Death*. Perhaps Shirley's most famous part was that of John Vassar, the soldier-politician hero of *The Fall of a Nation*, a 1917 Vitagraph production written by the Rev Mr Thomas Dixon, author of *The Clansmen* from which D. W. Griffith made his masterpiece *The Birth of a Nation*. A special musical score for *The Fall of a Nation* was composed by Victor Herbert. A dramatic photograph of Shirley as John Vassar was used as a patriotic poster in America during the Great War.

Side by side with movie-acting he ran a photography business at 6040 Hollywood Boulevard, and was a pioneer in the use of artificial lighting for portraiture, and three-dimensional rather than painted backgrounds. His portrait of Rudolph Valentino, then a dancing partner to Jean Acker in the Rose Room at the Alexandria Hotel, induced Rex

Ingram to screen-test and star Valentino in *The Four Horsemen of the Apocalypse* for Metropolitan-Mayer, forerunner of Metro-Goldwyn (Mr Goldfisch and Mr Selwyn)-Mayer.

After seven years of Hollywood experience and fame, Shirley returned to Sydney in 1921. He was thirty-five, and anxious to invest his money, talents, and knowledge in film production. He formed a company, Arthur Shirley Productions, and began to direct *The Throwback* in a studio at Rose Bay, Sydney. The company went into liquidation before the film was completed. An attempt by Ernest Higgins, the photographer, and Shirley, to finish the film—with Higgins as financier—failed. Higgins, religious to the point of Holy-Joe-ism, objected to the semi-nudes of a mural that gifted scenic artists, the Clint Brothers, had painted for a cabaret scene. He was equally aghast at the screen antics of Minnie Hooper's dancing girls. Arguments multiplied. Litigation began. Shirley and actress Vera Remee sued Higgins for salary. Higgins, in retort, kept the reels of film which have never been shown. Shirley's efforts to get the reels reduced him to a second bankruptcy. From the Hotel Australia he moved to less glamorous Cathedral Street, Woolloomooloo, close to Nellie Stewart's birthplace, where he took a room in a theatrical boarding-house run by the character actress, Cora Warner, who was to give a fine performance as Mother Guttersnipe in Shirley's next film, *The Mystery of a Hansom Cab*.

Despite the vicissitudes of *The Throwback* company, *The Mystery of a Hansom Cab* was substantially backed by a new company, Pyramid Pictures, and had its première at the Crystal Palace Theatre, Sydney, in 1925. Shirley wrote the scenario, directed the film, and played two parts. In the cast were Carleton Stuart, Godfrey Cass, Ronald Stavely, Leslie Woods, Sidney Sterling, Frank Barnes, Arthur Orbell, Charles Vincent, John Bruce, Grace Glover (who, as Grace Savieri, played the lead in Frank Hurley's film *The Jungle Woman* for J.C.W.'s), Cora Warner, Vera Remee, Isa

Crossley, and Isa Millett. The film took five months to photograph, many of the scenes being in Melbourne—on the steps of Parliament House, in the Fitzroy Gardens, and also St Kilda Road. Country scenes were shot on Scone Station, New South Wales, on lemon-tinted film—the first time this had been done in Australia. The film was also Australia's first ten-reeler, and the first to use double exposure. It cost £2,500 to make, and made a profit of £15,000. In 1925 this was an extraordinary gain for an Australian film—the American stranglehold was so powerful that in 1924-1925 only 426,742 feet of British film entered Australia, and 19,188,826 feet of American film.

In 1925 Australia had 1,200 picture houses, and an annual attendance of 66,000,000. The American rake-off from this "University of the Illiterate" was colossal. It was also free of income tax. Imploring government action of some sort against "the American octopus", and "anti-British and unclean movies", a motley crew vehemently ranted and wrote and lobbied—*The Bulletin,* leader-writers, a gaggle of archbishops, and Disgusted Parents, Mr Lang the Premier, Hugh D. McIntosh, the Returned Soldiers' League, Stuart F. Doyle, and many others more intimately connected with movie-making—Arthur Shirley, Harry Southwell, Franklyn Barrett, Beaumont Smith, the McDonagh sisters, Frank Hurley, Louise Lovely (in 1925 she and Wilton Welch were making *Jewelled Nights,* written by Marie Bjelke-Petersen), Raymond Longford, Scott Alexander (who had made the first English movie—a mayoral garden party at Reading—in 1894), and John F. Gavin. Gavin had played the villain in, and directed, *The Martyrdom of Edith Cavell* (cost £300); *Thunderbolt* (written by Bert Forsyth); three films written by his wife, Agnes Gavin; *Keane of Kalgoorlie* (by Arthur Wright), and several others, before going to Hollywood where he formed his own company, and made twenty-six Westerns, as well as playing the heavy with such silent stars as Warren Kerrigan, Stan Laurel, Anna Q. Nilsson, Charlie Chase,

Clyde Cook, Snub Pollard, Olive Borden, and Harold Lloyd. Back in Australia in 1925, to attempt film-making, he baulked. The odds were too great.

Against these odds, protests, commissions, parliamentary speechifying, and newspaper uproar were as nothing. *The Mystery of a Hansom Cab* had its unusual success, while its author, Fergus Hume, sixty-six in 1925, who had sold the book for fifty pounds, was living in poverty—even though he had published another 136 novelettes—on the outskirts of Hadleigh, a village in Essex. The Depression was drawing nearer. Shirley began his next film.

For Pyramid Pictures he wrote, directed, and starred in the seven-reeler *The Sealed Room* with George Bryant, Nellie Ferguson, Eric Harrison, Leslie Woods, Cecil Scott, Muriel Veck, Cora Warner, Grace Glover (Savieri), John Bruce, Henry Halley, and Walter Bentley. It was Shirley's last Australian picture. He appeared on the stage once more with Nellie Stewart in *Sweet Nell of Old Drury*, this time playing Sir Roger Fairfax at the Grand Opera House, Sydney. In 1927 he sailed for England to promote the two films he had made for Pyramid Pictures. After trying to establish a film company in Rhodesia, he studied film technique in Europe, and talking-picture production in Hollywood. He returned to Australia in August 1934. In 1935 the Cinematograph Films (Australian Quota) Bill was passed. Since this required the showing of a proportion of Australian films movie-makers began reckless planning. Despite the ominous fact that Eftee Film Studios in Melbourne had become a skating rink, and that the Australian talkies of 1934 were a seedy and unprofitable batch, Harry Southwell (for Film Players Corporation) set about directing and starring in *The Burgomeister*, derived from *The Bells*, which was shot in the Cinesound Studios at Waverley, Sydney. The cast included Janet Johnson, who had trained with Gregan McMahon, and the George Thirlwell Company, Lily Molloy, Gabriel Toyne, Bertie Wright, Harold Meade,

Muriel Meredith, Leslie Victor, and Ross Vernon. The film failed.

Arthur Shirley became involved, as their main stock-in-trade, with Australian National Feature Films (FROM AUSTRALIA TO THE WORLD was their slogan), the directors of which tried to whip up public support "to develop the Motion Picture Industry in Australia". Their efforts also failed, and with them Shirley's interest in films.

Now living in Sydney, Arthur Shirley has few regrets for his defeat by the forces of stage and movie cornering—his fate has been the fate of many talented Australians (and by-blow Englishmen and Americans) who had hoped and laboured to make good films in Australia. His main interests are archaeology, and ancient Egypt.

Also of a theatrical family was Madge Titheradge, daughter of George Titheradge. She was born in Melbourne, on July 2, 1887, at the beginning of the ten-year period her father spent with the Brough-Boucicault Company. When Titheradge returned to London in 1898 to support Mrs Patrick Campbell, Madge Titheradge was already versed in the lore of the theatre, and had played with the Brough-Boucicault and Bland Holt companies. She made her London début, at the age of fifteen, on December 18, 1902, as the Second Water Baby in the dramatization of Charles Kingsley's *The Water Babies*.

In April 1905 she was Mimi in *Trilby* at His Majesty's, London, in which theatre she played a succession of parts including Lisa in *Faust* (1908) and Katharine in *Henry the Fifth* (1908).

Pretty, well-grounded, and with exquisite diction, she went from success to success. Her photograph adorned cigarette-cards and postcards. She toured England and Canada between 1910 and 1911 in such parts as Roxalanne de Lavedan in *Bardelys the Magnificent*, and Mary Carlisle in *Monsieur Beaucaire*. Her first American appearance, on

September 7, 1912, was as Ruth Dix, in *Discovering America*, at the Thirty-Ninth Street Theatre, New York.

She next became leading lady in the Lewis Waller Company. Waller was one of the matinée idols of the pre-1914 era, his army of matinée girls calling themselves the K.O.W. Girls—the Keen On Waller Girls.

In 1913 Madge Titheradge returned to Australia with Waller in the presentation of a Shakespeare season which was rather overshadowed by the sumptuous productions, *Antony and Cleopatra* and *A Midsummer Night's Dream*, of the Oscar Asche–Lily Brayton Company.

Madge Titheradge was as versatile as many of the actresses of her time. Between starring in *Peter Pan* in 1914, and Desdemona in *Othello* at the Court Theatre, in London, in April 1921, she played Florian in the Drury Lane Christmas pantomime of 1916 (*Puss in Boots*); was in Hollywood films during 1919 and 1920; and back at Drury Lane Theatre in June 1920 as Domini Enfelden in *The Garden of Allah*.

Her appearance as Peter Pan in 1914 is historically interesting; she was the first and only Australian-born actress to have this almost legendary honour. The annual London production of *Peter Pan* is one in which all players with a feeling for theatrical ritual and stage tradition hope to appear. The list of world-famous actresses who have played Peter Pan is a glittering one, too long to give fully, but includes Nina Boucicault (1904), Pauline Chase (1913), Fay Compton (1917), Gladys Cooper (1923), Elsa Lanchester (Mrs Charles Laughton) (1936), Anna Neagle (1937), Glynis Johns (1943), Phyllis Calvert (1947), and Margaret Lockwood (1949). The list of Wendy's mothers is equally long and glamorous, and includes Zena Dare, Evelyn Laye, and the Australian-born Marie Löhr. Among the actors who have played the double part of Mr Darling and Captain Hook have been Gerald du Maurier, Seymour Hicks, John Mc-Callum, Boris Karloff, Cyril Ritchard, and Alastair Sim. In the year that Madge Titheradge played Peter Pan, one of the Lost Boys, Slightly, was played by Noël Coward.

Madge Titheradge's brother Dion, named for his father's friend, Dion Boucicault *fils*, was also born in Melbourne, on March 30, 1889. He, too, played a number of walk-on parts in Australia; travelled to England with his father, and made his English début in *The Woman of Kronstadt*, on March 2, 1908, at the Theatre Royal, Newcastle-on-Tyne. In 1910 he joined Lewis Waller's Company, and toured England, America, Australia, and New Zealand in a number of juvenile leads.

In 1912, he was playing *Henry the Fifth* at the Manhattan Theatre, New York; in 1916 he played Joseph Strangford with George Arliss in *Paganini*, and Leonard Brooke in *The Harp of Life*, at the Globe Theatre, New York.

Soon after this he devoted himself first to production, later to play-writing. Among the skilfully shallow, absolutely unrevivable comedy-dramas from his pen were *Jim the Rat*, *Peg for Short*, *A Girl of Today*, *A Wife's Dilemma*, and *Puppets*. He was also responsible for numerous film scenarios.

Ian Fleming was born in Melbourne on September 10, 1888, and educated at St Kilda. His début was made on May 1, 1904, at the Theatre Royal, Melbourne.

From 1904 to 1915 he toured the Australian provinces in Shakespeare, melodrama, Australianized melodrama, and the tattered but persistently popular blood-curdling minor classics of the nineteenth century.

His first London appearance was at the Lyric Theatre, London, on August 15, 1915, as Glover in *On Trial*.

Mignon O'Doherty was born in Brisbane on June 30, 1890, and was educated at the Royal School, Bath, England, and in Paris.

After two years of study at the Royal Academy of Dramatic Art, London, she made her first professional appearance, as Angélique in *Lady Frederick,* at the Globe Theatre, London, on April 6, 1913.

From then on she played a number of supporting rôles, particularly character parts. The following brief selection of some early performances shows her adaptability: Emily Rhead in *Milestones* (1914); Lucy in *The Recruiting Officer* (Haymarket Theatre, London, 1915); the Nurse in Eugène Brieux's *Damaged Goods* (St Martin's Theatre, London, 1917); and Maria in *Twelfth Night* (Court Theatre, London, 1918).

As Mignon O'Doherty's flair for characterization matured, and she herself grew older, she specialized in Irish character parts, and in unpleasant womankind in general—ill-tempered landladies, suburban gossips, and malicious harpies. These small but biting, and often very funny, character sketches have enriched stage, wireless, and television plays.

Marie Löhr was born in Sydney on July 28, 1890, the daughter of Kate Bishop, actress, who at one time ran a company in partnership with George Rignold. Lewis J. Löhr, her father, was treasurer of the Opera House, Melbourne. In 1894, when she was four, Marie Löhr made her first appearance, in Sydney, in *The World Against Her.* This was followed by appearances as a child in *Captain Fritz,* and in *Hans the Boatman.* In 1901 she made her London début at the Garrick Theatre in *Shock-headed Peter.*

Marie Löhr's career in hundreds of parts on the English stage and screen rather puts her, as it does the Australian-born Cecily Courtneidge, in the class of permanent expatriates. She has played with the Kendals, Beerbohm Tree, Sir John Hare, and numberless lesser lights such as Leslie Howard, Valerie Hobson, and Wendy Hiller. Her marriage to the theatrical manager Anthony L. Prinsep was dissolved in 1928. Her first film appearance was in 1932.

The Expatriates and the Stay-at-homes

Perhaps the most interesting part of her career was as manageress of the Globe Theatre, London, between the years 1918 and 1925, during which period she produced many plays with competence and finish. These included *Nurse Benson, A Voice from the Minaret, L'Aiglon,* and *A Marriage of Convenience.*

Clyde Cook was born in 1891, and, although his early training in Australia did include some small-part work, as in *A Message from Mars,* with Gregan McMahon and O. P. Heggie, his bent was hardly straight drama, either by inclination or preparation.

As a vaudevillean and a musical comedy dancer, his introductory career is not for detailed treatment here, but it can be outlined. He was a self-made comedian, and an acrobatic knockabout man.

Before the age of seven he was an expert Highland Fling dancer, and a tumbler; by Saturday, February 25, 1911, he had gained reputation enough to be cast as Our Sam (the Giant's myrmidon) in *Jack and the Beanstalk,* at Her Majesty's Theatre, Melbourne; by February 1918 he was partnering Maie Baird in eccentric dancing in *The Bing Boys Are Here* at Her Majesty's, Sydney.

He went to London, where his overnight success as a comedian at the Alhambra led to an engagement with the *Folies Bergère* in Paris. His next part was a slapstick one in *Happy Days* at the Hippodrome, New York.

Cook, a small man with a contortionist's body, and a face of great mobility, was seen in *Happy Days,* by William Fox, of Fox Films, who became enthusiastic about the Australian "Inja' Rubber Idiot", as Cook was billed. Fox saw a film possibility with something of the wistful quality of those great comedians Charlie Chaplin, Buster Keaton, and Harry Langdon.

He was launched in *Kiss Me Quick* (1921) and a series of Clyde Cook Comedies which were extremely popular until the capricious public tired of them. Although Cook, with his Chester Conklin moustache and his air of the victimized Little Man, appeared in a number of two-reelers crammed with side-splitting incidents and uproarious contretemps, he had not the art to make his name stick in the minds of the public. By the time sound came to the film, Cook was already rather *passé*, and his advertising captions had disappeared from the pages of theatrical magazines which, once proliferous, were themselves disappearing. (CLYDE COOK—THE ONE AND ONLY IN HIS LATEST RIBTICKLER. CLYDE COOK—HE'S TICKLIN' THE NATIONS INTO CONVULSIONS.)

No longer a star, Cook appeared in supporting parts, and in bit parts that grew smaller as the years passed, until they were no more than gone-in-a-flash appearances in such cockneyized and sickening travesties of Australia as *The Man from Down Under*, starring Charles Laughton and a pretty *ingénue* called Donna Reed.

Lottie Lyall, "a little lady, an elocutionist, and strictly religious", belongs to that group of film actresses and actors whose fame was purely local.

She was born in Sydney in 1891 and, because Raymond H. Longford starred her in so many films, can well wear the title of Australia's first film star. She can also be entitled Australia's—if not the world's—first female scenario writer. She and Longford wrote dozens of early film scripts. The films in which she appeared between 1910 and 1925 have already been listed. Almost always under the production of Longford she appeared with many of the toadstool film companies of her day. These were numerous: Fraser Films, Australian Life Biograph Company, Australian Photoplay, Australasian Films, Co-op. Films, Woods Australian Films, Australian Famous Players, Pugliese, Koala Film Company, Southwell Screenplays, Blue Bird Films, Gell and Brown, Crick and Jones, and the Lincoln-Cass Films Pty Ltd.

160

Forthcoming Events, including Arthur Shirley's
Patriotic Poster

TO-NIGHT. TO-NIGHT.

With Messrs. Ireland and Barry's Compliments.

Messrs. G. R. IRELAND & DAN BARRY'S
GRAND
Comedy Company !!

Stage Manager	Mr. G. R. Ireland
Business Manager	Mr. Dan Barry
Musical Directors	Mons. De Belville
Mechanist	Mr. Leonard
Agent	Mr. Chas. Moye

Comprising the well-known and most popular Actor,

MR. G. R. IRELAND,

The charming and gifted young Comedienne,

MISS KATE VINSON,

Supported by a Splendid Company, selected from the Sydney and
Melbourne Theatres, numbering

8 —— Talented Young Actresses —— 8
14 —— Clever Actors —— 14
22 —— Dramatic Artists, in all —— 22

PRONOUNCED by press and public to be by far the largest, most versatile, and powerful Theatrical organisation that ever travelled the provinces. This company has
been specially organised to produce in provincial towns, all the latest and most successful
Dramatic Novelties, from the Metropolitan Theatres, in a style of artistic and general
completeness fully equal to that which might be expected to be witnessed on the stage of
any first-class theatre in a capital city. No expense has been spared to gather together
the best available Dramatic Talent, and to Mount the pieces properly as regards costume,
scenery, and mechanical contrivances, the result being that the performances of this Company have been one series of Brilliant Successes in every town visited—crowded,
intellectual, and fashionable audiences, always greeting with enthusiastic applause the
programmes presented, in which will be found a happy blending of

Startling Novelty! Mirth!! Refinement!!! Sterling Merit!!!!

TO-NIGHT!
COMPLIMENTARY BENEFIT TO MR. G. R. IRELAND,
Under the patronage of the leading Residents of the Mount.

Grand production of the Celebrated Comedy Drama, with New and Beautiful
Scenery, Lime-light Effects, Novel and Startling Stage
Contrivances, Appropriate Music, Handsome
Costumes, with all its Touching,
Thrilling, and Humorous
Episodes entitled,

THE TICKET OF LEAVE MAN !
OR, THE CONVICT'S DESTINY
In Which Mr. W. H. ELLIS has kindly consented to appear in the Character of
BOB BRIERLY, the Ticket of Leave Man, the rest of the
Characters by the following Powerful Cast:—

HAWKSHAW (a detective, brave and true)	Mr. G. R. IRELAND
Tom Dalton (alias " The Tiger ")	Mr. DAN BARRY
Melter Moss (a fiery fence)	Mr. GEO. HERBERT
Mr. Gibson (a banker)	Mr. CHAS. MOYE
Maltby (landlord of the Bellevue Gardens)	Mr. SEARLE
Green Jones (first of the ladies')	Mr. ALLING
James (a pot boy)	Mr. W. H. MANNING
Sam Willoughby (a fast youth)	Mr. D'ANGELO
MAY EDWARDS (a singing girl)	MISS JOSEPHINE IRELAND
Mrs. Willoughby (who takes for steam)	MISS KATE VINSON
Emily St. Evremonde (with songs)	Miss DORA MORTIN
	Miss NITA STEELE

Guests, Waiters, Detectives, Policemen, Navvies, &c.

Doors Open at 7.15.   Performance to commence at 8.

USUAL PRICES OF ADMISSION.

Border Watch Print, Mount Gambier.

TO THE WHOLE OF THE
BLIC OF SANDHURST
AND OTHERS WHOM IT MAY CONCERN.

NOTICE!
MRS. HOLLOWAY

...ectfully to inform the Inhabitants of Sandhurst that her first Benefit takes place at
the Lyceum Theatre on Tuesday, February 4th, on which occasion

ARBLE HEART
Will be performed.

...he Committee, Peter Blankversus, Paul Transeversus, and Simon Reversus, do, by
...our office, for and in behalf of the said Mrs. Holloway, command that the whole
...edical fraternity be in attendance upon the evening of the above date, in case of a

URDER

...ce.) Lawyers are solicited to *witness* the deed, and we would recommend drapers
...their way to the Theatre and *endeavour to edge in*. We can rely upon the *major*
...shoemakers will be out there. Thus this, if you don't come, our case will be
...o press tailors is *needle-less*. If hatters don't come, their absence will be much
...istrates and Wardens will be in attendance, because much is depended upon their
Publicans ought to *drop in* as this is likely to turn out a *Drama* of spirit.
...opers must be there to draw out—if not they may depend upon a *pound-in*.
...ill, no doubt, do the *heavy* on this occasion—that is if it isn't wet. Printers are
...ill prepared to attend to this *matter* ; if they do it will cause a deep *impression*. As
...e *steak* our lives on them. It's *plane* carpenters will attend, unless they mean
...e *beneficiare* ; and we *augur* they won't do that. If cooks don't pay us a visit,
...will be in the fire. Ironmongers are not such *screws* as to withhold their support,
...makers don't make their appearance, we shall, it *seems* to us, be completely *sewn*
...stationers don't take a *seat* up stairs they deserve *kneeling down*. It is unnecessary
...kers they are *headed*—if they don't come it will make us somewhat *crusty*.
...expect you to lay of all hands above to get a *berth* aloft. If blacksmiths don't come
...ve a good *hammering*, and the worst we would say to them is such a case would
...be *blow* them. But if

HE LADIES,

One and all, will support us in our present endeavour, it will be

PRETTY AFFAIR.

	PETER BLANKVERSUS,
Signed,	PAUL TRANSVERSUS,
	SIMON REVERSUS.

April 7, 1917   MOTOGRAPHY

The Film of the Hour

★ Thomas Dixon's ★
Mighty Message of Warning

"THE FALL OF A NATION"
With Special Musical Score by Victor Herbert

In Seven
Tremendous Parts

An Awe-Inspiring Vision of
the Terrific Powers of An-
nihilation which America
May be Forced to Meet in
the World Struggle for a
Place in the Sun.

Show This
Master Spectacle
NOW—When National En-
thusiasm Is Running High
And Break All Box-Office Records

VITAGRAPH
V. L. S. E.

VICTORIA 🏛 THEATRE.

Lessee	...		Stage Manager	...	Mr. A. J. Solomon
Acting Manager	...	Mr. Shute		...	Mr. Young
Machinists	Messrs. Tongel and Garr		Propertyman	...	Mr. Weller
Prompter	...	Mr. Reading	Leader of Band	...	Herr S. chrade

THURSDAY AND FRIDAY, APRIL 25 AND 26,
The Performances will Commence with an Original Play in Three
Acts, full of Powerful Interest, Entitled

A BIRD IN THE HAND
WORTH TWO IN THE BUSH!

Roderick Praiseworthy	...	...	Mr. S. O'Brien
Reginald Prodigal			Mr. Morrison
Theodore			Mr. Andrews
Major Stormont			Mr. Musgrave
Capias Sharke		...	Mr. Charles Young
Pansey	...	...	Mr. J. B. Edouin
Button	...	...	Mr. Daniels
Champagne			Mr. Keets
Legs	...	...	Mr. Reading
Whipcord			Mr. Wells
Madame Reginald...			Mrs. H. J. Ray
Ellen Prodigal			Mrs. H. Jackson
Lettuce		...	Miss L. Arnot

Concluding with the Great Fairy Tale of Enchantment, entitled

THE ICE WITCH
Or, THE FROZEN HAND.

Harold		...	Mr. Stuart O'Brien
Sweno			Mr. Daniels
Gruthioff			Mr. Andrews
Tycho			Mr. Wells
Freyr			Mr. Morrison
Magnus Snora			Mr. Musgrave
Sterno			Mr. Ketts
Runic			Mr. Charles Young
Priest of Odin			Mr. Reading
Sprite			Mr. J. B. Edouin
Retainers of Guthioff			Retainers of Harold
Spirits of Ice.			Spirits of the Sun.
Drula			Mrs. Jackson
Hecla			Miss Tilly Earl
Edda			Miss Louisa Arnot
Finna			Miss Lester
Hilda			Miss Woods
Ulla			Mrs. Holmes
Minna			Mrs. Ray

Nancye Stewart, daughter of Nellie Stewart, and descended, therefore, from the great Irish actress, Mary Ann Yates, who was closely associated with David Garrick and the eighteenth-century Drury Lane Theatre, was born in Chingford, Essex, England, on June 19, 1893. When six weeks old she was brought to Australia in the S.S. *Doric*.

Since, during Nancye Stewart's childhood, her famous mother was so often on tour, she was educated by a governess who travelled with the company. Later, Nancye Stewart had five years at Lausanne, Switzerland, where she also studied piano-playing under Jules Nicati, director of the Zürich Conservatorium. She was taught dancing by Espinoza in London, and fencing by Frank Stuart in Sydney.

Her professional début was not as an actress, but as conductor of the orchestra on tour with Nellie Stewart in *Sweet Nell of Old Drury*. This tour, which lasted eight months, covered one hundred and nineteen towns in the eastern States of Australia, and the Northern Territory.

She did not make her début on the stage until 1914, when she was twenty-one, in The Firm's production of *Joseph and His Brethren*. This was directed by Sir Herbert Tree's director, Cecil King, and starred Frank Harvey. She then joined her mother's company on a tour of Australia and New Zealand with *Madame du Barry*, and *When Knighthood was in Flower*, playing five characters in the two plays.

Between 1915 and 1918 Nancye Stewart was constantly active on the stages of city theatres, and on tour. She played leading parts with Hale Hamilton, who was starring on a J.C.W. tour in *Seven Days' Leave, Kick In, It Pays to Advertise, Twin Beds*, and *Get-Rich-Quick Wallingford*; was in J. and N. Tait's first dramatic production, *Turn to the Right* (Palace Theatre, Sydney, and King's Theatre, Melbourne); and was understudy to Marie Tempest, and also playing parts, in Marie Tempest's season of *A Pair of Silk Stockings, Annabelle*, and *The Marriage of Kitty*. She next appeared with her mother in a most unusual form of stage

161

Scenes from "The Early Christian Martyrs", made in 1900-1
L

presentation—week by week Nellie Stewart played one act of *Sweet Nell of Old Drury* until the complete play was given. What was particularly unusual about this form of entertainment was that it was on a vaudeville bill, a Hugh D. McIntosh presentation at the Tivoli Theatres in Sydney and Melbourne.

In November 1918 Nancye Stewart was on the last leg of a tour (Sydney, Melbourne, Adelaide, Brisbane, New Zealand) with Margaret Wycherley in the first of all thriller dramas, *The Thirteenth Chair*. As the ship, the *Atua*, was returning from New Zealand to Sydney, pneumonic influenza broke out among the black crew. The cast, after acting as cooks and stewards for the sick and dying crew of the plague-ship, were quarantined at North Head, and spent the first Armistice Day there.

In 1919—year of the Actors' Strike, and Prohibition—she went to New York to play in the farce *Pretty Soft* at the Morosco Theatre. *Pretty Soft* was also pretty hot, and the police closed down the show. Nancye Stewart, in a vaudeville sketch, toured the camps for returned American servicemen. She then joined the Copley Repertory Players in Boston for five months, playing leading rôles under the direction of Australian Henry Jewett in a curious assortment of plays including Wilde's *A Woman of No Importance, Twelfth Night, Charley's Aunt, Pygmalion, As You Like It*, and *Hindle Wakes*. She also played a small part in a Marion Davies film, but finished up on the cutting-room floor.

In 1920, while on a six months' tour with George M. Cohan's *Genius and the Crowd*, she met her future husband, Mayne Lynton. She then toured the Middle West and the Eastern, and Southern States of America in *The Master of Ballantrae* with the Walker Whiteside Company.

She returned to Australia in 1922, and until 1929 appeared with Muriel Starr, Pauline Frederick, and Emilie Polini, and in *The Flaw*, which was written by Emilie Polini herself. In 1926 she was in the film *For the Term of His Natural Life*.

In 1929 she began her career as an actress on the air. Since then she has acted in more than five hundred broadcast plays, as well as a hundred and fifty stage ones. She and Mayne Lynton have also presented to the variety audiences of Brisbane and Sydney a programme of monologues accompanied by music.

Her numerous later stage appearances include *Black Limelight* (Comedy Theatre, Melbourne, 1944); *Who is Sylvia?* (Criterion Theatre, London, 1950); with the John Alden Shakespeare Company, 1951-1952, Goneril in *King Lear*, Mistress Page in *The Merry Wives of Windsor*, and Hippolyta in *A Midsummer Night's Dream; The Great Fog* (London, 1952), and *Hamlet* (The Edinburgh Festival, 1953).

In 1953-1954 she was with the Old Vic. Company in *King John, All's Well That Ends Well, Hamlet* (Richard Burton), *The Tempest*, and *Coriolanus*. She played Zürich and Copenhagen with the company, and appeared at the castle known as Elsinore in *Hamlet*.

In 1954-1955 she was with the Memorial Theatre Company, Stratford-on-Avon, in *Twelfth Night, All's Well That Ends Well*, and *The Merry Wives of Windsor*. During this season she played with Sir Laurence Olivier and Vivien Leigh in Peter Brook's productions of *Macbeth*, and *Titus Andronicus*. This last, which had not been revived within memory, was a particularly sensational production. She also played in plays for Bristol Television under the direction of Chlöe Gibson.

In 1956 she returned to Australia to act in *The Happiest Days of Your Life* (with Margaret Rutherford), and—for the Australian Elizabethan Theatre Trust—in *Ned Kelly* and *Witness for the Prosecution*.

She made many television appearances in plays and serials —*My Three Angels, Wuthering Heights, Blue Murder, No! No! Eugène!, Richard the Second, Peter Gray, Johnny Belinda*, and *Grey Nurse* (a play based on the Sydney Shark-

Arm Murder). She has been in sumless episodes of the A.B.C.
serial *Blue Hills*, playing the part of Mabel.

She is five feet four inches tall. Her hobbies are gardening,
dressmaking, travelling, an intense interest in the renovation
of old houses and old furniture, and reading. In this last
she is as eclectic as she has had to be in more than half a
century of playing everything from evanescent variety to the
unquenchable classics. Her favourite plays are Shakespeare's
The Tempest, and John Whitney's *Penny for a Song*.

J. Beresford Fowler was born in a suburb of Melbourne in
1893, the son of Ethel Adèle, an actress with the Brough-
Boucicault Company, who also played in J. C. Williamson
and early Gregan McMahon productions.

Fowler's first appearance on any stage, at the age of six,
was as Midshipmite in *H.M.S. Pinafore*, at the Elsternwick
Town Hall, Melbourne, in 1899. His first grown-up appearance was in 1911, as Vilhelm Foldal in Gregan McMahon's
production of Ibsen's *John Gabriel Borkman* at the Turn
Verein Hall, East Melbourne. The title rôle was played by
an intelligent young amateur actor who did not pursue the
stage further, but who became a doctor and head of the
Australian Army Medical Service—Major-General Sir Frank
Kingsley Norris. Olive Wilton played Mrs Borkman.

Fowler did more work with Gregan McMahon; this led
to an engagement in J. C. Williamson's 1914 production of
Joseph and His Brethren at the Theatre Royal, Melbourne,
in which he played several parts. His next J.C.W. part was
as Ginger, the Thames Embankment cockney, in *Sealed
Orders*. Later, he played with Nellie Stewart, with Allan
Wilkie, and in 1916 joined the Bert Bailey Company, appearing as Billy Bearup in the early productions of *On Our
Selection*.

His theatrical impulse had much in common with Allan
Wilkie's and Gregan McMahon's, or, more broadly, was
directed towards actor-managership in an age when actor-

managers were a dwindling race. In 1926 he bravely formed his own Art Theatre Players Company. Over a period of thirty years he produced more than a hundred plays at the Queen's Hall, Melbourne, this repertoire being composed of Shakespeare and the late-nineteenth and early-twentieth century playwrights, those whose works admonished, pilloried, and mocked society while entertaining society— Strindberg, Shaw, Galsworthy, Ibsen. These offerings were leavened occasionally and hopefully with the current "sparkling three-act comedy".

A glance at a usual week's repertoire played by Fowler's company will reveal his intentions:

Monday	Shaw's *Candida*
Tuesday	*The Merchant of Venice*
Wednesday ..	*Hamlet*
Thursday	Nöel Coward's *Hay Fever*
Friday	*Julius Caesar*
Saturday	Hermann Sudermann's *The Fires of St John*

This programme, smacking so much of the theatre in its heyday, was almost recklessly courageous for the second half of the twentieth century, but Fowler had always been recklessly courageous as, for example, in 1934, when he did a season of Strindberg and Shaw in Sydney, after eight years and two hundred and fifty performances in Melbourne. He also toured such provincial cities as Bendigo and Ballarat.

Among the more gifted players who worked for him were Ruby May, Peter O'Shaughnessy, June Clyde, Mollie Locke, Dulcie Bland, and Keith Eden.

J. Beresford Fowler's own favourite parts are Richard the Third, Iago, John Gabriel Borkman, Hjalmar Ekdal, John Tanner, and Burgess in *Candida*, which latter part was his most popular with the public.

He is author of a play, *A Heroine of Russia*, and has written a number of short stories and a book of theatrical reminiscences. He is a prominent member of the Players' and Playgoers' Association.

Elsie Mackay was born in Perth, Western Australia, in 1894. Her father was a wealthy squatter, her stepmother was Fanny Danger, the dancer.

After completing her education at a finishing school in Switzerland she made her first stage appearance in a walk-on part in Shaw's *Pygmalion* at His Majesty's Theatre, London, on April 11, 1914. Later that year, after apprenticeship as an understudy to Margery Maude, she took over from her the part of Virginia Bullivant in *Grumpy* at the New Theatre, London. Her poised performance gained her the respect of critics and public alike, and she became a leading player in Cyril Maude's Company. Throughout 1914 and 1915 she toured America with the company, playing Virginia Bullivant in *Grumpy*, Muriel Mannering in *The Second in Command*, and other such leading ladies as the repertoire called for.

In 1916 she joined Sir Herbert Tree's Company on its American tour to play supporting or leading ladies—Anne Bullen in *King Henry the Eighth*, Jessica in *The Merchant of Venice*, and a particularly charming Rosalind in *As You Like It*.

Among later parts, many of which she played under the direction of the forceful David Belasco, were: Ethel Newcome in *Colonel Newcome* at the New Amsterdam Theatre, April 1917; Dora in *Another Man's Shoes* at Thirty-Ninth Street Theatre, September 1918; Violet Pinney in *Clarence* at the Hudson Theatre, September 1919; Maria in *Poldekin* at the Park Theatre, September 1920; Marie Duplessis in *Deburau* at the Belasco Theatre, December 1920; and Jacqueline in *The Comedian* at the Lyceum Theatre, March 1923.

Elsie Mackay married Lionel Atwill, but left him to return to Australia with Max Montesole, a producer. She died in Melbourne in 1963.

If Lorna Forbes was Australia's great stay-at-home Shakespearian actress, Marie Ney was, of her era, the great expatriate one.

Marie Ney was born in Chelsea, England, on July 18, 1895, but was brought to New Zealand as a child before the nineteenth century was ended. She was educated at St Mary's Convent, Wellington. Her schooling over, she began to train as a kindergarten teacher, meantime playing in a number of amateur productions. She was, from the first, outstanding as an actress, and as a personality with something of the direct and fearless quality of Katherine Mansfield. Like Katherine Mansfield, she found little opportunity in New Zealand for the full expression of her abilities. Australia—where she arrived in 1916—was, although merely relatively, a place of more and greater opportunities.

A year earlier, 1915, Allan Wilkie had also arrived, and was now making the first moves in the establishment of a Shakespearian company. He perceived the possibilities of Marie Ney, and cast her as the Widow in *The Taming of the Shrew*, in which she made her début on November 4, 1916. Subsequently, she played Nerissa, Phoebe, the Player Queen, and Valentine in *Twelfth Night*. These were small parts, certainly, but parts in which to discipline her untrained abilities. Shakespeare was not, however, all. Wilkie was trying to do what Alfred Dampier and the earlier actor-managers had done. This was the sort of bifocal labour of making up what might be lost on the swings of Shakespeare and Sheridan, on the roundabouts of the "latest comedies" and "popular dramas". Wilkie was, however, facing extra competition—the Great War, moving pictures, and a theatrical atmosphere that was becoming increasingly addled. Moreover, Wilkie did not possess the touch for lighter works; on planes lower than Goldsmith and Sheridan he was earnestly heavy-handed.

Marie Ney, therefore, appeared in fairly disastrous Wilkie productions of *Seven Days' Leave* in which she played Lady

Mary, and *The Story of the Rosary* in which she was Princess Venetia. In January 1918, at the Princess, Melbourne, she was in the unsuccessful *For the King*, with Wilkie as "the evil Stephen Wenlock". Also in the cast were Arthur Styan, and—displaying "pretty feminine graces" as Mrs Clavering—Olive Wilton.

Marie Ney's talents had, however, not gone unnoticed, nor had her direct and inimitable charm. Between 1919, when she played the feminine lead in E. J. Carroll's film *Desert Gold*, with Claude Flemming, Bryce Rowe, and John Cosgrove, and 1921 when, on August 19, she appeared with Marie Tempest as Dinah in *Mr Pim Passes By*, she had been constantly in demand. During these three years she had played leading rôles in a stock company in Perth; had appeared in J. and N. Tait's presentations of *Peg o' My Heart, The Little Damozel, Kindling* (with Maggie Moore), and other lightweight plays. In July 1922 she doubled the parts of Liza and Mrs Collinson in *My Lady's Dress* for J. C. Williamson's, which was now controlled by its ex-rivals, J. and N. Tait. Encouraged by Marie Tempest, Marie Ney left Australia to seek her fortune and fame in England.

She made her London début, on August 27, 1923, at the Brixton Theatre, as Rosalie in *The Marriage of Kitty*, with Marie Tempest. In 1924, at the end of a tour of England as Lucy Shale in *The Lie*, she was invited to join the Old Vic. Company.

At the age of twenty-nine, and after eight years only of comprehensive experience, she appeared, in October 1924, as Desdemona in the Old Vic.'s *Othello*. Her brilliant success was followed by another as Helena in *A Midsummer Night's Dream*, and as Martha in *Hannele*.

With these three English successes behind her, Marie Ney can be said to have really begun her distinguished career as an outstanding actress, particularly as one of the great Shakespearians of her time.

Of the Australian actresses who reached film stardom over-seas—Mona Barrie, Enid Bennett, Mae Busch, Gwen Nelson, Dorothy Seacombe, Victoria Shaw—Louise Lovely was per-haps the most beautiful. At the height of her career she starred for such Hollywood companies as Universal, Fox, Goldwyn, and First National.

Originally Louise Carbasse, she was born in Sydney in 1896. Her mother, Madame Carbasse-Alberti, a prominent and forceful member of Sydney's French community during the late nineteenth and early twentieth centuries, arrived in Australia as a member of Sarah Bernhardt's Company in 1891.

Louise Lovely was a child actress who, by the age of fifteen, was playing leading-lady parts with the George Marlow Com-pany. At sixteen she was starred by the Australian Life Biograph Company in *Con, the Shaughraun* (from Bouci-cault's play), *Hands Across the Sea*, and *The Ticket-o'-Leave Man*.

In 1914, at the age of eighteen, she went to Hollywood where she signed a contract with William Fox Productions. During the next eight years she appeared opposite many of the film heroes of the day in such films as *Butterfly Man, The Lone Hand*, and *The Lone Star Ranger*. After playing a series of badgered heroines with clean-cut he-men of the William Farnum sort she returned to Australia. For a while she appeared with her first husband, Wilson Welch, in vaudeville sketches on the Harry Rickards Circuit. In 1926 she played the leading rôle in Welch's film production *Jewelled Nights*, and in 1927 in *The Last Warning*. At this time the Federal Government was conducting a Royal Com-mission on the worthiness or not of subsidizing moving pictures. On June 10, 1927 Louise Lovely gave level-headed and lucid evidence that *Jewelled Nights* had cost £8,016 6s. to produce, but would have cost much less had there been a properly equipped studio. She made a plea for Government subsidy during the initial stages of what could be a flourishing industry. Nothing came of the Commission: talkies and the Depression were already within earshot of ears attuned to such matters.

Louise Lovely's career has ended in retirement to Hobart where her second husband, Bert Cowan, manages the Prince of Wales Cinema.

Another film star of the 1920s was Lotus Thompson, who had appeared on the Fuller Circuit in 1919 and in several Australian films: Franklyn Barrett's *Know Thy Child* (1921), Longford's *The Dinkum Bloke* (1923), and Beaumont Smith's *Townies and Hayseeds* (1923). She attempted Hollywood. After a few minute parts, leg-show parts, Lotus Thompson, in despair, poured acid on her legs. What ability could not bring to pass notoriety did. She was given the lead in an inferior film, *The Yellow Back*, and in several films of equal inferiority. Within a couple of years the notoriety of the Grand Guignol gesture had faded to nothing, and her hopes of a Hollywood career with it.

Vera Spaull, who on the stage had played Tyl-Tyl in Maeterlinck's *The Blue Bird* and Miss Bobbie in *Seven Little Australians*, played Buster in J. C. Williamson Films production of *Seven Keys to Baldpate*, and the country girl in the Hayseeds series.

Adrienne Brune, born in Melbourne on October 27, 1897, and convent-educated, made her début in December 1904 at the Princess Theatre, Melbourne, as Mustard Seed in George Musgrove's production of *A Midsummer Night's Dream*. Her career was the minor one of a competent supporting actress. Her first London appearance, on December 30, 1922, at the Kingsway Theatre, was as Jenny Diver in *Polly*.

The Expatriates and the Stay-at-homes

There were some actresses of the nineteenth century who preferred to keep their years of birth misty. It seems a delicate enough mark of appreciation to fulfil their implied wish. Of these dateless women, Vera Pearce is the most famous.

She was born in Australia, and first appeared on the stage at the age of four, making thereafter an incalculable number of appearances, for well over half a century, in straight plays, vaudeville, musical comedies, pantomimes, and films.

Before the Great War, she toured England as a singing soubrette and in small comedy parts. She returned to Australia in 1914, and there, for the next seven years, she gave lavish demonstrations of her amazing versatility. There is space merely to indicate her range by selection from the scores of parts listed in *Who's Who*. In November 1915 she starred in *The Tivoli Follies*, at the Tivoli Theatre, Sydney; in 1916, played Edith Cavell in the Australian film *The Martyrdom of Nurse Cavell* with Harrington Reynolds and Percy Walshe, and starred in *The Shepherd of the Southern Cross* (Fraser Films) with Tien Hogue and Arthur Shirley; in 1917 she appeared in *The Beauty Shop*; in the 1918 Christmas pantomime at His Majesty's Theatre, Melbourne, she was Principal Boy in *Dick Whittington*. By 1922, when she returned to London, she had played in the musical comedies *My Lady Frayle* and *The Officers' Mess*, with Claude Flemming, at the Sydney Tivoli, and, as Zahrat-al-Kulub in *Chu Chin Chow*, with Oscar Asche and Lily Brayton. In short, she had given samples of her ability as an effervescent vaudevillean, as a musical comedy and pantomime star, and as a deft actress in more serious vein on stage and screen.

This flexibility, this width of range, was neither to crumple nor diminish throughout more than fifty years on the stages, not only of London (London Hippodrome, Shaftesbury Theatre, Drury Lane Theatre, Piccadilly Theatre, Empire Theatre), Edinburgh (Empire Theatre), and New York

(Majestic Theatre, Henry Miller Theatre), but in provincial theatres throughout Great Britain and America. It is not the purpose of this book to follow her well-lit career of musical comedy successes, which were innumerable, and, more innumerable, when she was younger, than her successes on the straight stage and in films. She made her first appearance in an English film (*Yes, Mr Brown*) in the same year as Marie Löhr did, and has since then made many film appearances in supporting rôles which, in her hands, have been flawless comic vignettes.

Among the more recent parts played by this brilliant all-rounder have been Mrs Edgoose in *Bob's Your Uncle* (May 1948, Saville Theatre); Violet Binder M.P. in *The Party Spirit* (September 1954, Piccadilly Theatre); and Madame Boniface in *Hotel Paradiso* (April 1957, Henry Miller Theatre, New York).

Essie Jenyns was outstandingly beautiful even among the many gloriously beautiful Australian actresses of the late nineteenth and early twentieth centuries . . . Myra Kemble, Violet Varley, Marion Dunn, Nellie Stewart . . . and out-shone many of the later beauties although these included Jean Anderson, Jessica Harcourt, Diana Parnham, Mary Mac-Gregor, Margaret Vyner, Louise Lovely, and Eve Grey.

In 1881 she created the character of Babs Berkeley in George Darrell's five-act *The Sunny South*, which left scarcely a melodramatic stone unturned. Essie Jenyns was intelligent as well as beautiful, and by 1888 was leading lady for W. J. Holloway's Company, which had its headquarters at the Bijou Theatre, Melbourne. She played a number of heroines, and played them with luminous poise—Parthenian in *Ingomar the Barbarian*, Rosalind in *As You Like It*, Beatrice in *Much Ado About Nothing*, and a particularly dazzling Portia in *The Merchant of Venice*.

Darrell's *The Sunny South* was a vehicle in which many actresses other than Essie Jenyns travelled some of the way along the path to fame. Katie Towers, who had been on the boards since she was five, and who reached the heights of her abilities later, playing leads in *Madame X* and *Lilac Time*, was in the production of *The Sunny South* at the Garrick Theatre, Sydney, during October 1891. She played Rebecca (H)Ann (Reared in the Kitchen).

Hilda Spong, in 1898, created the part of Imogen Parrott in the New York première of *Trelawney of "The Wells"*. In Australia she played a long series of badgered and harassed Bland Holt heroines and, at a higher level, Rosalind in *As You Like It*, and leading parts in the 1912 productions of *The Blue Bird*, and *Everywoman*.

Betty Ward was born in Sydney, and was educated at the Sydney University. In 1909 she completed a year's study at the Royal Academy of Dramatic Art, London, and was immediately drafted into F. R. Benson's Number Two Company, making her début during January 1910 at Barrow-in-Furness, as Mistress Quickly in *The Merry Wives of Windsor*. She graduated from the provinces to her first London part, that of Jane Pratt in *Susan's Embellishment*, at the Palace Theatre on December 23, 1912. Her first big success with the general public was as Miss Deacon in *Poached Eggs and Pearls*, in November 1916. She had a happy touch in light parts, but committed herself adequately as Hippolyta in *A Midsummer Night's Dream*, Mrs Candour in *The School for Scandal*, and the Duchess of York in *Richard the Third*.

Lizette Parkes, born in Sydney, was a skilled and charming actress much in demand by producers during the first two decades of the twentieth century. In 1905 and 1906 she was playing *ingénue* leads for William Anderson. Honora in *Nobody's Daughter*, and Ellean in *The Second Mrs Tanqueray* are exactly the type—wistful and sensitive daughters of sophisticated and dashing parents tangled in the purple velvet mesh of Edwardian high-society scandals. Her first bill-heading part was as Peter Pan in J. C. Williamson's tour of New Zealand in 1907. By 1921 she was accounted by some critics "the leading Australian-born actress before the Australian public".

She appeared for J. C. Williamson's with Julius Knight in a long line of his dressy triumphs: *The Lion and the Mouse, The Third Degree, The Silver King, The Sign of the Cross, The Scarlet Pimpernel, Monsieur Beaucaire, A Royal Divorce,* and *Under Fire.* When Frank Harvey stepped smoothly into Knight's smooth shoes, Lizette Parkes continued to play with him the charming ladies she was adept in playing so competently and so stylishly.

Eve Grey was born in Birmingham, England, but was brought up in Australia. A beautiful woman, her major successes, both overseas and in Australia with The Firm, were in musical comedies. She starred in many during the 1920s and 1930s. She had, however, gained a helpful background in straight plays, her first notable success, in 1922, being as Phyllis Beaton in the Hugh J. McIntosh presentation of *Bulldog Drummond.*

Dorothy Brunton was, like Eve Grey, a star whose reputation was made in the musical comedy world. Her glittering career was cut short at its height when a heavy fire-curtain fell on her. She was born in Melbourne, where her father was a first-rate scenic artist, and was educated at the Presbyterian Ladies' College in that city, and at Alford House, Sydney. Before her singing voice and musical comedy technique had reached their full development, she had made a number of appearances under such painstaking actor-managers as Bland Holt, and in the film *Seven Keys to Baldpate.* Her London début was made at Drury Lane Theatre, on August 28, 1918, as Fan Tan in *Shanghai.*

The Expatriates and the Stay-at-homes

Nellie Bramley, born in Melbourne, was, at the peak of her powers, one of those rare enough beings—a kind of Woman's Woman of the Stage—who inspire the useful idolatry of the Gallery Girls. The precise reasons for this worship of woman by women are difficult to pin down, particularly when one assesses the difference in the external qualities of the various goddesses the Gallery Girls have set up. The common factor entrancing to women is elusive if one lumps together the goddesses—Tittell Brune, Gertrude Lawrence, Gladys Moncrieff, Tallulah Bankhead, Marion Dunn, Josie Melville. Whatever the quality, the response to it was a practical one expressed in gifts of the most useful sort: women do not waste long-stemmed roses, orchids, and bottles of Chanel Cinq even on their idols.

As a child, Nellie Bramley studied voice production and dramatic technique under Daisy Belmore of Melbourne. At fourteen, after learning the part of the maid in the short notice of eight hours, she made her début . . . with an inevitability that appears almost orthodox for the era . . . in *East Lynne*. Several years later, partly because her hair was black and short and curly, but also because her ability was patent, she was cast in the name rôle of *The Squaw Woman*. From her success in this part she did not look back.

As leading lady for Fuller's Dramatic Players at the Palace Theatre, Melbourne, she played in a number of parts, and toured extensively. Her popularity was such that she held the record for unbroken runs at one theatre, in each of the cities of Melbourne, Brisbane, Adelaide, and Perth—a two-year run in Brisbane; sixty-seven weeks without a break in Melbourne, at the Palace Theatre.

Campbell Copelin, who joined the Nellie Bramley Company at Melbourne's Playhouse in the early 1920s, and became the leading man in her stock company at the Sydney Opera House later in the same decade, summed up what many who have played with her express in many admiring ways. "She was", said Copelin, "one of the smoothest per-

175

formers to work with . . . a trouper in every sense of the word."

Although her most "lovable" parts were in such *soufflé* offerings as *Daddy Longlegs, Brown Sugar, Sunday, Polly with a Past, Smilin' Through,* and *Peg o' My Heart,* she was trained and gifted enough to be convincing in less saccharine characters: as leading lady in *The Last of Mrs Cheyney* and *Camille;* as Rosalind in *As You Like It;* and as Juliet in *Romeo and Juliet.* One of her last appearances, at the Minerva Theatre, Sydney, was in support of the Welsh actress, Megs Jenkins, in *The Late Christopher Bean.*

Earlier, in 1918, she played the "sweet heroine, Lady Raa, in an awful piece of bother," *The Woman Thou Gavest Me,* which was a pretty ineffectual dramatization of Hall Caine's ineffectual novel of the same name. About this time she also appeared as leading lady in an Australian film financed by Cozens Spencer. This was a version of *The Bells,* Henry Irving's *tour de force,* and was photographed by Australia's most gifted cameramen of the time, the Higgins Brothers—Ernest, Arthur, and Tasman.

She married Billy Russell, theatrical manager for such heterogeneous luminaries as Julius Knight, Madge Fabian, Anna Pavlova, Marie Tempest, and Lady (Gertrude) Forbes-Robertson.

Cecil Kellaway spent much of his life between 1918 and 1938 in Australia, and most of that period on the musical comedy stage. A South African by birth, he is the godson of his namesake, Cecil Rhodes, who was his father's lifelong friend. Playing comedy and character parts, he toured North Africa, South Africa, China, Japan, Siam, Borneo, and Malaya, and arrived in Australia in 1918, where he joined J. C. Williamson's. Since leaving Australia in 1938 he has been seen in a variety of exquisitely performed character parts in films, and on television. He is the only non-Jew to play the part of Mawruss Perlmutter in *Potash and Perl-*

mutter. His portrayal of the leprechaun in the film *The Luck of the Irish* won him an Academy Award.

In private life he is a landscape painter, an intellectual, a gambler, and a collector for his personal museum, which contains such nostalgic relics as the Derby hat Chaplin wore in *The Gold Rush*; the leopard skin once slung about the torso of Elmo Lincoln, the first film Tarzan; and the Arabian head-dress worn in *The Sheik* by Rudolph Valentino.

Cyril Ritchard, whose brief biography is the last in this chapter, was born in Sydney in December 1898, ten months after Judith Anderson, whose biography is first in the chapter. Although much of his work was done on the musical comedy stage, and his main fame in Australia, particularly with middle-aged playgoers, is based on his and his wife Madge Elliott's light-hearted and graceful appearances there, he has successfully played many straight parts.

After leaving school, Cyril Ritchard was a medical student at Sydney University, but was unable to resist the lure of the stage. His first appearance was at Her Majesty's Theatre, Sydney, in December 1917, in the chorus of *The Waltz Dream*. This long-running musical comedy was one of the numerous shows of which Dorothy Brunton was the star. It was about the core of her voice and abilities that the New Comic Opera Company, a J. C. Williamson enterprise, had been built.

While Cyril Ritchard was dancing and singing in Sydney, Judith Anderson was leaving Sydney for America because she had correctly foreseen that Australia was not, theatrically, a place where she could display her particular cold art. It was otherwise for the Cyril Ritchard of that era. A tidal wave of musical comedies and lush revues was already rising to wash over the Australian theatrical scene in the years after the Great War. Cyril Ritchard, in constant employment with The Firm from 1917 to 1924, was the chorus-boy bound to make good. Tall, debonair, good-looking in the shirt-collar-

M

advertisement style of musical comedy juveniles, slender, nimble-footed, and with a light, flexible singing voice, he was soon out of the chorus. After progressing step by step through such melodious pain-killers as *The Pink Lady, The Bing Boys Are Here* (this had, in 1921, the record for the second longest run ever in London, with *Chu Chin Chow* holding the record for the longest), *Kissing Time,* and *So Long, Letty.* By 1925 his elegant appearance, pleasant voice, and limber dancing, and the pinch of insouciance he gave to the fantastically absurd lines that have to be uttered by the puppets of musical comedy and revue, had engaged the attention of a London entrepreneur. He was given the second lead in *Bubbly,* after which he played in many revues in London, and on tour throughout Great Britain.

His first film appearance was in 1929, in *Piccadilly*. Gradually, it was realized that he had gifts in less frivolous arenas than that of musical comedy, as a comedian of the "sophisticated" Noël Coward kind, adept in timing, able to carry white tie and tails with an air, or silk dressing-gowns and Sulka cravats. His successes in this genre—it goes without saying—included the part of Algernon Moncrieffe in Oscar Wilde's *The Importance of Being Earnest* in 1942, and Eliot in Coward's *Private Lives*. By this time, Cyril Ritchard and his stage-partner wife, Madge Elliott (who died in 1955), were famous enough to be shuttling from leading parts in London to leading parts in New York, and to make money-spinning tours every now and then—as with *Private Lives* in 1951—to his homeland, Australia.

In 1954, at the Winter Garden, New York, he played the two parts of Mr Darling and Captain Hook in *Peter Pan*. Theatrical tradition has it that these parts are always played by the one actor, just as the part of Peter Pan is always played traditionally by a woman. Other curious conventions of the kind insist that the Principal Boys of pantomime, the Prince Charmings, Aladdins, and Sinbads, are played by women, whereas the pantomime Dames, the Widows

Twankey and the Ugly Sisters, are played by men. When Cyril Ritchard played Captain Hook in 1954 he played opposite Mary Martin, who thus joined the long queue of famous actresses who have cropped their hair, soared towards the flies on unseen wires, and implored audiences to clap so that the life of a fairy could be saved.

In 1958, at the age of sixty, Cyril Ritchard had his greatest success, and a brilliant New York run of four hundred and seventy-four performances, in the leading rôle of *The Pleasure of His Company*, a part in which he toured Australia in 1960.

Fifi (Yvonne) Banvard was born in Pasadena, California, U.S.A. Her father was one of the Flying Banvards, trapeze artists. Her mother, a male impersonator, and riflewoman, toured as dancing mistress with Pollard's Lilliputian Opera Company. This extraordinary and—to modern sensibilities —disturbing organization, with child performers dressed as miniature men and women, has left records of itself on the handbills and programmes which it scattered over much of the globe.

NOVEL THEATRICAL ATTRACTION!

The Pollard Lilliputian Opera Company is without doubt the most unique operatic organization in existence today. It is composed entirely of Australian children. (Not dwarfs or little old people as the little would imply.) The productions by these Juvenile Artists are complete in every detail, the costuming and scenic investiture of each opera presented comparing more than favourably with a majority of the high-class adult companies. Fathers and mothers who take their little ones to see the Pollards, instead of being bored as they might fear, soon find themselves laughing at and applauding the comedy, vocalization, dancing and acting of these small but experienced operatic artists.

The Company has achieved unqualified success in every part of the globe during the period of its career, which is just thirty years. The Company was originally organized in Melbourne for a tour of the Australasian colonies, and so great was its success that it extended its itinerary to Java, India, China, Japan, Africa, the Philippine Islands, Canada and other portions of the British Dominions, and are now in America for the fourth time. The children are recruited in Melbourne and its surrounding country. They are carefully trained by a dramatic instructor who has been associated with the Pollards for twenty years. When, in his opinion, they are proficient, they are allowed to take part in the regular performances. In their travels the girls are under the charge of four governesses who see that they receive proper educational advantages. The boys receive the same attention from male tutors.

The above blurb is from an American handbill *circa* 1900. The repertoire included *Floradora, A Gaiety Girl, The Toy-maker,* and *In Town* (with Act One set in the Vestibule of the Caravanserai Hotel, and Act Two set in the Green Room of the Ambiguity Theatre). The programme for the 1900 season at the Town Hall, Penang, for *The Belle of New York,* was—as programmes in the East often were—scented, and gave the age of each performer:

ICHABOD BRONSON	President of the Young Men's Rescue League	Willie Pollard	9
HARRY BRONSON	His Spendthrift Son	Lily Thomson	13
KARL VON PUMPERNICK	A Polite Lunatic	Harold Hill	12
DOC SNIFKINS	The Comic Opera Queen's Father	Emma Thomas	13
BLINKY BILL McGUIRE	A Mixed Ale Pugilist	Irene Goulding	11
KENNETH MUGG	Low Comedian, Comic Opera Co.	Fred Stewart	11
COUNT RATSI RATATOO	Portuguese Twins	George Moore	8
COUNT PATSI RATATOO		Willie Thomas	8
MR TWIDDLES	Harry Bronson's Secretary	Alice Turner	12
MR SNOOPER	A Newspaper Reporter	Myrtle Trott	8
MR PEEPER	A Photographer	Bennie Musgrove	9
WILLIAM	A Butler	William Thomson	9
VIOLET GRAY	A Salvation Lassie (The Belle)	Minnie Topping	12
FIFI FRICOR	A Little Parisienne	Madge Williams	6
KISSIE FLITZGARTER	A Music Hall Dancer	Ivy Trott	12
CORA ANGELIQUE	The Comic Opera Queen	Agnes Turner	7
MAMIE CLANCY	A Pell Street Girl	Ivy Trott	12

MYRTLE MINCE		May Topping	8
QUEENIE CAKE		Ruby Moore	11
BIRDIE SEED		Alice Bennetto	13
GLADYS GLEE	Cora's Bridesmaids	Daphne Trott	5
DOROTHY JUNE		May Thorn	12
MARJORIE MAY		Bella Thomson	12
LITTLE MISS FLIRT		Ethel Bennetto	7

Chas. A. Pollard and Mrs N. Chester were "sole owners" of this incredible company ("To belong is not only a distinction but an advantage which results in benefit to its members long after they have retired from it.") in which Yvonne Banvard, aged seven, made her début as Fifi Fricor, a part she played so often that Fifi became her pet name and, later, her stage and broadcasting one. A Lilliputian's day was long: morning lessons, afternoon rehearsals, shows at night. It was also hard, and at times hazardous. Once, on tour, the nine-year-old Fifi Banvard had her dress clawed through the bars of a cage by a panther also on tour. Her screams brought her mother plus rifle to her aid. Once only did she have two steady years at one school, in Seattle. Her Lilliputian days over, she studied ballet dancing with Pavlova, and came to Australia with her father in the same ship as John McCormack. After appearing, at the age of seventeen, in the title rôle of *Madame X*, she pursued a many-angled career. The earlier part of this was spent with the Reynolds and de Tisne New Theatre Royal Stock Company, which was based at the Theatre Royal, Brisbane, playing ingénue and comedy rôles in such plays as *Fair and Warmer, Peg o' My Heart*, and *Within the Law*, as well as Viola in *Twelfth Night*. In 1921, with her first husband, Eddie de Tisne, a violinist, she was on the Fuller Vaudeville Circuit in a song-and-dance act—Fifi and Her Excess Baggage. In 1922, as Fifi de Tisne, she played a harem-trousered and bepearled Fatima in Sir Benjamin and Mr J. Fuller's pantomime *Bluebird*. This was at the Princess Theatre, Melbourne, and the cast included Eddie de Tisne (Demon Discord), Jim Gerald (Sister Mary), and Frank Neil (Rastus).

In May 1923, at the Brisbane Theatre Royal, she played the Slavey in Jerome K. Jerome's *The Passing of the Third Floor Back* with Harrington Reynolds, Gerald Harcourt, Robert Fairfax, and Tom Cosgrove. By 1925 J.C.W.'s had cast her as Lady Jane in *Rose Marie* to play alongside the beautiful Jean Robertson, and Lou Vernon, George Bryant, and Reginald Dandy. About this time she introduced the Charleston and the Black Bottom to Australia, and was the model for black-and-white artist Brodie Mack.

In February 1931 she returned from several years on the American variety stages to tour with Clem Dawe in "gay and sparkling" shows of the *Honeymoon Girl* sort. Clem Dawe's *Midnight Frolics* had its hundredth performance in 1933 at the Theatre Royal, Hobart, which theatre was, nearly twenty years later, to play an important but frustrating part in Fifi Banvard's life. In 1934, wearing a wig of platinum blond corrugations, she played June East—an imitation Mae West—with Roy Rene in Cinesound's *Strike Me Lucky*. In September 1939, on the night war was declared, she was appearing in *Why Men Leave Home* at her old stamping-ground, the Theatre Royal, Brisbane.

While her second husband, Charles Kilburn, was at the war, Fifi Banvard lived at Berowra Waters, New South Wales, meantime developing a career as a "Radio Personality". She appeared on the Bob Dyer Show as leading comedienne, as well as playing leads in broadcast farcical comedies such as *Cradle Snatchers* (1944), with Dorothy Dunckley and Queenie Ashton, and *Meet the Wife* (1945).

After the war, the Minerva Theatre, King's Cross, Sydney, which had been built by entrepreneur David N. Martin in 1939, became the centre of her activities, first as an actress, but also, increasingly, as a producer.

Fifi Banvard's numerous Minerva experiences include parts in the revue *Sweetest and Lowest* (1947), with Max Oldaker, Sumner Locke-Elliott (playwright of *Rusty Bugles*), Gordon Chater (ex-medical student of Cambridge

University who had made his Minerva revue début with Wee Georgie Wood), and Margaret Rainer; and a number of plays which she directed for Whitehall Productions. Among them were: *Ah, Wilderness!* with Trader Faulkner, Lou Vernon, Therese Desmond, and Bebe Scott; *The Streets of London* (December 1948), with Grant Taylor, Lola Brooks, Nellie Bramley, Lou Vernon, Marie Bremner, Gwenyth Friend, and Bebe Scott; Noel Langley's *Little Lambs Eat Ivy* (May 1949), with Richard Parry and Gordon Chater; *See How They Run*, with Gwen Plumb, Daphne Winslow, Richard Parry, Aileen Britton, Lou Vernon, and Alan Herbert; *Dream Girl*, with June Clyde, and a badly written Max Afford play, *Dark Enchantment*, with Neva Carr Glyn, Grant Taylor, and Georgie Sterling.

Fifi Banvard's acting was—in the field she chose—forceful, dominating, and vital. Her ability as a director included these qualities, and the dangerous one of sparing-no-expense.

In 1949 she and Gwenyth Friend formed a company, Fifi Banvard Productions. Gwenyth Friend, sister of artist Donald Friend, had done theatrical work in Sydney with Thea Rowe, and with Whitehall Productions. Although she appeared successfully in a number of stage plays (John Henry in *Member of the Wedding*, Mrs de Winter in *Rebecca, See How They Run, Love From a Stranger*), and in numerous child parts on the air, her main theatrical interests lay in backstage work, and in making puppets and masks.

Fifi Banvard Productions leased the Theatre Royal, Hobart, and established there a basic company of mainland professionals supplemented by talented Tasmanians. Fifi Banvard and Gwenyth Friend were to find, as the heroic Mrs Clarke had found a century earlier, that this theatre was a perilous proposition. Before the company was financially wrecked, however, it competently—and, considering the small population, too lavishly—presented a number of popular comedies and dramas: in 1949, *See How They Run*, with

Daphne Winslow, and *On Monday Next*, with John Moore; in 1950, *Ladies in Retirement*, with Freda Elliott and Daphne Winslow, *Love From a Stranger*, with Aileen Britton (who had trained with Allan Wilkie), Neva Carr Glyn, John Tate, and Gwenyth Friend, *The Gioconda Smile*, with Lloyd Lamble, Lesley Jackson (Mrs Lloyd Lamble), and Edwin Finn, *Clutterbuck*, with John Tate, and *Pygmalion*, with Lloyd Lamble; in 1951, *Night Must Fall*, with Fifi Banvard as Mrs Branson, *Rain*, with Laurier Lange, John Moore, and Fifi Banvard as Sadie Thomson, *Susan and God*, with Eric Reiman, Marie Austin, Daphne Winslow, and Spencer Teakle (who had acted on Broadway, and in the film *Lloyds of London*), *Arsenic and Old Lace*, *Rebecca*, and *I Killed the Count*.

Despite heartbreaking and purse-draining efforts the company was compelled to disband in 1952. After an attempt to establish a theatrical guest house in Hobart with a small theatre attached, Fifi Banvard returned to Sydney. The ghost which is said to haunt the Theatre Royal, Australia's oldest theatre, and to make its presence felt as signal of successful ventures, did not do this enough times for Fifi Banvard Productions.

One of the last plays in which Fifi Banvard played a leading part was *Nude with Violin* (1961), with Robert Helpmann, Bettina Welch, Minnie Love, and Campbell Copelin. In the cast as juvenile lead was Pamela Greenall who has since advanced her career in England, starring in more than a hundred plays with provincial repertory companies—Leatherhead, Wolverhampton, Worthing, Glasgow, and Dundee. The plays included *Hedda Gabler*, *The Glass Menagerie*, *Private Lives*, *Candida*, *The Millionairess*, *Billy Liar*, *Heartbreak House*, *The Miser*, and *A Taste of Honey*. Also in *Nude with Violin* was Alistair Roberts, who lectured on drama in Occupied Japan in 1947, and played leading rôles in *Young Woodley*, *Rusty Bugles*, *The "Caine"*

Mutiny Court-Martial, and *The Rivals* in which his performance as Bob Acres for the Australian Elizabethan Theatre Trust won the Sydney Critics' Award.

Fifi Banvard's last stage appearance was as Mae Peterson in *Bye Bye Birdie* in J.C.W.'s production at the Majestic Theatre, Sydney, in October 1961. She died in Sydney in 1962.

CHAPTER SEVEN

THE TWENTIES—AND THEIR
AFTERMATH

THE first twenty years of the twentieth century seem, at a glance, to have offered opportunities galore for home-grown players on stage and screen. As well there were opportunities for home-grown playwrights. The better actor-managers were avid for Australian plays. Bland Holt commissioned a fashionable socialist writer, Henry Lawson, to write one. Lawson, who had been paid in advance, shillied and shallied, for he was unreliable as well as being unequal to the task. The grisly result, which would have taken three weeks to play, was unrevisable even by Holt, a master of revivifying inferior works.

Gregan McMahon encouraged Australians by producing their plays. Among the more dramatically sound were: *Dead Timber* (Louis Esson), *Whither?* (Mary Wilkinson), *The Taint* (E. H. Oliphant), *The Image Breaker*, and *The Sacred Flame* (Alfred Buchanan), *Mrs Pretty and the Premier* (Arthur H. Adams), *The Children's Bread* (Blamire Young), *The Only Game* (William Moore), and *The Climax* (Edward Dyson).

Australian film-makers were working in advance of any in the world, and with more verve. Joseph Henry Perry, born in Birmingham, England, in 1862, who came to Australia as a young man, made the world's first motion picture play. It was filmed and edited in 1899, two years before the film generally accepted as first—a fantasy *A Trip to the Moon* made in 1901 by a Frenchman, George Melies. Melies's film had a conglomeration of characters, some straight from Hieronymus Bosch, and others—full-hipped ladies of the chorus—who could have come from some *boîte de nuit* on the buttes of Montmartre. It contained also a shot of the globular earth as presumably seen from the moon, forerunner of scores of such shots in later pseudo-scientific films.

Perry's film, *The Early Christian Martyrs*, made for that lively institution the Salvation Army, was filmed by daylight —artificial light was not used in films until 1920—on the tennis courts of the Salvation Army Home for Girls, in Dandenong Road, Murrumbeena, Melbourne. This production was of incredibly high standard with a cast of six hundred, the leading rôles being performed by players from William Cole's Dramatic Company. The problems of cinematically illustrating the showier sufferings of the martyrs were cunningly and convincingly solved. The film went to London to be hand-coloured, and had its première at the Melbourne Town Hall on September 13, 1900, by which time Perry, who died in Sydney in 1943 at the age of eighty-one, was working on his next film, also for the Salvation Army, called *Soldiers of the Cross*. Nothing daunted him. Christ was depicted writhing on the Cross; Stephen was stoned to death; Nero illuminated his garden by setting staked Christians alight.

Perry's three sons, Reginald H., Stanley W., and Orrie G. —especially Orrie G.—followed in their father's footsteps and, in a St Kilda studio, photographed a string of films. *The Story of the Kelly Gang*, with O. G. Perry as cameraman for J. and N. Tait, was the world's first feature-length film. It was made less than a year after the American film, *The Great Train Robbery*, which is carelessly accounted the first film-with-a-real-plot ever made. Among their films was Nat

Gould's *The Double Event* (1909), for which the racing scenes were shot on the notorious and powerful John Wren's Ascot racecourse.

In 1907, Perry *père* and his sons made *The Scottish Covenanters* in a studio the Salvation Army had built for them at Caulfield, Victoria, with players from the Cullinan-Grant Company.

Much of Australia's lead in film-making was due to a neurotic London showman, Cozens Spencer, whose real name was Spencer Cozens or Cousins. He came to Australia in 1904 exhibiting *The Great Train Robbery, A Trip to the Moon*, and that primitive ancestor of a sumless and apparently indestructible breed called simply *Cowboys and Indians*.

Cozens Spencer sized up Australia's entertainment-loving and money-squandering possibilities. By becoming a monopolistic agent for overseas film releases, by backing a number of rough-and-tumble films, largely about bushrangers, and by building a moving-picture studio at Rushcutters' Bay, Sydney, Spencer was, come 1912, a wealthy man, first of the movie moguls. By 1918 he was also a nervous wreck and, in an attempt to escape the perils of multiplying riches and increasing neuroses, retired to a ranch in Canada. In 1933 his body, with a revolver near by, was found on the banks of a stream by an officer of the Canadian Mounted Police.

Associated with Spencer were the Higgins brothers, Ernest, Arthur, and Tasman, all cameramen. Raymond Longford was Spencer's producer. Their films have already been mentioned.

In 1909 Franklyn Barrett produced the first Visitor-from-Outer-Space film, *A Message from Mars*.

While film companies sprang up, and 1914 and cataclysm were drawing inexorably nearer, babies who were to become actors and actresses continued to be born. Between 1900 and the Sarajevo assassination, an assortment of infants, bonneted, and booteed, mittened, long-robed, and beribboned, one by one made first public appearances in cane and sennit perambulators—Jos Ambler, and Hal Percy (1900), Gus Bluett (1902), Agnes Dobson (1904), Max Oldaker, John Alden, and Dick Bentley (1907), Chips Rafferty, Robert Helpmann, and Errol Flynn (1909), Russell Napier (1910), Neva Carr Glyn, and John Sherman (1911), Coral Browne (1913), and Merle Oberon, Margaret Vyner, and Lloyd Lamble in 1914. Some were to have a limited and local fame, others were of the wide world.

Hal Percy, born 1900, spent his patchwork career in concert work, musical comedy, wireless production, and the amateur theatre, but he has done enough straight acting to justify mention. At seventeen he joined the Australian army, went overseas, and worked with a concert party behind the lines. He made sufficient impression on the organizer of the Co-Optimists to be offered a part. This he turned down and, the war over, went back to Australia, where after an attempt to study commercial art, he joined the Philip Lytton Touring Tent Show Company. At the end of two years on the road he appeared at the Princess Theatre, Melbourne, in pantomime and musical comedy. He was next with the Harry Greig Company at the Athenaeum Theatre, Melbourne. Finally, he became a juvenile lead with J.C.W.'s, remaining with them for twelve years, constantly touring, and appearing with such favourites of the 1920s as Leon Gordon and Maurice Moscovich. By 1931 he felt confident in his powers to produce, and with Brett Randall formed the Little Theatre Company. With scarcely any more backing than enthusiasm and optimism, Percy and Randall launched the company on December 2, 1931, at the Central Hall, Melbourne, with Miles Malleson's *The Fanatics*.

Brett Randall was born in London, on September 15, 1884, of theatrical parents, members of the D'Oyly Carte Company. He appeared on the stage from earliest boyhood and, as a boy, waiting for his father outside the Adelphi Theatre, London, on December 16, 1897, witnessed the stabbing to death of William Terriss, who was entering the Adelphi to play in *Secret Service*. The assassin was a madman, Richard Prince. After playing numerous parts in England, Randall came to Australia in 1925.

The Little Theatre Company is now a flourishing group with a splendidly appointed theatre, St Martin's, in South Yarra, Melbourne. The mission of the Little Theatre Company was "to present plays of both literary and entertainment value, and to offer scope for Australian authors". This was early accomplished: in the first six months the company had produced six overseas plays and four Australian ones. Brett Randall died in 1963.

Productions by Hal Percy included *The Second Man* and *The Circle of Chalk* (1932), *Cock Robin* (1933), *The Crime of Margaret Foley* (1947), *The Mocking Bird* (1948) and *Grand National Night* (1949).

He was Acting Director of Variety for the Australian Broadcasting Commission, Sydney, when he died in 1950.

Agnes Dobson was born in Sydney on December 30, 1904. Her father, Collet Barker Dobson, was a Shakespearian actor-manager, handsome, dashing, and a swordsman—qualities which, when he was younger, made him the ideal choice for Mercutio, Romeo, Hotspur, and Richmond. Among other parts he played Claude Melnotte, Judas in Maude Williamson's production of *Barabbas*, many parts with the tragedian George Miln, and some with Maggie Moore. As Agnes Dobson was growing up he was producer for C. E. King's Royal Dramatic Company. One of his productions was *Dinna Forget*, a play he wrote in 1911.

With her parents often on tour, Agnes Dobson was "brought up in theatre trunks, cradled on the hat-rack of trains", and was once carried on stage as an infant. When this infant Dobson wailed, a voice from the gallery shouted, "Jeez, it's alive! Feed it, missus!"

Billed as Little Agnes, she ran the gamut of child parts— Little Willie in *East Lynne*; Little Eva in *Uncle Tom's Cabin; Little Lord Fauntleroy; The Little Girl God Forgot;* and the girl in *No Mother To Guide Her.*

She was rigorously trained. She studied Shakespeare with her father, fencing at a gymnasium, piano-playing with Victor Vizer, painting with Vida Lahey, and dancing with Dora Leslie. Her dancing teacher, who could stand on her head at the age of sixty-four, was the sister of Fred Leslie. He and his partner Ivy Schilling were the Astaires of their day.

During a long and multicoloured career, Agnes Dobson has worked with a number of notable people, on the stage, and in Australian films: Joe E. Brown, Robert Morley, Lesley Adrienne, Sir Lewis Casson, Dame Sybil Thorndike (Agnes Dobson played the Nurse to Dame Sybil's Medea for the A.B.C., Melbourne), Tom Keene, Ron Beck (who played in the 1937 production of Agnes Dobson's own play, *Dark Brother*, a prize-winner in the Adelaide *Advertiser* Centenary Play Competition), Lewis Shaw, Bob Dyer, Frank Royde, and Nellie Ferguson. Nellie Ferguson also began as a child actress, growing up to play Ophelia to Allan Wilkie's rather beefy and moon-faced Hamlet, Lady Isabel in *East Lynne*, and a coven of villainesses.

Selections from Agnes Dobson's lengthy and many-branched repertoire give the graph of her career. In 1914, at the Royal Theatre, Brisbane, billed as Little Agnes, she played in the tear-inducing *A Girl Without a Home*. In 1918 she appeared in Sydney in *Rasputin* and, with Nellie Bramley in the lead, in *The Woman Thou Gavest Me*. In 1919 Agnes Dobson made her leading-lady début, after being on the stage since babyhood, in *While London Sleeps*, at the Majestic Theatre (later the Elizabethan Theatre), Newtown, Sydney. In this play she walked, encumbered by a child in arms, a hazardous tight-rope every night of the play's run.

During the 1920s, a slender reddish-brunette, five feet five inches tall, with green eyes, she was "the darling of the stalls", and was constantly busy playing leading rôles in *Camille; Young Woodley* (in which she wore Judith Anderson's superb wardrobe from *The Green Hat); Number Seventeen* (with Brett Randall as hero); *Charley's Aunt; The Sign of the Cross* (she played a wide-eyed Mercia to the Marcus Superbus of English actor Guy Hastings); and the comedy *Almost a Honeymoon* at the Criterion Theatre, Sydney, with Frank Neil, Hal Percy, and, as the vamp, Fifi Banvard.

She played in Australian films: in *The Hayseeds* series; in 1919 in *The Face at the Window*, with D. B. O'Connor, Claude Turton, and Gerald Harcourt; and in *Barry Butts In*, in which she cavorted opposite the English comedian Barry Lupino, and for which the hilarious chase scenes, involving Tin Lizzies, a scooter, and a hansom cab (the last in Sydney), were shot in Macquarie Street, Sydney, in the early morning.

When the bottom fell out of stage work she taught drama and voice-production at girls' schools, wrote scripts for broadcasting, was Talks Presentation Officer for the A.B.C. during World War II, and then principal of the Crawford School of Broadcasting. She appeared in sketches with George Wallace. She wrote and produced her second play, *Immortal Road*. She produced for the Independent Group, Adelaide, in 1937, a lofty selection of works including *Mary Stuart* (Swinburne), *Physician in Spite of Himself* (Molière), *Lady from the Sea* (Ibsen), *The Oresteia* (Aeschylus), *As You Desire Me* (Pirandello), *The Playboy of the Western World* (Synge), and *The Girl Who Didn't Want to Go to Kuala Lumpur* (Bridie). She played, and continues to play, Mrs Sharpshot in the A.B.C.'s long-running *The Village Glee*

Club with Colin Crane, who created a furore singing "Old Man River" in the first Australian production of *Show Boat*.

Agnes Dobson is a widow who has been married three times, and has one son. She has always had high theatrical ideals and—while believing that the professional must adapt and be prepared to give immaculate performances no matter what the material—is adamant that sincerity and naturalism should be the actor's goal. She feels that "acting is an inspired and inspiring business", and inclines to be a devotee of Stanislavski and, so far as the voice is concerned, of Dr Aikin whose voice-training methods were used by John Gielgud and Sir Laurence Olivier.

Her father, Collet Barker Dobson, produced and played for C. E. King's Royal Dramatic Company, based in Brisbane, and for Fuller's Dramatic Players at the Palace Theatre, Melbourne, an interminable list of melodramas: *From Shopgirl to Duchess, The Coal King, Night Birds of London*, Hall Caine's *The Christian* (this was filmed in 1909), *Nick Carter, The Sorrows of Satan*, with George Cross as Prince Lucio; *Rasputin* (written by John Cosgrove and Benjamin Fuller); Walter Melville's *The Female Swindler*, and *The Girl Who Wrecked His Home; While London Sleeps, The Girl Who Knew a Bit, The Bad Girl of the Family*, with Lorna Forbes as Bess More; *A Sailor's Sweetheart*, and *The World Against Her*.

His casts included Elsie Prince, Molly Mead, Effie Rowlands, Edna Waters, Mabel Lynne, Olga Agnew, Rutland Beckett, Harrie Collet, Athena Claudius, John Barker, Gladys Auchter, Florence Richter, Rose Knight Phillips, Gilbert Emery, Lorna Forbes, Claire Duggan, Charles Villiers, Austin Milroy, Marie Ilka, Doris Mills, D'Arcy Kelway, Nellie Ferguson, George Harpur, Lillian Wiseman, Augustus Neville, Stanley Robinson, Paul Devere, Violet Minty, and "the young man who plays old men so well", Tal Ordell.

Agnes Dobson and her father are descendants of the well-known explorer after whom Mount Barker in South Australia is named.

Max Oldaker was born in Devonport, Tasmania, on December 17, 1907, and educated there. After leaving school he studied music and sometimes sang at concerts. At one of these, in 1930, he was heard by Edward Branscombe, an English entrepreneur responsible for bringing Maud Allan, Sousa's Band, the Scarlet Dandies, and the Cherniavsky Trio on Australasian tours. Having "discovered" Max Oldaker, Branscombe, who was piloting the Westminster Glee Singers on a world tour, invited him to join the company of which, in 1930, Wilfred Thomas was also a member. Max Oldaker, therefore, after a professional début at the Palace Theatre, Sydney, travelled with the Glee Singers to Peking. In the Yellow Sea the ship was trapped in pack-ice, through which it laboriously ploughed towards an opening night in Tientsin. The Glee Singers returned south by the Shanghai Express which, in those pre-Communist days, was crammed with wealthy Chinese in fur-lined robes who expectorated copiously in the elaborate spittoons in the dining car. Max Oldaker was stranded in Singapore, "the actors' graveyard". He reached England with £8.

For the next eight years, until the outbreak of World War II, he went through the theatrical mill of the Depression years, mainly in musical comedy, comic opera (with the D'Oyly Carte Opera Company), floor shows, and concert parties.

By 1934 he had a part in *The Three Sisters* (Oscar Hammerstein II and Jerome Kern), which opened at the Drury Lane Theatre on April 9, 1934, and, despite Stanley Holloway and Charlotte Greenwood being in the cast, was an expensive failure with the shortest Drury Lane run for ten years. For the rest of 1934 Max Oldaker worked, first for two weeks as second pianist (he had won a scholarship at the

Royal Academy of Music, and the Sir Arnold Bax Prize for singers who could play the piano), and "pop" vocalist with Joe Loss and his band at the rather *louche* Kit Kat Club. This stint was followed by five months with a summer concert party in Aberystwyth, Wales, as a Jack-of-all-trades—actor, singer, handyman, light comic, second pianist, and stooge for the first comedian.

In 1935 he sang Walther Von Stolzing to Sir John Barbirolli's conducting of Wagner's *Die Meistersinger* and later played many parts in Birmingham Repertory's *1066 and All That*, which afterwards transferred to the Aldwych Theatre, London.

The year 1938 found him playing in *Operette* the part of Paul Trevor which Noël Coward had written for him. It was his first West End part, in a cast headed by Lynn Fontanne and Alfred Lunt. In the same year he played second juvenile to Bobby Howes in *Bobby Get Your Gun*. In the cast were Diana Churchill, Bertha Belmore, and Wylie Watson.

When war came in 1939 he worked with Beatrice Lillie and Jeanne de Casalis in entertaining the troops. In 1940 he returned to Australia to play all the important tenor rôles for a J. C. Williamson's season of Gilbert and Sullivan.

During the remainder of the 1940 decade he interspersed recurring Gilbert and Sullivan appearances with leading man rôles in musical comedies: 1942, Baldasarre in *Maid of the Mountains* with Gladys Moncrieff; 1943, in *The Merry Widow*, as Prince Danilo; 1944, Baron von Schober in *Lilac Time*; 1945, The Red Shadow in *The Desert Song* with Joy Beattie; and, in January 1946, Jim Kenyon in *Rose Marie*. He was the most popular of matinée idols, six feet tall and handsome, and was showered with gifts by his fans, and with praise by critics . . . "a dashing and romantic figure", "his fans almost raised the roof when he entered on a handsome white charger", "charming and debonair".

In June 1946, with Viola Wilson as Maria, he starred as

Rudi Kleber in Ivor Novello's *The Dancing Years*, his favourite rôle in Australia, a non-singing part in which his "combined vivacity and pathos" were applauded by fans and critics alike.

On April 6, 1949, he played Rudi Kleber opposite Victoria Campbell in an English tour of *The Dancing Years*, produced by Australian Freddie Carpenter. Back in Australia, he played the murderer, Dr Jeffries, in *Bonaventure* at the Theatre Royal, Sydney, during October 1950.

After another prolonged Gilbert and Sullivan season on tour, he joined the John Alden Shakespearian Company which opened in Melbourne on December 5, 1951, with *Lear*, Alden playing Lear, and Max Oldaker the Duke of Albany. The Alden Company then made an expensive zig-zag tour until November 1952—Sydney, Melbourne, Adelaide, Brisbane, Toowoomba, Canberra, Perth, Hobart, Launceston—with Oldaker playing Polixenes in *A Winter's Tale*; Fenton in *The Merry Wives of Windsor*; Bassanio in *The Merchant of Venice*; and, in *A Midsummer Night's Dream*, opposite Neva Carr Glyn's Titania, an Oberon which was played as "a laughing playboy with a respect for poetry".

After appearing in *White Horse Inn*, Offenbach's *La Belle Hélène*, with Marie Collier, and *Maid of the Mountains*, he joined William Orr's Company at Phillip Street Theatre, Sydney, in January 1955, and gave, until July 1957, a series of smooth comic characterizations in *Hat Trick* (1955), *Two to One* (1955), *Round the Loop* (1956-1957), and *Alice in Wonderland*.

In July 1957 he was in England, to play Zoltan Karpathy in *My Fair Lady* at Drury Lane Theatre, and to understudy Rex Harrison as Professor Henry Higgins. On the occasions when he took over Harrison's part it was with applauded distinction.

Since 1959, when he was recalled to Tasmania and his invalid parents, of whom he is the only son, he has appeared rarely on the more brightly lit theatrical planes, but has worked with enthusiasm in Tasmania on television, wireless, stage production, script-writing, and theatrical criticism.

His hobbies include restoring old furniture, reading, and redecorating his Hayloft Studio in Launceston, which is something of a *salon* for visiting actors and musicians.

Sophie Stewart, born in Crieff, Perthshire, Scotland, has made an unusual reversal of the cliché pattern of the unknown Australian actress making a name overseas. Her stage and film careers were long and well established before she settled in Australia where she has starred (with Robert Morley) in *Edward, My Son* (1949-1950), *Dear Charles* (1954-1955), *Not in the Book* (1958-1959), *Shadow of the Vine* (TV, 1961), and *Fly By Night* (TV, 1962). During 1963, at the Old Tote Theatre, Sydney, she played Madame Ranevsky in *The Cherry Orchard,* Queen Gertrude in *Hamlet,* and Lady Bracknell in *The Importance of Being Earnest.*

She was educated at Morrison's Academy, Crieff, and studied ballet dancing with Enrico Cechetti, and stage technique at the Royal Academy of Dramatic Art, London. After playing many parts at the Plymouth Repertory Theatre (destroyed by bomb during World War II), including the title rôle in *Mary Rose,* Lady Babbie in *The Little Minister,* and Pollyanna in *Peg o' My Heart,* she made her professional début at the New Theatre, Oxford, on November 16, 1925, with Lyn Harding in *His Highness Below Stairs.* Her London début was in the title rôle of *Marigold* at the Kingsway Theatre, London, in 1927. Since then she has created a theatrical record as star of *Marigold* in its multiple metamorphoses: in 1930 on Broadway, and on tour of Canada and America; in the wireless and television adaptations (*Marigold* was the first play ever to be televised, in 1936); in the 1938 film; and in the musical comedy version in 1959.

Among the numerous plays she starred or co-starred in were: *The Sleeping Clergyman,* with Robert Donat, 1933, Piccadilly Theatre, London; *Marriage is No Joke,* with Ralph Richardson, 1934, Globe Theatre, London; *The Maitlands,* with John Gielgud, 1935, Criterion Theatre, London; *Twelfth Night* (as Olivia), with Helen Hayes, 1940, on Broadway; *Life with Father,* with Leslie Banks, 1947-1948, Savoy Theatre, London; and *The Human Touch,* with Alec Guinness, 1949, Savoy Theatre, London.

Her career as a film actress began in 1935 opposite Eric Portman in *Maria Martin,* and included contract work for Sir Alexander Korda in England, and for R.K.O. and United Artists in Hollywood. Among films she played leading rôles in were *City of Beautiful Nonsense,* with Emlyn Williams, *As You Like It* (as Celia), with Elisabeth Bergner and Laurence Olivier, *Things to Come,* with Raymond Massey, *The Man Who Could Work Miracles,* with Roland Young, *Under the Red Robe,* with Conrad Veidt, *Nurse Edith Cavell, My Son, My Son, The Lamp Still Burns, Yangtse Incident,* and *Uncle Silas.*

She married the actor Ellis Irving on April 14, 1940, in Hollywood, and lives at Church Point, Sydney.

John (Gordon Buchanan) Alden was born at Taree, New South Wales, in 1907. A subtle and dramatic Shakespearian actor, his most convincing performances were as Othello, Shylock, and King Lear. His major contribution to Australian theatre was his courageous foundation, in 1948, of a permanent Shakespearian group of players, based somewhat on the lines of the Old Vic. Company, which toured widely. He died in 1962.

Chips Rafferty was born John William Pilbean Goffage on March 25, 1909, at Broken Hill, New South Wales, birthplace also of June Bronhill, the singer (whose stage-name Bronhill is derived from the name of her native city), and of film star Dorothy Alison.

He received the final years of his education at Parramatta Commercial High School. Considering that he had abilities as a painter, he began to study art at the Royal Art Society, Sydney. This studentship did not last long. Chips Rafferty's life as a young man was one of fits and starts: an apprenticeship as an iron-moulder at Clyde Engineering Works; cellarman to a wine-and-spirit merchant; and a mish-mash of labouring jobs in the outback of New South Wales and Queensland—clearing, fencing, opal-gouging, gold-fossicking, droving, and kangaroo-shooting. After he married Ellen K. Jameson, on May 28, 1941, he and his wife ran an ice-cream parlour where they sold sweets and toffees made by themselves, and Rafferty's water-colours. Just before this, at twenty-nine, he had made his film début.

His first part was in a minor Australian talkie called *Ants in His Pants* (1938), which starred the vaudeville comedian Will Mahony. Next year, 1939, Rafferty played his second film role, in *Dad Rudd, M.P.*, in which Bert Bailey, at the age of sixty-seven, and after more than a quarter of a century of it, was still doing what he had first done at the age of forty.

Other Rafferty films were *The Lives of Joanna Godden*, with John McCallum and Googie Withers; *Eureka Stockade* (1949, Ealing Studios); and *Bitter Springs*, a Michael Balcon production, with Tommy Trinder and Michael Pate. This was the last and most absurd attempt of Ealing Studios to depict pioneer Australia. Two other "Australian" films, made by London Films and Twentieth Century-Fox, were *Smiley*, with Colin Petersen, Sir Ralph Richardson, and John McCallum; and *Smiley Gets a Gun*, with Keith Calvert and Dame Sybil Thorndike. In 1951 Rafferty appeared as Trooper Leonard in *Kangaroo*, with Maureen O'Hara, Peter Lawford, Finlay Currie, Richard Boone, Letty Craydon, Charles Tingwell, and Ron Whelan. In 1952 Rafferty and several other Australians went to Hollywood to sell such dinkum-Aussie verisimilitude as they could to *Desert Rats*. In the same year he founded Platypus Films with Lee Robinson, a director of film documentaries. He appeared in the first production *The Phantom Stockman* (1953), with Henry Murdoch and Max Osbiston.

Forming another company, Southern International Films, which worked hand-in-hand with outside companies to produce B class work, Rafferty next appeared in a colour film shot on the Barrier Reef, *King of the Coral Sea* (1954), with Ilma Adey and Charles Tingwell. Later productions in which Rafferty took part as actor or producer were *Walk into Paradise* (1955), with a French unit, Discifilm; *Dust in the Sun* (1957), with Jill Adams, Ken Wayne, Maureen Lanigan, James Forrest, Reg Lye, and the aboriginal, Robert Tudawali; and *The Stowaway* (1958).

In 1959 Lee Robinson produced *The Restless and the Damned*, with Edmund O'Brien, Richard Basehart, Andrea Parisy, Reg Lye, and Nigel Lovell.

During World War II Chips Rafferty was a flying officer with the Royal Australian Air Force. He records swimming, golf, and chess as favourite relaxations.

An interesting comparison in venues can be made between selections from works of two of the busiest directors of the talkie period—Kenneth G. Hall (mainly for Cinesound) and Charles Chauvel.

Hall's and Cinesound's attempts to meet a wary public half-way were an almost unbelievable revelation of timidity, pinheadedness—or stale cunning. Old tales were retold, tales that had barely warranted the first telling: *On Our Selection* (1932); *The Silence of Dean Maitland* (1934); *Orphan of the Wilderness*, and *Thoroughbred* in 1936; *It Isn't Done*, and *Tall Timbers* in 1937; *Let George Do It* (George Wallace), *Lovers and Luggers, Mr Chedworth Steps Out*, and *The Broken Melody* in 1938, and much Dad-and-Davery with Bert Bailey. In 1946 Hall directed, for Columbia Pictures, the film *Smithy*. It had some freak value because William Morris Hughes, and the aviators P. G. Taylor and John T. Stannage, played themselves. Other players were Ron Randell (Kingsford Smith), Muriel Steinbeck (Mary), John Tate (Ulm), and Joy Nichols (Kay).

It has already been noted that Australian film-makers were quick off the mark. Even in 1914 *Australia's Response to the Empire's Call* was flickering away for audiences lined up on kauri benches at threepence a head for "back stalls", sixpence a head for "front stalls". In 1913 John F. Gavin had produced an imitation Chaplin in *Charlie at the Show*. Second and even third versions of *The Kelly Gang, Mutiny of the "Bounty", For the Term of His Natural Life, The Silence of Dean Maitland,* and *The Mystery of a Hansom Cab* appeared. Francis Birtles, ex-airman and explorer, produced travelogues. So did Frank Hurley. In 1917 Hugh McCrae, the poet, appeared in Bert Ives's *The Life of Adam Lindsay Gordon,* and in 1921 Henry Lawson made an untidy *ave atque vale* appearance in the prologue of Beaumont Smith's *While the Billy Boils*.

In 1925 Charles Chauvel directed his first film, *Moth of Moonbi*, featuring Arthur Tauchert, and in 1926 his second, *Greenhide*.

In 1927 Chauvel made the third, and best, £60,000 version of *For the Term of His Natural Life* with an Anglo-American-Australian cast—Hollywood's Eva Novak (Silvia Vickers), George Fisher (Rufus Dawes), Dunstan Webb (Lieutenant Frere), the beautiful Australian Jessica Harcourt (Sarah Purfoy), Mayne Lynton (Rev. Mr North), and Gerald Kay Souper (Major Vickers). It made the box-office record of its period for an Australian film; was further distinguished by having the author's daughter, Marion Marcus Clarke, play Rufus Dawes's mother; and inspired a melancholy theme-song which cinema pianists played at the film's more depressing moments:

201

For the term of his natural life,
To be an outcast for ever,
Weighed down with fetters of grief and shame,
Innocent, yet taking all the blame . . .

Marion Marcus Clarke, daughter of Marcus Clarke and actress Marion Dunn, trained with Bland Holt, making her début in two small parts, an old woman, and a nursemaid, in *The Price of Peace*. By 1906 she was a character actress in America with the Fred Niblo Company, which lost everything in the San Francisco earthquake. She then worked with the George Howard Company, which played in Alaska where the old dance-halls of Dawson City had been transformed into theatres. Touring this new world she preferred Canada, which did not allow Sunday performances, to western America, where Sunday was a gruelling day with a matinée and a change of bill. When she returned to Australia from Vancouver via Honolulu in 1927 she did not stay long —The Firm's domination dismayed her. After touring Australia in the stage presentations that accompanied the first showings of *For the Term of His Natural Life* she returned to America.

Eva Novak stayed in Australia to star in another film, *The Romance of Runnibede*, supported by Gordon Collingridge, Claude Saunders, Ronald Conway, and Dunstan Webb.

Jessica Harcourt appeared again, in 1928, in *The Russell Affair*, with Aidre Stewart, Roylie Payne, and Arthur Clarke. Two other 1928 films, *The Birth of White Australia* and *The Devil's Playground*, were among the last Australian silent films.

Australian producers were slower in taking to production of talkies than they had been to productions of silents, but before he retired the veteran Beaumont Smith had his Hayseeds talking, in 1933, and directed *Splendid Fellows*, his final talkie, in 1934, for J.C.W.'s.

Kenneth G. Hall had a coarse-grained cinematic liaison

with elderly vaudevilleans. Charles Chauvel had a more perceptive and creative one with loftier ideas and a wider canvas.

Chips Rafferty performed with both Cinesound and Chauvel. In 1941 he was in *Forty Thousand Horsemen,* with Grant Taylor playing a lead. The film was Chauvel's account of the Palestine Campaign of the Great War, and had a Cecil B. de Mille cast of actors supplied by the Australian army authorities, who gave lavish co-operation. In 1944 Chauvel made *The Rats of Tobruk,* with Peter Finch as star, and Chips Rafferty playing Chips Rafferty as a laconic Aussie hard-doer. He was next in *The Overlanders,* with Daphne Campbell. This Ealing Studios film, directed by Englishman Harry Watt, took advantage of the wartime necessity of overlanding southwards vast herds of cattle from North Australia because invasion by the Japanese army was more than a possibility. Watt had been sent from England by Ealing Studios, who were investigating the potentialities of profitable film-making in Australia. In 1947 the J. Arthur Rank Organization had the same idea, which resulted in *Bush Christmas,* a direct and charming picture in which Chips Rafferty, whose name had become household and box-office, was a star. Rafferty played with John Fernside, a "frank and manly" actor, who first drew the attention of J. and N. Tait when he took over from leading man Cyril McKay, victim of laryngitis, the part of Jimmy Fitzpatrick in *De Luxe Annie,* an Emilie Polini play. He played numerous parts with players of the calibre of Frank Harvey and Olive Wilton.

Bush Christmas had more success in London than films produced in Australia, which mostly deserve little success because their vitality is forced, their Aussie-ism distorted to burlesque, and their content immature. Even the half-polished amateurism that is the standard today in Australian stage and television presentations is lacking in these films which blunder to THE END—ill-written, ill-acted, ill-timed, ill-cut—with an abundance of embarrassing and misplaced sincerity.

Charles Chauvel's works include: *In the Wake of the "Bounty"* (1933), starring Errol Flynn; and *Heritage* (1935), which was written, produced, and directed by Chauvel, filmed by cameraman Tasman Higgins, and included in its cast Margot Rhys, Peggy Maguire, Franklyn Bennett, Joe Valli, Frank Harvey, Norman French, Victor Fitzherbert, and Ann Wyn. In 1936 he was connected with *Uncivilized, The Flying Doctor* (Margaret Vyner and Charles Farrell), and *Rangle River*, the latter two directed by imported men. *Forty Thousand Horsemen* was made in 1941, *The Rats of Tobruk* in 1944. In 1949 he was producer and director, and part-author with his wife, Elsa Chauvel, of *Sons of Matthew*. In the cast of O'Riordans were John O'Malley (Matthew O'Riordan), Thelma Scott (Jane), Michael Pate (Shane), Ken Wayne (Barney), Tommy Burns (Luke), John Unicomb (Terry), and John Ewart (Mickey). Non-O'Riordans were played by Wendy Gibb and Betty Orme.

Perhaps Chauvel's greatest and most integrated film was *Jedda*, produced in 1953-1954 in colour. Once more the screenplay, beautifully simple, was written by Charles and Elsa Chauvel. The parts of the aboriginal lovers were played by Ngarla Kunoth, now a nun, and Robert Tudawali, who became a victim of alcoholism. Betty Suttor, George Simpson-Lyttle, and Paul Reynell were also in the cast.

After Harry Watt had finished *Eureka Stockade* in 1949, Ealing Studios recklessly decided to establish a permanent unit in Australia, with studios at Pagewood, New South Wales, and sent Ralph Smart to produce *Bitter Springs* in 1950. Neither film was, understandably, profitable. Ealing Studios retreated from Australia.

Michael Pate, born in Sydney, sang, danced, and acted in his native city during the late 1920s and early 1930s. He acted in many broadcast plays, and on the stage, and belonged to an Entertainment Unit in the South-west Pacific during World War II. His Australian film experience included rôles in *Forty Thousand Horsemen, Sons of Matthew,* and *Bitter Springs.* In 1950 he went to Hollywood to play in the film *Bonaventure,* in which he had appeared on the Sydney stage. Since then he has starred or featured in more than fifty films, including *Julius Caesar, Face to Face, Sergeants Three, P.T. 109,* and two hundred-odd television plays. William Holden starred in *Rope's End,* one of Pate's screenplays. In 1959 he toured Australia in *Tunnel of Love.*

Footlights or klieg lights, no two public or private careers could have been more diverse than those of Chips Rafferty and Robert Helpmann, whose births were a mere fortnight apart.

Robert Murray Helpman was born on April 9, 1909, at Mount Gambier, South Australia, eldest son of a stock and station agent and an actress interested in ballet. The extra "n" was added early in his career. He was educated at Prince Alfred College, Kent Town, Adelaide. Trained in ballet, then known as Fancy Dancing, by Nora Stewart, from the age of six, he made his amateur début as a solo dancer in *The Ugly Duckling,* at the Theatre Royal, Adelaide. He was thirteen. When Anna Pavlova was on her 1926 Australian tour, Helpmann's father was able to persuade her to accept his seventeen-year-old son as a student. For a year Helpmann toured Australia and New Zealand with the Pavlova Company as a bit-part boy. He considers Pavlova the most inspired of ballerinas.

In 1927 he began a five-year career as principal dancer in J. C. Williamson musical comedies. In 1927 he danced in three Charles Wenman productions: *Frasquita, Tip Toes,* and *Queen High;* in 1929, *This Year of Grace, The New Moon, The Merry Widow,* and *Katinka;* in 1931 he and Frances Ogilvey danced the Spider and the Fly dance in the Christmas pantomime, *Sinbad the Sailor,* at the Theatre

Royal, Melbourne. During the Great War he had seen Fred Leslie and Ivy Schilling do the same dance at Adelaide's Theatre Royal, in *Come Over Here,* on a rope spider-web hung from the flies above the proscenium arch. He and Frances Ogilvey danced on the same web in Melbourne.

Helpmann's ambitions were pitched above musical comedy and, even so early, were forked ones: he had actor yearnings. Margaret Rawlings, the English actress, touring Australia in *The Barretts of Wimpole Street* in 1932, gave him the small part of one of the Barrett sons, Septimus, in which he made his début in Sydney in 1932.

This book does not intend to refer except *en passant* to the rest of his career as dancer and controversial choreographer (*Hamlet, Comus, The Birds, Miracle in the Gorbals, Adam Zero*) with the Sadler's Wells and the London Ballet companies, or to his career as a producer of plays (*Murder in the Cathedral* in March 1953, with Robert Donat as Thomas à Becket; *The Tempest; As You Like It*) and of operas (*Madama Butterfly,* and *Coq d'Or,* at the Royal Opera House, Covent Garden, in 1950). Since it was through ballet, however, that he came to acting, it is necessary to indicate that Margaret Rawlings recommended him to Ninette de Valois, director of the newly constituted Vic. Wells Ballet Company. In April 1933 his family staked him a birthday trip to London, where he became, at thirty shillings a week, a member of the Vic. Wells's *corps de ballet.* By September he had a summer engagement in Nigel Playfair's *The Fantasticks* at the Lyric Theatre, Hammersmith. De Valois, who was later to make Peggy Hookham into a star and Dame Margot Fonteyn, nudged Helpmann towards stardom with the important rôle, at £2 10s. weekly, of Satan in her ballet *Job.*

The quality of acting revealed in Helpmann's character dancing engaged the interest of producers of highly coloured plays. In April 1938 he appeared at the Playhouse, London, in Nancy Price's production of *The Insect Play* by Karel

Capek. He played three parts—Felix the Butterfly, Mr Cricket, and the sinister Chief of the Yellow Ants.

Helpmann had to contend with a light and affected voice which gave a petulant note to his characterizations, thus weakening them. His voice did not match the studied flamboyance of his appearance, and the deeper intention of his conceptions. Often, too, his gestures, although perfectly disciplined for ballet, intruded, even in costume plays, which can often support larger-than-life gesturings. As the years passed he controlled his vocal cords, and modified the balletic posturing. His performances improved.

Among his parts were: Gremio, and the Tailor, in *The Taming of the Shrew*, in 1939; the screen part, played in Dutch, of the Quisling, De Jong, in *One of Our Aircraft is Missing* (1942); the title rôle in Tyrone Guthrie's 1944 *Hamlet*; and the comic villain, Wyecroft, in the film *Caravan*.

In 1946 he formed a company with Michael Benthall, to produce *The White Devil*. With Margaret Rawlings as Vittoria, it opened at the Duchess Theatre, London, in March 1947. Later that year, Helpmann played the Clown in Tyrone Guthrie's production of Andreyev's *He Who Gets Slapped*. During 1948 he was busy with rôles in ballet and, at the Stratford Festival, in playing—baroquely and vixenishly—the lead in Benthall's presentation of *King John*; Shylock in *The Merchant of Venice*; and *Hamlet* in Benthall's version, presented in a Victorian setting. Robert Helpmann and Paul Scofield alternated the playing of a frock-coated Hamlet. Neither Hamlet nor *Hamlet* was outstanding.

Since Helpmann's first appearance of importance in 1937, as Oberon, in an Old Vic. production of *A Midsummer Night's Dream*, his interest in acting has increased. His ballet appearances have become fewer. By the mid-1950s he had virtually retired as dancer, but not as choreographer. His ballet, *The Display*, danced by the Australian Ballet

Company, and based in part on the mating antics of lyre-birds he had observed in Sherbrooke Forest, Victoria, Australia, had its world première at the Adelaide Festival of Arts in March 1964.

In 1951 he was Apollodorus to Laurence Olivier's Caesar and Vivien Leigh's Cleopatra in *Caesar and Cleopatra*, and an icy Octavius in *Antony and Cleopatra*, both at the St James's Theatre, London. Later parts were: 1952, the Doctor, opposite Katharine Hepburn, in Shaw's *The Millionairess*; another Oberon, in 1954, for the Old Vic. Company's *A Midsummer Night's Dream*, at the Empire Theatre, Edinburgh; and, during the same company's Australian tour in 1955, Petruchio to Katharine Hepburn's Katharina, Angelo to her Isabella, and Shylock to her Portia.

In 1957 he played a subtle Launce in *The Two Gentlemen of Verona*, Saturninus in *Titus Andronicus*, and a fantastic Dr Pinch in *The Comedy of Errors*, in which another South Australian, Keith Michell, played Antipholus of Ephesus.

Helpmann's sensitivities may be razor-edged but lack width. While there is always a *trompe l'œil* side to his performances, he is, nevertheless, too good an actor to waste his decorated skill on such sludge as Noël Coward's *Nude With Violin*. As a character actor Helpmann is at his peak in parts where a sort of clownish craziness and grotesque poetry is required. It is only a disciplined, detail-loving, and intelligent player—which he is—who can make such characters credible.

He is five feet ten inches tall; weighs ten stone seven pounds; eats one meal a day; smokes heavily; considers Sir John Gielgud the greatest actor he has seen; and in 1964 in Honolulu sang a Stomp song called "Surfer Doll". This was recorded, to be sold to those who buy such recordings.

He is justifiably appalled at the decline of Australian theatre, and particularly appalled that a generation has grown to adulthood without any theatrical education and with no chance, in the future, of getting that education.

Agnes Dobson, with D. B. O'Connor and Gerald Harcourt,
in a shot from "The Face at the Window"

Miss Dobson, with Barry Lupino, in the film "Barry Butts In"

His brother, Max Helpmann, born in 1914, is a professional actor who lives in Canada. His sister Sheila, now retired, also had an acting career, mainly with the Edwin Styles Company in the 1940s, when she toured in such plays as *The Man Who Came to Dinner* and *Reunion in Vienna*, in supporting rôles to Diana Parnham and Edwin Styles, in casts that included Ruby May, Roger Barry, and Hilda Scurr.

An actor is apt to find ballet mannerisms—over-definition in miming—hard to shake off. It is fascinating to see how much of Helpmann's early life comes out in his present performances, how much of Rafferty's early knockabout life comes out in his performances, how much of the swashbuckling of Errol Flynn's younger days coloured his film acting.

Errol Leslie Flynn was born in Hobart, Tasmania, on June 20, 1909. His father was Dr T. T. Flynn, who seems to have been as footloose as his notorious son was later to be. Errol Flynn's education was, therefore, a thing of shreds and patches, as he moved from Hutchins School, Hobart, to St Paul's School, London, to South-West London College, and back across the equator to North Shore Grammar School, Sydney.

At fourteen Flynn was earning his first money as second cook on a schooner. By the time he was nineteen he had his own trading schooner, and in 1929, at the age of twenty, was appointed a patrol officer in the waters about New Guinea. He also prospected for gold in the Wau and Bulolo areas. In this year, too, he made his first film appearance, as an oceanographer in a German documentary film about New Guinea. In 1932 he became a member of the Hong Kong Volunteers.

Tales of Flynn's adventures, misadventures, and misfortunes in the New Guinea area are many, and have assumed the proportion of libellous legends. Most of these tales, con-

George Coppin as Milky White   *Agnes Dobson*

"The Great Millionaire"—Bland Holt

o

sidering his later successes as leading man in *Captain Blood* and *Robin Hood*, have a prophetic tinge, for they imply that Flynn's life was scarcely within the law, larded with unconventional *amours*, and of a piratical nature in regard to financial obligations. Estimable and hard-bitten men who had dealings with him at this stage of his life do not discuss him with affection.

In 1933 Charles Chauvel gave Flynn his authentic chance in films in Chauvel's first talking picture, *In the Wake of the "Bounty"*. Flynn, tall and handsome, was seen to be star material of the lady-killing sort. He had, moreover, a pleasant voice, and an accent that was not brutally Australian in the mock-butch manner.

With the idea of adding value to his physical attractions, he shrewdly went to England to make some study of acting, and played small parts in touring companies, his first being at the Malvern Festival in 1934. With this limited but useful experience to back up his good looks and his undentable self-possession he sailed for America. In 1936 he was on the payroll of the Warner Brothers Picture Corporation.

He was cast, generally, in the sorts of devil-may-care, game-cock rôles that had brought fame and wealth to Douglas Fairbanks. Flynn was a better actor than Fairbanks but did not possess the absurd and lovable *élan* of the older man. Fairbanks was burlesqued by Will Rogers in a series of Hal Roach Comedies in which, among others, Rudolph Valentino and his *Blood and Sand* performance were satirized. Flynn had a deadpan quality not easy to ridicule; he played his plume-hatted and rapier-brandishing athletes with care. He spent the greater part of his career in faultlessly tailored costume or uniform of this or that cinematically romantic period. He carried these trappings easily and, as Douglas Fairbanks had done in his day, out-fenced adversaries in baker's dozen batches, and out-leapt from riggings, out-climbed from balconies, and out-loved under blossom-laden branches all other males in the cast. If he did not have

Fairbanks's jack-in-the-box zest which made film unreality so much more unreal that it was stimulating, he did have the ability to portray the lover with conviction. Fairbanks always side-stepped, or absolutely eschewed, amorous by-play or the burning kiss. Flynn's tender moments on the screen made unreality seem more warmly real. In the few parts where he was enabled to act a credible character, Flynn revealed a talent for sensitive, witty, sincere, and down-to-earth portrayal.

Most of his films were, however, no more than melodramatic costume pieces in which he competently fulfilled the functions of a latter-day Julius Knight: *Captain Blood, The Charge of the Light Brigade, Robin Hood, The Private Lives of Elizabeth and Essex,* and, in more modern setting, *Dive Bomber, The Edge of Darkness, Uncertain Glory,* and *Objective Burma.*

Errol Flynn's private life was scarcely circumspect, and was encumbered with marriages, divorces, and unseemly *affaires* in the Hollywood tradition of vulgarity and indiscipline.

Some of the facts of his earlier life can be glimpsed between the lines of his books: *Beam Ends* (1937), *Showdown* (1946), and *My Wicked Wicked Ways.* He died of a heart attack in Vancouver, British Columbia, on October 14, 1959.

Neva Carr Glyn was the daughter of theatrical parents who spent their life on the move. Her father, Arthur Carr Glyn, was an actor; her mother, Marie Dunoon, was both actress and singer, and it was while they were on a J.C.W.'s tour with the Fred Niblo Company that Neva Carr Glyn was born, on May 10, 1911. Her stage début was made in New Zealand when Fred Niblo carried her, aged four months, on to the stage. When she was four years old she was put in boarding school, at Parramatta Convent, New South Wales. From then on she was, as she says, "in and out of convents all over Australia", and her "happiest childhood memory was of being able to stay for three uninterrupted years at the same school". Meantime, training towards a stage career began.

At the age of eight she became a pupil at the Minnie Hooper School of Dancing in Sydney. Her first public display in ballet was when she was eleven, in an exotic extravaganza called *The Queen of Sheba*, at the Town Hall, Sydney.

Arthur Carr Glyn died when she was twelve. Neva Carr Glyn left her final convent the next year, and took her first job, as a chorus-girl for the Fullers (Sir Benjamin Fuller and John Fuller) in a pantomime at the Majestic Theatre, Newtown, five miles from Sydney. Later, the Australian Elizabethan Theatre Trust companies were to have their headquarters at the Majestic.

This theatre, seating fifteen hundred, opened on June 2, 1917, with the revue *Then They Woke Up*. Bert le Blanc was leading comedian. The cast included Jack March, Carlton Chase, and Nellie Fallon. Within the first six months the Majestic housed a conglomeration of entertainments: revues; silent films; Phil Percival in *Sexton Blake, The Great Disinfectant*—Sexton Blake was the Sherlock Holmes of the period; and Kate Howard's Company in *The Outcast of the Family*. This chameleon existence of revue, variety, farce, melodrama, and film continued for a decade or so. In 1928 the Fullers presented Allan Wilkie's Shakespearian Company there in a season of more than a hundred performances, the hundredth being a special Souvenir Programme performance of *Henry the Eighth*, on July 18. Ultimately the Majestic became a cinema.

On July 1, 1955, with the financial coddling of the State Government of New South Wales, and the Sydney City Council, the Australian Elizabethan Theatre Trust took an eight and a half years' lease of the Majestic, which they found it necessary unnecessarily to rename the Elizabethan, and necessarily to renovate. Donations were sought in the sacred name of culture, and freely given by those blinded with faith—the furnishings of three dressing-rooms, a piano, a crystal chandelier, a neon sign, and five hundred and fifty seats in the stalls at a tenner each.

On July 27, 1955, Garnet H. Carroll presented for the Trust the opening play, a piece of cream-puff nonsense by Terence Rattigan, *The Sleeping Prince*, later to be filmed with Marilyn Monroe, Sir Laurence Olivier, and Dame Sybil Thorndike. Dame Sybil also appeared in the Trust's cultural sunrise, and spoke the Prologue which had been especially written by that demi-Ern-Malley, James McAuley:

> Here Drama used to live; and now once more
> She breathes, she wakes, far lovelier than before.
> Years past as Melodrama she held sway
> With NELLIE BRAMLEY and with MARIE NEY;
> Then, Virtue wept, while Villainy leered and frowned
> Until the Hero dashed him to the ground.
> Later, when ALLAN WILKIE stamped the boards
> She rendered Shakespeare to the restless hordes
> Of lolly-chewing children from the schools.
> Another time (what memories!) those great fools,
> JIM GERALD and GEORGE WALLACE, won her heart
> And turned her to the vaudevillean art:
> A comic hoyden, pert from top to toe,
> She giggled helpless in the hands of MO.
> But then times changed. Alas, she had to go,
> To make room for a moving-picture show:
> For crooners, cops and cowboys, and (O bliss!)
> The glutinous splendours of a GARBO kiss.
> So living Drama slept. The wise foretold
> She'd waken only to a flow of gold
> From private cheque books and the public purse.
> Who worked this wonder and removed the curse?
> Our Royal Patron, she alone had power:
> Timing her Progress in a lucky hour,
> She broke the spell, she summoned up delight,
> And led us to the triumphs of this night.

In the cast with Dame Sybil were Sir Ralph Richardson, Sir Lewis Casson, and Meriel Forbes. Terence Rattigan was in Sydney to see *The Sleeping Prince,* as well as *Separate Tables,* another play of his that played alternately with *The Sleeping Prince.*

Thirty years earlier, in 1925, when Neva Carr Glyn was beginning her career at the Majestic, it was not the home of an organization pretending "to concentrate on raising the standards of Australian theatre to that of the finest overseas companies".

After her Majestic début, she joined the ballet of Fullers' 1925 *Band Box Revue* which toured Australia and New Zealand. The tour over, Sir Benjamin Fuller drew up a five-year contract for the fifteen-year-old Neva. In 1926 she made her first important appearance at the National Theatre, Sydney, as Principal Girl in *Robinson Crusoe.* For the next five years she was always busy—with the Jim Gerald Company; with George Wallace; teamed with Charles Megan in a dancing-singing-comedy act; as Principal Boy with Sid Beck in *Aladdin* at the Majestic Theatre, Sydney; at the Tivoli Theatre, Melbourne, in *The Vanities* (1928), with Leyland Hodgson, Marie la Varre, and Hugh Steyne; and, at the King's Theatre, Melbourne, with Ann Penn and Roy Rene in *Clowns in Clover* (1929) for the Frank Neil Company. In December 1929 she left with Sir Benjamin Fuller's blessing and the Frank Neil Company for a prolonged tour of South Africa. She played leading rôles in many a feathery comedy of the ilk of *Up in Mabel's Room, Why Men Leave Home,* and *This Thing Called Love.*

In the New Year of 1931 Neva Carr Glyn got to London, and four days after her arrival was cast as second lead for Lee Ephraim in an operetta, *Nina Rosa,* which starred Harry Welchman and Robert Chisholm, and was produced by Carol Reed, later Sir Carol Reed, the director of such masterpieces as *The Third Man, Odd Man Out,* and *The Outcast of the Islands.*

At the end of 1931 she joined the Firth Shephard and Leslie Henson Company with which she spent seven years, appearing at the Strand and Aldwych theatres, London, in shows which indicate their type by their titles—*It's a Boy, It's a Girl, Living Dangerously*, and *Night of the Garter*. Her co-players included Jack Hawkins, Alice Delysia, George Robey, Leslie Henson, Robertson Hare, Godfrey Tearle, Sir John Martin Harvey, and Sydney Howard. She played with Sydney Howard again in a British and Dominion Film, *Girls Please*. In a London Films Production of *The Squeaker*, directed by William K. Howard, she played Minnie Trent. Other members of the cast were Ann Todd, Edmund Lowe, Robert Newton, and Sebastian Shaw.

In 1938, with her reputation as a skilful all-rounder well established, she returned to Australia for a visit. After playing at the Tivoli Theatre, Sydney, with Ella Shields and Jim Gerald, and on contract for the A.B.C. opposite Peter Finch in several productions, she was about to return to England when war was declared.

In 1940 she married John Tate. In 1942 their one son, Nicholas, was born. He is now following in the footsteps of his parents and of his maternal grandparents.

Neva Carr Glyn's innumerable assignments on stage, on the air, and on television include *The Laughing Woman*, with Peter Finch (A.B.C., 1941); leading lady at the Minerva Theatre, King's Cross, Sydney, in *Love From a Stranger*, with Grant Taylor, *Clutterbuck, Storm in a Teacup, Separate Rooms*, and J. B. Priestley's *Dangerous Corner*. In 1944 she toured New Zealand for J.C.W.'s as leading lady of a repertoire including *Susan and God* and *The Man Who Came to Dinner*.

In 1951 the John Alden Shakespearian Company opened a season at the Comedy Theatre, Melbourne. In *The Merchant of Venice* she played Portia; in *A Winter's Tale* Paulina; and in *The Merry Wives of Windsor* Mistress Ford, with William Rees playing Falstaff, and Nancye Stewart as Mistress Page. In 1958 she joined the Australian Elizabethan Theatre Trust Players.

In 1950, and again in 1951, she won the Macquarie Award for Actress of the Year, the only actress to win this broadcasting award twice running. In 1964 she played the part of Mrs Gillipop in a television serial for children, *The Gillipops*.

Coral Browne (Coral Edith Brown) was born on July 23, 1913, at Footscray, Victoria. The "e" was a 1936 professional addition.

While a student at the National Gallery Art School, Melbourne, Coral Browne made her amateur début, directed by Frank D. Clewlow in Shaw's *You Never Can Tell*, at the Garrick Theatre, Melbourne. Her performance of Gloria was immediately seen to be that of an actress who would travel far and fast. Clewlow described the seventeen-year-old actress as "a rare find". Gregan McMahon said, "She cannot escape success", and launched her professionally as Margaret Orme in *Loyalties* at Melbourne's Comedy Theatre on May 2, 1931. The leading man was Frank Harvey, who was born in Jersey in 1885. He made his début when nine, in 1904, at the Devonport Theatre Royal, Tasmania, in *The Executioner's Daughter*. After London experience he played numberless leading rôles for J.C.W.'s between 1914 and 1926. He returned to London, and was there from 1927 to 1930. Since then he has worked in Australia. Among the several plays he has written, *The Last Enemy* (1929) and *Forlorn Hope* (1930) are the best.

Campbell Copelin was juvenile lead in *Loyalties*. Copelin played with Coral Browne again in the farce *Warm Corner*, with Cecil Kellaway, and in other productions, for he was the most capable and catholic of juvenile leads during the 1920s and 1930s. It will be useful—as a sketch of the scene Coral Browne was to disappear from in 1934—to outline Campbell Copelin's career.

An Englishman who had "drifted towards the stage via school dramatic societies, and concert parties entertaining servicemen of the Great War", Campbell Copelin arrived in

Australia in 1921. During the twenties he worked with many companies: the Philip Lytton Players in *The Rosary* and other dramas; the Nellie Bramley Company, which he was to rejoin in the 1930s as leading man; the English Players, who worked in the Athenaeum Theatre, Melbourne, and with whom he played Tom Prior in a notable production of *Outward Bound*, with the great character actress Henrietta Cavendish; and, finally, J. C. Williamson's. In this organization he played with Lady (Gertrude) Forbes-Robertson, Dion Boucicault, Irene Vanbrugh, and Sir Seymour Hicks (*Old Bill*). He supported Pauline Frederick in *Spring Cleaning*. In this play a young Australian actress, Thelma Burness, had her greatest success as the sophisticated and bemonocled young woman.

During the 1930s he added considerably to his reputation as a sterling actor under managements which, despite the Depression, were still active enough—Gregan McMahon, Nellie Bramley, F. T. Thring, J. C. Williamson's. He appeared with Leon Gordon in *The Trial of Mary Dugan*; Bunny Coutts; Betty Tait, daughter of John Tait; George Wallace; Mona Barlee (daughter of Phil Smith), later called Mona Barrie on the American screen; Kenneth Tuckfield, a promising actor killed in World War II; Enid Hollins, the actress who became a playwright; Frank Harvey, with whom he played in *Rope*, by Patrick Hastings, and, as the detective Kelly, in *On the Spot*, to Harvey's Tony Perelli. Campbell Copelin's greatest experience during this period was to be leading man, in *Mother of Pearl* and *Her Past*, to the fascinating French actress, Alice Delysia, for whom his admiration as an artist remains undiminished. *Mother of Pearl*, by A. P. Herbert, was that theatrical oddity, a play with music.

A list of a few of the plays in which Copelin acted will indicate something of the public taste of the time: *Autumn Crocus, When Knights were Bold, The Calendar, Bird in Hand, Smilin' Through, Command to Love, Scandal, To What Red Hell, The Streets of London, A Message from*

Mars (with Beatrice Day), and, at the Princess Theatre, Melbourne, F. T. Thring's presentation of *Collitt's Inn*, in which Copelin, no singer, sang.

He returned to England in 1938, after playing in *Lover's Leap* at the Theatre Royal, Sydney, with Enid Hollins, Betty Tait, Kenneth Tuckfield, and Sydney Wheeler. Throughout the 1940s and 1950s he had a variety of engagements in London, under contract to H. M. Tennent (*Grand National Night*, Apollo Theatre), and to other managements—Robert Sherwood, Daniel Mayer, and Tom Arnold. Between 1947 and 1950 he played film parts in Hollywood. In 1956 he was with Robert Helpmann and Fifi Banvard in *Nude with Violin*. On Friday, May 22, 1964, he appeared at the Comedy Theatre, Melbourne, in Freddie Carpenter's production of *Never Too Late*, with Mary Orr, Margaret Reid, and Kenric Hudson.

Coral Browne, having been launched by McMahon in 1931, was in constant demand, and appeared during the next three years in a score of productions by him and others. Among the parts she superbly played were: Suzy Courtois in *Topaze*, Orinthia in *The Apple Cart*, the title rôle in *Hedda Gabler*, Alice Dearth in *Dear Brutus*, and the schoolmistress in *Children in Uniform*, with Phyllis Best as the tragic schoolgirl. In *Command to Love*, in which she worked with Copelin once again, she was cast opposite the handsome but hysterical Theo Shall, a Viennese actor whose backstage tantrums outmatched Oscar Asche's, and far outran other displays of temperament by visitors such as Diana Barrymore, Mischa Auer, and Sir Seymour Hicks—all firebrands of one sort or another.

In the winter of 1934, Australian laurels thick upon her, she sailed in the *Ormonde* for England. She was immediately given work as understudy to Nora Swinburne, in *Lover's Leap*, at the Vaudeville Theatre, London. From this point on her career has been wide in range, and exhilarating to theatre and cinema audiences. As Gregan McMahon had

218

prophesied, with her flamboyant personality and great gifts she could not escape success. Before the beginning of World War II she had already stolen scenes from accomplished scene-stealers: Laurence Olivier, Marie Tempest, Robert Newton, Victor McLaglen, Elissa Landi, Gordon Harker, and Gracie Fields. Her portrayals of the intenser women of Ibsen stirred the Berlin Ibsen Organization to make the unique gesture of inviting her to play with their company, one dedicated to the point of obsession.

Her genius was a supple one. In 1942 she played Maggie Cutler to Robert Morley's Sheridan Whiteside in *The Man Who Came to Dinner*, a slick American comedy and a far cry from the middle-class anguishes of Ibsen. Coral Browne was as sleek a comedienne as she was an intimidating tragedienne; she could be a blood-chilling Regan or Goneril, and as subtly funny as she when acting Rosalind Russell's champagne-tippling actress friend in the film version of *Auntie Mame*.

Flexibility of talent, and power of attack were not the only traits she had in common with actresses of an earlier day. She had also their grand manner. It was a manner that did not suggest, as the manner of many present-day actresses does, that they are hash-cooking *hausfraus* with an accidental flair for acting, or that, seductive as they seem from the dress circle, they are at heart suburban girls-next-door, readers of light romances, and drinkers of fizzy fluids permeated with sulphur dioxide. Coral Browne had presence on and off stage. She dressed the part. The public could see where its money went. Norman Hartnell of Bruton Street, London, dress designer for the Royal family, announced her to be "the most beautifully dressed woman on the London stage". When she visited Australia in April 1948 she travelled with a wardrobe that had cost four thousand pounds.

On June 26, 1950, she married Philip Westrope Pearman. At the Old Vic. Theatre, in 1951, she played Emilia in *Othello*, and Regan in *King Lear*.

In 1956 she played Lady Macbeth, Queen Gertrude in *Hamlet*, and Goneril in *King Lear*. In 1958, at the close of the Stratford-on-Avon season, she starred in the Shakespeare Memorial Theatre Company when it toured to Moscow and Leningrad. In 1960 she played Albertine Prine in *Toys in the Attic*.

Coral Browne was fortunate that her endowments were perceived early. These endowments were nurtured by Gregan McMahon with the sort of training no longer obtainable in Australia. Producers in Australia today, although in a position to offer some opportunity to younger people, scarcely have the authority—or knowledge—to lead the tiro beyond a certain point.

Players trained by craftsmen of McMahon's kind have, of course, fled from Australia quite as readily as the quarter-trained players of a later generation have fled, and keep on fleeing. The pity is that, of the many who did not flee and will not flee, the trained players are retiring or dying off or have been dehydrated by disuse, while the quarter-trained are increasing in number. The most dangerous attribute of these virtual amateurs—players and producers with a thin gloss of what they imagine to be experience—is that they regard themselves as professionals. In this climate of self-infatuation, the standards of acting and production, already low, yearly become lower.

Among players of quality to be seen during the 1920s and 1930s, there are those who remained in the game, and are still being heard of, as well as others who gave up, or were forced by the perilous times to give up, promising stage or film careers for less scarifying occupations—housewife, nine-to-five businessman, or other forms of mundane security. The following selection from those whose names were on programmes of the Roaring Twenties and the Depression Decade has, therefore, some interest. It intends to be no more than partial.

Scott Alexander; and Jos Ambler. Ambler was born in Melbourne on June 23, 1900, and educated at Melbourne Grammar School. His earliest professional appearances were made with the Brandon Thomas Repertory Company in Edinburgh and Glasgow, but much of his later career was in English films. He played character parts in more than eighty. He began working with the British Broadcasting Commission in 1949, and appeared in many television plays. Bonita Appleton; Leslie Barry, a handsome juvenile lead in demand during the twenties; Roger Barry (*East of Suez*, 1924; *The Poppy God*, 1930, with Leon Gordon and Hal Percy); Phyllis Best (*The Last of Mrs Cheyney, Children in Uniform*, with Coral Browne); Dulcie Bland; Frank Bradley; Sylvia Breamer (the film *The Blood Barrier*); Ella Bromley who, although a beauty of the chiselled sort, was a warm and skilful actress; and Gwen Day Burroughs.

Gwen Day Burroughs, born in Melbourne, began as an *ingénue* with Marie Tempest, and received good notices in May 1918 when she played with Marie Tempest in a farce—"a silly little snivel" wrote one acute reviewer—called *A Pair of Silk Stockings*. Marie Tempest encouraged her to go overseas. Gwen Day Burroughs appeared in England and America with such stars as Ivor Novello, Diana Wynyard, and Gladys Cooper, whom she supported in *Dodsworth* in 1936. After 1941 Gwen Day Burroughs played characters for the B.B.C. Mae Busch, Hollywood star of *The Triflers*, and many other films; Dick Bentley, born in Melbourne on May 14, 1907, who began acting in 1929; Pirie Bush; Zillah Carter; and Mary Charles.

Born in Maryborough, Queensland, Mary Charles, daughter of a pastoralist, played with Allan Wilkie in Sydney before going to the Royal Academy of Dramatic Art. She played leading rôles on repertory tours in *Tovarich, The Dominant Sex*, and *The Shining Hour*, Elizabeth Barrett in an Edinburgh production of *The Barretts of Wimpole Street*, and has done English film work, and B.B.C. plays.

Terence Crisp; George Cross; John Darcy; Betty D'Arvall (in Vaughan Marshall's film *Environment* with Hal Percy); Daphne Deane; Leal Douglas (who appeared in English films, and with George Robey, between 1913 and 1929); Catherine Duncan; Geoff de Fraga; Ena Gregory; Ada Guildford; Joy Gwyn; Loveday Hills; Keith Johns, Arthur Keane; Cyril Keightly; Fred Macdonald, and Mary McGregor.

Mary McGregor, a beauty with a red-gold shingle, the daughter of a Brisbane barrister, began her career in her native city in Barrie's *Quality Street*, in which she later played the lead at the Theatre Royal, Sydney. After a hard apprenticeship with the Sydney Repertory Company she was conspicuously successful as the daughter in *A Bill of Divorcement*. This success led J.C.W. to engage her for *The Skin Game, So This is London, The Admirable Crichton* (as the Tweenie), and, opposite Maurice Moscovich, in *The Fake* and *The Ringer*.

Russell Napier, born in Perth on November 28, 1910, abandoned law in 1935 to appear on the stage in Australia, New Zealand, and England. He has also appeared on television and in plays for the B.B.C.

Frank Neil; Joy Nichols; Peter O'Shaugnessy; Diana Parnham; and Jerome Patrick. Patrick, who played small parts only in Australia, mainly with Julius Knight, was in more demand, as a personable juvenile lead, by Belasco, Ziegfeld, and Hollywood.

David Reid; Harry Roberts; Jean Robertson, "a well-bred, poised, outstanding personality with a full and melodious voice, and features that cannot easily be forgotten", was particularly praiseworthy as Lalage with Maurice Moscovich in *The Outsider*, during early 1925.

Eileen Robinson; Milton Sands; and John Sherman. Sherman, Melbourne-born on June 2, 1911, was one of the earliest wireless announcers. He became a character actor in 1935. From 1938 he appeared with the Minerva Theatre Players, Sydney, and, after a number of sound performances with this company, went to England, where he has played minor parts in stage, film, and B.B.C. productions. In Hollywood he has appeared in such offerings as Metro-Goldwyn-Mayer's *The Knights of the Round Table.*

Wilfred Spargo played Fiers in *The Cherry Orchard*, and Satin in *The Lower Depths*, at the Garrick Theatre, Melbourne, in Dolia Ribush's productions in the manner of Stanislavski. Leonard Stephens, Charles Villiers, and John Wiltshire.

Junee Cornell, daughter of Olive Wilton, was born in Toorak, Melbourne, and taken to Hobart, Tasmania, as a child. Her initial dramatic training was in her mother's drama school, and her début, at eight, in May 1922 was as Jill in Olive Wilton's production of A. A. Milne's *Make Believe* at the Theatre Royal, Hobart. From time to time during her education at Clemes College, Hobart, Junee Cornell was allowed to play small rôles. It was not, however, until November 1931, at seventeen, that she played—and brilliantly—a large part, that of Tessa in Margaret Kennedy's *The Constant Nymph*, again at the Theatre Royal. She then went to London to study for a year at the Royal Academy of Dramatic Art. On her return to Tasmania she earned her living as an actress under contract to the A.B.C., and satisfied her need to play parts of dramatic and intellectual value by appearing frequently with the Hobart Repertory Society.

In 1947 she went to Sydney and, in the same year, played her first part there, Bronwen, in J. B. Priestley's *The Long Mirror* with Peter Finch's company at the Phillip Street Theatre. In 1948 she made her professional début for Whitehall Productions as Mrs Gardiner in *Pride and Prejudice*. From then on, meantime earning ample money as an actress in steady demand by broadcasting stations, Junee Cornell appeared in leading rôles with professional and semi-professional companies. Her flawless diction, her sensitivity of perception, allied to her close and intelligent study of character, resulted in immaculate performances.

Her professional performances included the Duchess in *The Duchess of Malfi* for Cavalier Productions (Independent Theatre, Sydney, September 1948), Miss Pierce in *Bonaventure* for The Firm (Theatre Royal, Sydney, October 1950), Harriet in *Dragon's Mouth* (Mercury Theatre, Sydney, October 1953), Catherine Sloper in *The Heiress* (Theatre Royal, Hobart, May 1955), Mrs Sowter in *The Happiest Days of Your Life*, with Margaret Rutherford (Elizabethan Theatre, Newtown, Sydney, November 1957), Hilda Prescott in *The Poltergeist* (Theatre Royal, Hobart, April 1959), and Miss Madrigal in *The Chalk Garden* (Phoenix Theatre Company, Playhouse, Hobart, February 1961).

One of the more curious aspects of Australian theatre is the overlapping of the purely professional and that strange area, the semi-professional, in which much of the best theatrical work is done. Junee Cornell's comment on her experiences in the semi-professional theatre is interesting. "In semi-professional theatres such as the Sydney Independent," she said, "I was sometimes paid as a guest artist, sometimes not, according to a peculiar method all the Independent's own."

Among her outstanding rôles for the Independent Theatre were Miss Sheily in Ruth Park's *Harp in the South* (1949), with Ethel Gabriel as Grandma, the star rôle in *The Old Maid* (1949), with Diana Perryman, and the prostitute in Eugene O'Neill's *S.S. Glencairn* (1950).

Her favourite rôle is the Duchess of Malfi, a most challenging part at every level, and one she would like to attempt again now that she has "gained in maturity as a person and an actress". Catherine Sloper, a psychologically superb study of female responses to circumstance, runs the Duchess a close second in Junee Cornell's choice of parts worthy of the attention of the dedicated player.

She has some justifiable pride in the fact that, between

Nellie Stewart as Prince Charming
in "Cinderella"   *Keith Michell*

A model of the set in Act I of "Riding to Win"
[Photo Leonie Mills

THEATRE ROYAL

Lessees   Messrs. Harwood, Stewart, Hennings and Coppin.

V.   R.

GRAND COMMAND NIGHT

HIS EXCELLENCY SIR GEORGE BOWEN, G.C.M.G.,
GOVERNOR OF VICTORIA,
AND LADY BOWEN.

The Performance will commence, at Half-past Seven, with the Comedietta of a

HAPPY PAIR

Mr Honeyton   ...   Mr F. C. APPLETON
Mrs. Honeyton   ...   Miss ELEANOR CAREY

To be followed by the Entirely New and Original Fairy Comedy in Three Acts, by
W. Gilbert, Esq., entitled,

THE WICKED WORLD

Fairies.

Ethais	Mr G. R. IRELAND
Phyllon	Mr. F. C. APPLETON
Lutin	**Mr. G. Coppin**
Selene (A Fairy Queen)	Miss ELEANOR CAREY
Darine	Miss HATTIE SHEPPARDE
Zayda	Miss EMMA AUSTIN
Leila	Miss BROWN
Neodie	Miss JENNY BRYCE
Locrine	Miss KATE DOUGLAS
Ena	Miss MARSH
Colombe	Miss SCOTT
Camilla	Miss HOLMES
Lena	Miss WATSON

Mortals

Sir Ethais	Mr G. R. IRELAND
Sir Phyllon	Mr F. C. APPLETON
Lutin (Sir Ethais Henchman)	**Mr. G. Coppin**

NO DELAYS BETWEEN THE ACTS.
Visitors are requested to keep their seats

DURING THE EVENING THE BAND WILL PLAY.

Overture—" Die Felsenmuhle "	Reissiger
Valse —" Leila "	Coote
Polka—" Excelsior " (Cornet Solo)	Frevin
Quadrille—" Cox and Box"	Verdi

To Conclude with the Popular Farce,

A BILIOUS ATTACK

Mr Job Jinniwin (a Bilious Subject)	Mr JOHN DUNN
Captain Marmaduke Myrtle (of the " Royal Berkshire Plungers")	Mr J. MUNRO
Mrs Jinniwin	Miss K. DOUGLASS
Betsey Jane	Miss JENNY BRYCE

Azzoppardi, Hildreth & Co., Steam Printers, Post-office Place, Melbourne.

1945 and 1962, when she married to settle down in Sandy Bay, Hobart, she earned a comfortable living from playing in broadcast productions as well as in the theatre proper.

Merle Oberon (Estelle Merle O'Brien Thompson) was born on February 12, 1914, at St Helens, a village overlooking the black mud flats of George Bay on the north-east coast of Tasmania. She lived in Tasmania until she was seven. She was taken to live in Bombay, India, where her education was continued, and completed in Calcutta. As an adolescent she displayed an enthusiasm for acting, and acted *ingénue* parts with THE CATS—the Calcutta Amateur Theatrical Society.

At the age of seventeen she went to England and worked as an extra in films. Her first part was in a Gaumont-British comedy called *Alf's Button*. Her efficient acting in other small parts, and her face with its slightly Oriental cast, drew the attention of Alexander Korda—later Sir Alexander—and London Film Productions. At the age of eighteen, in 1932, she signed a five-year contract with them. Seven years later, on June 3, 1939, she married Sir Alexander Korda in the south of France, at Antibes. This marriage lasted for no more than five years.

Her initial success on the screen was as Anne Boleyn in *The Private Life of Henry the Eighth*, a part the scenario-writer had imbued with such unhistorical pathos that she almost stole the film from Charles Laughton who, as a Tudor monarch given to tossing gnawed bones over his shoulders at royal guzzlings, also caught the fancy of the wider, less choosy public. Two film careers were established.

Merle Oberon starred in many English films, and in far more American ones. Among the earlier was *The Lodger*, based on Mrs Belloc Lowndes's conception of the Jack the Ripper mystery which, in a silent version, had been one of the few outstanding films made in England, and had starred Ivor Novello.

It wasn't such a bad world

P

Merle Oberon's other films include: *Wedding Rehearsal, Private Life of Don Juan, The Scarlet Pimpernel, The Dark Angel, Beloved Enemy, A Song to Remember, Wuthering Heights, Berlin Express, Deep in My Heart, Price of Fear, Désirée, Dark Waters,* and *Of Love and Desire.*

Her acting, even at moments of emotional upheaval, was never overwhelming. It had a cold core, and a brittle quality, a kind of over-bred restraint. This dead-ashes coolness may sometimes have been required in a portrayal; it can scarcely have been always required.

In 1945 Merle Oberon was a June bride for the second time, when she married Lucien K. Ballard. Her third marriage, to G. Bruno Pagliai, broke the June pattern, for she was married on July 28, 1957. In 1963 she made a comeback in *Of Love and Desire.*

Merle Oberon's hobbies are listed as reading, golf, and swimming, but embrace the garnering of diamonds; her collection of diamond ornaments—rings, bracelets, necklaces, ear-rings and the like—being famous. She also owns a vast avocado-growing ranch in California.

Lloyd Lamble, born in Melbourne in 1914, was educated at Wesley College there. As a child he was trained to be a concert pianist, but on leaving Wesley College, where he had been a successful athlete, this form of public exhibition received little more of his consideration—he turned to acting. His first part, in 1931 at the age of seventeen, was as a juvenile lead in *Fresh Fields,* with the Grace Lane Company. He later appeared with Katie Towers in the play at the Theatre Royal, Hobart.

During the rest of the Depression Thirties he played in a number of rather blues-tinged and edgy plays—*Idiot's Delight; Dinner at Eight; Yes, My Darling Daughter; While Parents Sleep;* and *Gaslight.* Other plays included *Elizabeth the Queen, Twelfth Night, The Merchant of Venice,* and— pallid carbon-copy of the times—*Love on the Dole.* He also played Lennie in *Of Mice and Men*. Many of his portrayals were for Gregan McMahon, who finally cast him in the part by which he first really impressed public and critics. This was Danny the page-boy murderer in Emlyn Williams's *Night Must Fall*, which opened at the Comedy Theatre, Melbourne, in November 1938. After appearances in *Claudia*, and *The Man Who Came to Dinner*, he produced and starred in six J.C.W. plays on tour in New Zealand, where he met the actress Lesley Jackson whom he later married. He starred in Aldous Huxley's *The Gioconda Smile* in 1950.

Lamble now lives in England, where he pursues a successful career on the stage, in English films, and television plays.

Margaret Vyner, one of Australia's more notable beauties, was born in Armidale, New South Wales, on December 3, 1914. She was educated at Doone Kindergarten and, later, at Ascham, where Jocelyn Howarth, another distinctively good-looking Australian woman, was also educated. Jocelyn Howarth played the heroine in the 1933 Cinesound film of *The Squatter's Daughter*, with Grant Lyndsay, W. Lane-Bayliff, John Warwick, Dorothy Dunckley, and Fred Macdonald. In 1934 Jocelyn Howarth was also in Kenneth G. Hall's *The Silence of Dean Maitland*. She went to St Gabriel's after Ascham; Margaret Vyner went to Doone Finishing School where, she says, Miss Jean Cheriton taught her "some of the most useful lessons I have ever learned, or will ever learn. I owe her a great deal".

Thus fortified, she left her finishing school to work as a junior salesgirl in the dress department of David Jones's departmental store in Sydney. This venture into commerce was, she says, "a dismal and unqualified failure". In 1933 she was chosen, along with five other current beauties, all of them absolutely ignorant of stage matters, to form the sextet for a production of *Floradora*. *Floradora* had originally been brought to Australia in 1901 by the enchanting Grace Palotta, who starred in it, supported by Hugh Ward and George Lauri.

After *Floradora*, Margaret Vyner was taken up by Cyril Ritchard and Madge Elliott, and toured Australia in 1932 with them in *Blue Roses, The Merry Widow, Follow Through*, and *The Quaker Girl*. She then went to France where, in 1934, she joined the staff of one of the great dress designers, Jean Patou, "first of all", she says, "as dog's body, and, finally, as his top mannequin". During this period Margaret Vyner studied French, and colour design, at night classes, and wrote articles for Australian newspapers and magazines. She returned to Australia for a Christmas visit in 1935, and remained long enough to appear in a film, *The Flying Doctor*, with Charles Farrell. Back in England, she played in several English films, two with Jessie Matthews, one with John Loder, and one with Pat Barr; and in a number of plays.

On New Year's Eve, 1937, while sailing to New York to play in the Frederick Lonsdale comedy *Once is Enough*, she met Hugh Williams, who was cast in the same play as leading man opposite the American comedienne, Ina Claire. They were married in June 1940.

In 1938 she toured Canada and America with a valuable collection of Norman Hartnell clothes, after which she returned to England to appear in more plays and films. When World War II began, Hugh Williams joined the Territorials, in September 1939, and served throughout the war. Meantime, Margaret Vyner did car-driving for the Home Service, now and then making a quick film. Her first son, Hugo, was born in 1942. Another son, Simon, was born in 1946, and a daughter, Pollyanna, in 1950.

Since 1948 she and Hugh Williams have collaborated in the writing of successful plays—*The Plaintiff in the Pretty Hat, The Happy Man, The Grass is Greener, Double Yolk, The Irregular Verb to Love*, and *Past Imperfect*.

In her last film, in 1952, *The Ant and the Grasshopper*,

from a Somerset Maugham story, she played opposite Nigel
Patrick, who directed *Past Imperfect*, in which Hugh Williams starred with Susan Hampshire. This play opened in
the West End on June 24, 1964. Hugh Williams has played
leading rôles in three other of the Williams-Vyner plays;
Margaret Vyner has not appeared on the stage since 1954,
when she was in a George Barraud comedy. Between play-
writing and work with Norman Hartnell, Margaret Vyner
gardens and goes bird-watching. She admires, at present, the
paintings of Celso Lagar and Sidney Nolan, and would like
to own an island. As most expatriates do, she thinks nostal-
gically of Australian sunshine, but makes do with summer
holidays in France, Greece, or her favourite Spain.

Australia's talkies, many of them made by overseas companies, have none of the rough-and-ready gusto of the purely
native silents.

Although *The Cheaters*, made by the McDonagh sisters
in 1926, was dubbed with sound and dialogue in 1930, the
first complete talkie was *Out of the Shadows* (1930), with
William Greene, Edna Lyall, Paul Plunkett, and Syd
Hollister. Efftee Films produced some, all rather shoddy:
Diggers, 1930; *Co-respondent's Course*, and *Haunted Barn*,
1931; *The Royal Highness*, and *The Sentimental Bloke*,
1932; *Harmony Row*, 1933; *A Ticket in Tatt's, Clara Gib-
bings*, and *Streets of London*, 1934.

Pat Hanna directed *Diggers in Blighty*, 1933; and *Waltzing
Matilda*, 1934. A. R. Harwood directed *Isle of Intrigue*,
1930; *Secret of the Skies*, 1934; *Something Different*, 1935
(Alfred Frith); *Show Business*, 1936; and *The Avenger*,
1937. Zane Grey produced *White Death* in 1936.

Among the longer productions were *The Kangaroo Kid*
(1950), with Jock O'Mahoney, Veda Ann Borg, Douglas
Dumbrille, Martha Hyer; *The Glenrowan Affair* (1951),
with John Fernside, Alma King, Bob Chitty; *Wherever She
Goes* (1951), featuring Eileen Joyce, with Suzanne Parrett,

Nigel Lovell, Muriel Steinbeck; *Long John Silver* (1954), with Robert Newton, Rod Taylor, Connie Gilchrist; *Captain Thunderbolt* (1955), with Grant Taylor, Charles Taylor, Harp McGuire; *Robbery Under Arms* (1957), with Peter Finch, Ronald Lewis, David McCallum; *The Shiralee* (1957), with Peter Finch, Dana Wilson, Rosemary Harris.

Smaller films included *Fellas, The Adventures of Dot, Showgirl's Luck, Spur of the Moment, The Man They Could Not Hang, Two Minutes' Silence, When the Kellys Rode, The Burgomeister, Mystery Island, Seven Little Australians, Wings of Destiny, The Power and the Glory, Racing Luck, That Certain Something, A Yank in Australia, Red Sky of Morning (Escape at Dawn), Time Off, Always Another Dawn, Into the Straight, Strong is the Seed* (The Farrar Story), and *They Found a Cave.*

There were also many documentary films of varying quality, and several films made by outside organizations—*On the Beach, Summer of the Seventeenth Doll, The Siege of Pinchgut,* and *The Sundowners*—which, despite expensive intentions, failed to portray either Australians or their background convincingly.

CHAPTER EIGHT

YOUNGER REPUTATIONS

PETER FINCH (Peter Ingle-Finch) was born in London on September 28, 1916. His father was Professor George Ingle-Finch, F.R.S., scientist, physicist, and mountaineer.

When Peter Finch was nine his grandmother apprenticed him to a Buddhist priest in India. After a period of this kind of education, he received some other kind of education in France and, finally, in Australia, at the North Sydney Intermediate High School. When he left school he led a rackety life, attempting to earn his living in jobs, including those of journalist, waiter, sheep-hand, and—his first steps in the arena of entertainment—as stooge to a second-rate variety comedian.

He joined George Sorlie's Tent Theatre Company, which toured the backblocks of Queensland and New South Wales with the kinds of acts considered suitable for the inhabitants of remote regions. Peter Finch's first straight acting was as Jerry in *While Parents Sleep*, in 1935. He served with the Australian army in World War II.

Back in Australia, he formed, in collaboration with John Wiltshire and John Kay, a company which had its head-quarters in a matchbox of a theatre, the Mercury, in Phillip Street, Sydney. He also engaged in an Uplift-for-the-Moron-Masses activity by performing the less intellect-teasing portions of Shakespeare and Molière on the spot for factory-workers disinclined to visit a theatre. It was while Peter Finch was performing in Molière's *Le Malade Imaginaire* at a factory canteen that Laurence Olivier and Vivien Leigh saw him, and suggested that he go to London.

He made his début there on March 23, 1949, at Wyndham's Theatre, as Ernest Piaste, in *Daphne Laureola*, supporting Dame Edith Evans. Since that début he has played some other rôles on the English stage: Henry Adams in *Damascus Blade* (on tour, 1950); Professor Winke in *Carvallo* (St James's Theatre, June 1950); Iago in *Othello* (St James's Theatre, October 1951); Papa in *The Happy Time* (January 1952); Mercutio in *Romeo and Juliet* (Old Vic. Company, September 1952); Monsieur Beaujolais in *An Italian Straw Hat* (Old Vic. Company, November 1952); and Jerry Ryan in *Two for the Seesaw* (Haymarket Theatre, December 1958, for H. M. Tennent).

He has appeared in a score of films since 1953: George Carey in *Elephant Walk*, with Elizabeth Taylor (Paramount, 1953); Ryland in *Passage Home*, with Diane Cilento, 1954; Simon in *Simon and Laura*, 1955; Joe in *A Town Like Alice*, 1955 (his performance as Joe won him the British Film Academy Award for the best British actor seen in 1956); Langsdorf in *The Battle of the River Plate*, 1955; *Windom's Way*, 1956; *Robbery Under Arms*, 1956; and Johnny Byrne in *No Love for Johnnie*, 1960. The last seven of these were J. Arthur Rank productions—Finch had signed a five-year contract with the Rank Organization. He has played in two Warner Brothers films: *The Sins of Rachel Cade*, 1959, and, a year earlier, in 1958, *The Nun's Story*, as Dr Fortunati. Dorothy Alison, the Australian actress, played in the same film. She also played a character part in Ealing Studios' king-size failure, *Eureka Stockade*, of which Finch was assistant director.

For Metro-Goldwyn-Mayer he starred in *The Shiralee*, in 1956, and, in 1962, in *I Thank a Fool*, in which he once again appeared opposite Diane Cilento. In 1959 he was Alan Breck Stewart in a Walt Disney version of *Kidnapped,* and in 1960 played Oscar Wilde in *The Man With the Green Carnation,* for Warwick Film Productions.

Although his film parts have been varied enough Peter Finch has, more often than otherwise, been cast as the tough and agonized male with a chip on his shoulder, unshaven, brimming with whisky, and weak beneath the knobbled hide. He plays these parts with conviction.

He married ballerina Tamara Tchinarova on April 21, 1943, and has one daughter. He is director of Peter Finch Enterprises, and has stated that his favourite recreations are painting and swimming.

Hugh Hastings, born in Sydney in 1917, made his début in *Cat's Cradle* in 1935. Between 1938 and 1940 he played in Great Britain with the Dundee Players, and St Andrew's Repertory Company. He served in the Royal Navy during World War II. His London début was in 1946 in *Sweetest and Lowest,* after which he acted in and directed many stage productions. He has written three comedies: *Seagulls Over Sorrento* (1949), *Red Dragon* (1950), and *Pink Elephants* (1955).

John Neil McCallum was born in Brisbane, Queensland, on March 14, 1918, and was educated at Knox Grammar School, Wahroonga, Sydney, and the Brisbane Church of England Grammar School. His father, John Neil McCallum, owned and operated the Cremorne Theatre, Brisbane, where Gus Bluett, the comedian, began his career, and players as various as Maud Fane, Marie Ney, Arthur Riscoe, and Claude Dampier performed.

It was at his father's theatre, on August 16, 1934, that the sixteen-year-old McCallum made his début in *Henry the Eighth.* A year later, at the Scala Theatre, Brisbane, he appeared in *Hamlet,* and *Richard the Second.*

After a course at the Royal Academy of Dramatic Art, London, in 1937, he acted in repertory at the People's Palace, Mile End, next at Tonbridge, at Stratford-on-Avon, and with the Old Vic. Company. His last part, before serving with the 2/5 Field Regiment, Australian Imperial Forces, in World War II, was as the ex-officer in *Cornelius*, at the Westminster Theatre, London, in 1940.

He returned to Australia to appear at the Theatre Royal, Sydney, as Baldasarre in *The Maid of the Mountains*, and as General Esteban in *Rio Rita*. At the same theatre he directed his first play, *The Wind and the Rain*, before returning to England to begin, in 1945, a film career. Since then he has played leading rôles in twenty-two films, among them: *It Always Rains on Sunday*, *The Loves of Joanna Godden* (with Googie Withers and Chips Rafferty), *Traveller's Joy*, *Miranda* (with Glynis Johns, Googie Withers, and Margaret Rutherford), *The Calendar*, *Melba*, *Valley of Eagles*, and *The Woman in Question*.

In June 1949 he appeared as Tony Macrae in *Western Wind* at the Q Theatre, London, and at the Piccadilly Theatre when the play transferred there in September 1949.

Other parts were Sir Philip Hayes, K.B.E., in *View Over the Park* (Lyric Theatre, Hammersmith, August 1950); Jules Manning in *Waiting for Gillian* (St James's Theatre, London, April 1954); Simon Foster in *Simon and Laura*, and Freddie Page in *The Deep Blue Sea*, on a tour of Australia and New Zealand in 1955 (he also directed these two productions); Mr Darling and Captain Hook in *Peter Pan* (Scala Theatre, London, December 1956); Gill in *Janus* (Aldwych Theatre, London, April 1957); and Lord Dungavel in *Roar Like a Dove* (Phoenix Theatre, London, September 1957). After *Roar Like a Dove* had run for nearly a year he left the cast, and returned to Australia as assistant managing director of J. C. Williamson's Theatres Limited.

In March 1959 he directed *Roar Like a Dove*, again playing Lord Dungavel, at the Comedy Theatre, Melbourne. At the same theatre, in September 1959, he directed *Piccadilly Bushman*. In 1960 he directed a second company in *My Fair Lady* at Her Majesty's Theatre, Melbourne. The same year he was appointed joint managing director (with Sir Frank Tait) of J. C. Williamson's.

His recreations are gardening, cricket, and golf. He is a member of several clubs, including the Savile, London, and the Melbourne Club. His wife is the English film and stage actress, Googie Withers. They have three children, Joanna, Nicholas, and Amanda.

Margaret (Annette McCrie) Johnston was born on August 10, 1918, in Sydney. After making appearances there on the amateur stage, the first in 1936, she sailed for London, where she studied at the Royal Academy of Dramatic Art, and with Dr Stefan Hock.

In November 1939 she made her London début at Wyndham's Theatre, playing the parts of Jean, and the waitress, in *Saloon Bar*. After playing repertory seasons at Worthing and Coventry, she was once again at Wyndham's, understudying Elizabeth Allan as Janet Royd in *Quiet Wedding* (1940).

During 1941-1942 she was in several plays at the Q Theatre, including *To Fit the Crime*. This play, renamed *Murder Without Crime*, transferred to the Comedy Theatre, London, and ran for a year, during which Margaret Johnston played Jan.

In June 1944 she appeared at the Phoenix Theatre, London, as Angele Kernhan in *The Last of Summer*; at the Lyric Theatre, Hammersmith, as Susanna Willard in *The Shouting Dies*, in October 1945, and—at the same theatre —in February 1946, in William Saroyan's *The Time of Your Life*, as Kitty Duval.

In May 1948 she opened at the Garrick Theatre as Elizabeth Barrett in *The Barretts of Wimpole Street*, then played Laurie Phillipson in *Always Afternoon*, at the Embassy

Theatre. In July 1950 *Always Afternoon* moved to the Garrick, and she went with it. During October 1950 she toured with *Chuckeyhead Story*, in the part of Rita.

A disciplined and subtle player, Margaret Johnston has been cast, enough times for repetition to suggest a particular quality of her talent, in the rôle of a woman beneath whose restrained, refined, and even diffident manner a passionate nature dangerously simmers. She was, for instance, the more reckless of the two middle-class sisters in the film *A Man About the House*. She played, with moving conviction, the part of the preacher's daughter, Alma Winemiller, in the Peter Glenville production of *Summer and Smoke*, by Tennessee Williams, which opened on Thursday, November 22, 1951, at the Lyric Theatre, Hammersmith. Megs Jenkins played the childishly dotty kleptomaniac Mrs Winemiller; the young doctor, John Buchanan, was played by William Sylvester. Margaret Johnston also played Alma Winemiller at the Duchess Theatre, London, in January 1952. In September 1952 she was appearing as Miranda Bolton in *The Second Threshold* at the Vaudeville Theatre; in April 1954 she played Gelda in Christopher Fry's *The Light is Dark Enough*, at the Aldwych Theatre.

By 1956, her abilities having ripened, she played with the Stratford-on-Avon Company at the Shakespeare Memorial Theatre as Portia in *The Merchant of Venice*, Desdemona in *Othello*, and Isabella in *Measure for Measure*.

Parallel to her stage career has run a successful film career. Among her more notable films were *The Rake's Progress, A Man About the House, Magic Box, Portrait of Clare, Summer and Smoke, Touch and Go*, and *Knave of Hearts*.

Her most recent stage appearance was in 1963, at the Royal Court Theatre, Sloane Square, opposite John Fraser in Donald Howarth's production of his own play *Sugar in the Morning*. She is married to Al. Parker, and lives in Park Lane, in the West End of London.

236

Ron Randell (Ronald Egan Randell) was born on October 8, 1918, and educated at St Mary's School, Sydney, and Clunes High School, Victoria. At fourteen he began work as office boy in a Sydney financier's office, a job he did not keep long. He began working in a Sydney broadcasting station. For the next twelve years he remained in this occupation, either in Sydney or Melbourne. Within this period he made his stage début at the Minerva Theatre, Sydney, in 1940, in *Quiet Wedding*, in which he also played, at King's Theatre, Melbourne, during June of the same year. He appeared in several equally flimsy pieces—*Voice of the Turtle*, at the Minerva Theatre, was one of them.

It was not until 1946 that he had the opportunity to be anything more than a juvenile lead in short-lived mediocre comedy-dramas but in 1946 he was starred in *Smithy*, a Columbia film directed by Ken G. Hall, presenting a version of Sir Charles Kingsford Smith's life. In the same year he starred in *A Son is Born*. Some quality in Ron Randell's acting or, more likely, in his screen image with its sex-appeal possibilities, stirred the attention of Columbia Pictures, with whose organization the twenty-eight-year-old Australian signed a contract at three hundred and fifty dollars a week. Ron Randell went to Hollywood, where during the next several years he played in a number of second-rate films adorned by the presence of established screen women, among whom were Ginger Rogers, Rita Hayworth, Susan Peters, and Olivia de Haviland. In 1949 he returned to the stage in New York productions by Maurice Evans, and played for him in Terence Rattigan's *Double Bill*.

In 1952, at the age of thirty-four, he made his first London appearance in *Sweet Peril*. Since then he has divided his time between England and America. In 1955, for example, he co-starred in an English film, *I am a Camera*, and played leading rôles in London plays *Sabrina Fair* and *Fifth Season*, and was in the Hollywood film, *Desert Sands*. Latterly most of his engagements have been in America, where he starred on

Broadway, in 1958, in his greatest success, *The World of Susie Wong*. In America he has also appeared in a television series. On July 27, 1957, he married Laya Raki. He confesses to an enthusiasm for walking and, as so many other Australian actors do, for swimming.

Colin Croft was born at Kogarah, Sydney, New South Wales, on March 21, 1919. His theatrical training began when he was five. At seven he was singer, dancer, and comedian with the Young Australia League Boys' Band, and toured Australia, New Zealand, and South Africa for seven years. He was one of four boys chosen to represent Australia in the British Empire Boys' Band. Although this was under the patronage of the Duke of Gloucester, the notion that the four boys could be exploited caused the Education Department to refuse them permits to travel. Colin Croft then joined the Australian and New Zealand Boys' Band until 1940, by which time, being twenty-one, he was scarcely a boy. After three weeks in David Jones's store in Sydney, he worked on the Macquarie Network as a comedian partner to Joy Nichols.

In December 1942 he joined the Second A.I.F. as a driver in the Army Service Corps, but was transferred into Army Amenities Service to appear in dramas and musical comedies until May 1946. He saw active service in Bougainville, New Guinea, and New Britain.

Demobilized, he joined the Tivoli Circuit in Sydney, in Jim Davidson's *Clambake* on June 24, 1946. During the next two years a contract with Tivoli Theatres kept him regularly on the light-hearted stage, hand-in-glove with such entertainers as Tommy Trinder, Ella Shields, George Wallace, Lilian Roth, Will Mahony, and Clem Dawe.

He became a J. C. Williamson's man, his début for The Firm being at Perth on April 5, 1948, in *No, No, Nanette*, with Pat Keating and Fred Murray. Thenceforth he appeared in many musical comedies, including *White Horse Inn*, with

Miriam Lester, and *Viktoria and Her Hussar* with Gladys Moncrieff.

On September 19, 1949, he sailed for England in the *Ormonde*, in which, fifteen years before, Coral Browne had sailed towards a more single-minded future than Croft's. For a decade he ran the theatrical gamut, including near-starvation in the early Oscar Asche manner. His first job was in B.B.C. variety *(Starlight Hour)*; his next, in March 1950, was in the play *Pommy* for Stanley French. After that he appeared at night clubs (Ciro's, Churchill's), in revues, variety, television plays, stage plays, films, and musical comedies, once achieving the hat-trick of being featured in three places at once—in *Wonderful Town*, with Pat Kirkwood, at the Princess Theatre, London; at Churchill's Club in *Pot Pourri*; and in a leading rôle in the film *Rock, You Sinners* at the Pavilion Theatre. Once, he was a real-life hero. He had been playing Luther Billis in *South Pacific* at the Drury Lane Theatre from May 2, 1953, and, a year later, on tour with the same show, had reached Stratford-on-Avon —which does not feed on Shakespeare alone. On May 19, 1954, he saved the house Shakespeare was born in by extinguishing a fire that threatened to destroy it.

Besides *Rock, You Sinners*, he made a number of other films: *Tread Softly*, with Frances Day, 1952; *Kiss of Death*, 1956; *The Traitor*, filmed in Berlin, 1957, and in the same year *Lady of Vengeance*, with Dennis O'Keefe; *African Patrol* and *Jungle Boy*, filmed by Americans in Kenya, 1958; *High Hell*, with John Derek, for Paramount Pictures, 1958; and *The Heart of Man*, with Frankie Vaughan, for Herbert Wilcox, also in 1958.

Among the television plays he appeared in were *The Schirmer Inheritance, A Dram of Death, Policy for Love, Portrait in Black, It Pays to Advertise, The Sound of Death, Death has Three Faces, The Franchise Affair*, and *Dixon of Dock Green*. His last television appearance before returning to Australia was in *Wedding Day*.

239

He arrived in Sydney on July 27, 1959, accompanied by two Cairn terriers named Angus and Mumtaz. His first appearance on his return was on tour in Tasmania in the revue *Trunkline*, with Queenie Ashton, who is best known in today's Australia for her portrayal of Granny Bishop in the infinite serial *Blue Hills*, written by Gwen Meredith, and produced by Eric John for the Australian Broadcasting Commission.

Born in London, Queenie Ashton made her first public appearance as a singer at the age of three, but did not begin to learn dancing until she was four. Her professional début was at the Prince of Wales Theatre, London, in *Happy Family* in a singing and dancing duet with Noël Coward. At sixteen, she began to study drama and voice production at the Guildhall School of Music, and was coached in operatic technique by the bass-baritone Dinh Gilly. She sang in B.B.C. recitals; played leading rôles at the Winter Garden Theatre, Drury Lane, in the musical comedies *Tell Me More*, and *Kid Boots*; and appeared in several films before coming to Australia to star in *Sunny* at the Empire Theatre, Sydney. She appeared in a number of revues and musical comedies for Ernest C. Rolls, who had imported her.

Her later parts have included many in A.B.C. plays, films, and stage plays such as *John Loves Mary*, with June Clyde and Hartley Power, at the Theatre Royal, Sydney, and *The Glass Menagerie* at the Palace Theatre, Sydney. She won the Macquarie Award for her supporting rôle in *Edward, My Son*. She is married, and has two children.

Colin Croft has appeared in variety shows with Sheila Bradley, Lorrae Desmond, and Shirl Conway; in the musical comedies *The Student Prince* and *Show Boat*; in ballets with Ruth Galene (*The Tell-Tale Heart, Overture for Dancers, The Genius*); and poetry readings. A.B.C. television plays in which he has taken part are *Blue Murder*, with Ric Hutton; *Divide and Conquer; Whiplash; Scent of Fear; Off Centre*, with Nigel Lovell; *The Patriots*, in which he acted Colonel Shadforth; and *Red Peppers* and *Family Album*, attempting the original Noël Coward parts opposite Lorrae Desmond attempting the original Gertrude Lawrence ones.

Unmarried, he lives with his mother and a sister at French's Forest, New South Wales. His recreations are yachting, and, perhaps inevitably, swimming. In March 1964, in partnership with Barry Wayne, he formed Crane Productions, a company designed to promote entertainment in any of the many fields he has himself performed in from the age of seven.

Leo McKern (Leo Reginald McKern) was born at Petersham, New South Wales, on March 16, 1920.

McKern was educated at Randwick Public School, and later at Sydney Technical College. He displayed an early interest in painting. He was later to work as a commercial artist. Following, however, in the footsteps of his father, who was an engineer, he was apprenticed, at fifteen, to an engineering shop. Here he had an accident which, even after he had spent eighteen months in hospital, resulted in the loss of one eye.

During World War II he served with the Australian army, and was discharged in 1944, when he worked as a commercial artist in Sydney, and devoted his leisure to amateur acting. His début was in May Hollinworth's production of Thornton Wilder's *Our Town*, at the Metropolitan Theatre, Sydney, in 1944. Later that year he played the chemist in *Uncle Harry* for J. C. Williamson's, and some small parts in other productions for The Firm.

In 1946 he sailed for England, and on November 9, a fortnight after his arrival there with no more than £3 left, married Jane Southall (Holland) whom he had followed from Sydney. In London, he tried many jobs—furniture salesman, commercial artist, cleaner in a grocery shop, and factory hand in an artificial jewellery factory—until his wife got him the job of stage manager for *Easy Money*, in which she was on

Q

tour. This connection with the world of entertainment led to other things. Between 1947 and 1949 he travelled to Germany with the Combined Services Entertainment Unit; fulfilled touring engagements with the British Arts Council Theatre Company; and, with the Nottingham Repertory, made one-night stands throughout Wales and the Midlands.

In 1949 he began a fruitful association with the Old Vic. Company which was, that season, starring Michael Redgrave in *Hamlet, She Stoops to Conquer, Love's Labour's Lost,* and *The Miser.* McKern played small parts, and understudied Tony Lumpkin. He continued to work with the Old Vic. Company for five years, by which time he had risen to playing important parts, and his salary had risen to £15 a week. He next spent two years at the Shakespeare Memorial Theatre with the Stratford-on-Avon Company. During these years he played in *Lear* (the Fool, 1950), *Twelfth Night, Henry the Fifth, The Merry Wives of Windsor, Electra, Othello* (Iago, 1952), *As You Like It* (Touchstone, 1952). In the plays with which the Stratford Company toured Australia in 1953 he played Iago, Glendower, Touchstone, and Northumberland.

At Christmas 1954 he was acclaimed for his delightful performance as Toad in *Toad of Toad Hall* at the Princess Theatre, London. Throughout the years in England he had appeared in small film parts, the first being in 1951. In 1955 he was co-starred with Ann Todd and Michael Redgrave in *Time Without Pity.* In 1956 he was invited to Australia to play the title rôle in Douglas Stewart's *Ned Kelly.* Leo McKern is five feet six inches tall; Kelly the killer was six feet two and a half inches.

The production was sponsored by the Australian Elizabethan Theatre Trust, an over-subsidized, wasteful, and generally ineffectual organization. The producer was John Sumner, who had had experience with the Dundee Repertory Company, Scotland. Supporting McKern as Ned Kelly were a number of Australians, most of whom were expensively brought back from England for the occasion. Each had stage experience.

Frank Waters, who played Joe Byrne, was a South Australian amateur actor who became prominent in the Sydney broadcasting world, and appeared often at the Minerva Theatre. His performance of Willy in *Death of a Salesman* impressed Anthony Quale, and led to an engagement for the 1954 season of the Stratford-on-Avon Company. In 1956 Waters received the Sydney Critics' Award for his acting in the Independent Theatre's *Winter Journey*.

Kevin Miles, who played Dan Kelly, was born in Melbourne, and acquired his technique in a series of rôles with the Melbourne Little Theatre. His professional début was with the Stratford Company on its 1953 tour of Australian cities. He then played in J. C. Williamson's *Seagulls Over Sorrento* and *Reluctant Heroes*, before spending two seasons with the Stratford-on-Avon Company in England in a number of smaller Shakespearian parts. During the 1955 season, which starred Laurence Olivier and Vivien Leigh, Miles played in *Titus Andronicus, The Merry Wives of Windsor, All's Well That Ends Well,* and *Macbeth.* Nancye Stewart and Keith Michell were also in the company. While in England Kevin Miles had film and television experience.

Lloyd Cunningham, who played Steve Hart, began work as a Western Australian farmer who rode steers in rodeos as a sideline. In search of an even more public expression of his talent he entered the theatrical field and, starting with backstage work, presently graduated to appearances in *A Streetcar Named Desire* and *Worm's Eye View*. In 1953 he sailed for England, and had all-round experience in touring with repertory companies, as well as appearing in television plays, and in small parts in films such as *Dial 999*, with Gene Nelson.

Other players in the cast of *Ned Kelly* were Bunney Brooke (the barmaid), a Victorian with wide experience in Australia and England; Frank Lloyd (Mackin, Curnow), a Sydney-born actor who had played in London, Rome, and Paris, and had appeared in films with Errol Flynn, Jean Kent, and Arlene Dahl; Peter Wagner (a lounger), who was born in Queensland, and whose initial amateur career, from 1946 to 1954, with the Brisbane Twelfth Night Theatre, was topped by two years as a student at the Royal Academy of Dramatic Art, London; Collins Hilton who had trained and worked with Gregan McMahon; Robert Levis and Ron Shand, who had both performed with the John Alden Shakespeare Company; and Benita Harvey, who had been launched by Fifi Banvard at the Theatre Royal, Hobart.

Special backdrops were painted for the occasion by Kelly-enthusiast Sidney Nolan, an Australian painter with a high reputation among certain art-fanciers. Music was composed by John Antill, an Australian composer. Seats in the stalls of the Elizabethan Theatre, Newtown, Sydney, where the *Ned Kelly* season began on October 3, 1956, had been donated, at a cost of £10 each, by the well-meaning. An audience, however gypped by a Trust presentation, could derive comfort of a sort from occupying seats given by conspicuous victims of being conspicuous: Dick Bentley, Sir Lewis Casson, Noël Coward, Sir Eugene Goossens, Kathleen Gorham, Oscar Hammerstein II, Katharine Hepburn, Robert Helpmann, Vivien Leigh, John McCallum, Sir Laurence Olivier, Gwen Plumb, Terence Rattigan, Anna Russell, Sophie Stewart, Mayne Lynton, Googie Withers, Ray Lawler, Helene Kirsova, Nancye Stewart, and Thelma Scott.

When *Ned Kelly* closed down with a loss of £9,317, Leo McKern was invited to produce and play in *The Rainmaker* for the Trust. The play lost £17,118 for its open-handed sponsors. McKern returned to England. The Trust then lost £36,051 on its Mozart Opera Season of *Figaro, Don Giovanni, Cosi Fan Tutte,* and *The Magic Flute.*

In 1958 McKern played Big Daddy in *Cat on a Hot Tin Roof.* In 1959 he starred in *Rollo,* and was called by a critic "the new Goon"; played a newspaper's science correspondent in *The Day the Earth Caught Fire*; and had his second production failure at the Duke of York Theatre when *The Shifting Heart* was withdrawn after three weeks. In 1962 he played the title rôle in *Peer Gynt* and, in 1963, one of his two favourite rôles, Iago (Nym is the other) in *Othello*. Both plays were at the Old Vic. Theatre.

His recreations are fishing, shooting, painting, and photography. His daughter Abigail was born in 1955.

Allan Cuthbertson was born in Perth, Western Australia, on April 7, 1920. His mother was Isobel Ferguson Darling, member of a South Australian pioneer family; his father, Ernest Cuthbertson, who died in 1934, came from Newcastle-on-Tyne, England, at the age of sixteen, to be a jackeroo. Ernest Cuthbertson's career followed a course from jackeroo to farmer to city businessman with a flair for acting, singing, and musical comedy production—Allan Cuthbertson's earliest memory is of being backstage at His Majesty's Theatre, Perth, to watch his spotlit father singing a Lionel Monckton song. Allan Cuthbertson and his brother Henry (Director of Drama for the A.B.C., Melbourne) were both intensely interested in matters theatrical from boyhood.

Allan Cuthbertson was educated at Hale School, Perth, and during his nine years there was not only a leading light in the school drama society, but played child rôles with the Perth Repertory Club, and (at seven-and-six an episode) with broadcast children's serials. Cuthbertson's father and two brothers—Henry and William—were pioneer broadcasters with the A.B.C. in Perth.

Leaving school he became a bank clerk. This did not impair his fervour for drama: A.B.C. rôles; Perth Repertory rôles; scene-painting; the writing of one-act plays, and farcical sketches. By 1939 he had salted down £600 towards an assault on England and the Old Vic. Drama School. His assaults were elsewhere. As an R.A.A.F. pilot he flew Catalinas in the Pacific area—New Guinea, the Celebes, Borneo, the Philippines—until 1945.

After demobilization, Cuthbertson joined the George Edwardes Company in Sydney, playing in such soap operas as *Dad and Dave,* and *Martin's Corner,* and for the Lux and the Macquarie broadcast theatres. He appeared with Madge Ryan in Lee Thompson's *Murder Without Crime* in 1946, and then left for London, travelling in the same ship as his future wife, Dr Gertrud Willner, a Czechoslovak refugee to Australia in 1938. They married in London, and have one son, John, born in 1949.

Within a fortnight after arriving in England in 1947 Cuthbertson had a leading part in a Philip Johnson play with the Palmer's Green Repertory. A season with Bexhill-on-Sea Repertory followed. From this he went to the rather *recherché* try-out theatre, Bolton's, Kensington, to play Romeo to Isobel Dean's Juliet and the Nurse of Eileen Thorndike (Dame Sybil's sister), in *Romeo and Juliet.* He had, thereafter, personal successes in Peter Glenville's unsuccessful production of Coward's *Point Valaine,* playing opposite Mary Ellis; in the unsuccessful tour of *Little Holiday*; in Leonov's *The Apple Orchard* for the Bristol Old Vic. Company; and in *Hamlet* (Old Vic. production), at the now demolished St James's Theatre, as Laertes in a cast which included Paul Rogers, Robert Eddison, Catherine Lacey, and William Devlin. His next engagement was for eighteen months with the Theatre Royal, Windsor; thence to the Lyric Theatre, London, to play Aimwell in Farquhar's *The Beaux' Stratagem* with John Clements. This production, which ran for six hundred performances, holds the long-run record for the revival of a costume play. His next part— the soppy Octavius in Shaw's *Man and Superman*—lasted for a year, opening at New Theatre before transferring to Prince's Theatre.

Even in plays which flopped, Cuthbertson had received increasingly laudatory reviews, and was now cast in the part which was to change somewhat the direction and tone of his career. The Mask Theatre Company presented a new play by Dorothy and Campbell Christie, *Carrington V.C.*, with Alec Clunes playing the title rôle, and Allan Cuthbertson having an outstanding success as the villainous army grotesque, Colonel Henniker. This play also ran for a year. Anthony Asquith asked him to repeat the rôle in his film of the play with David Niven and Margaret Leighton. Since then—1954—Allan Cuthbertson has appeared in more films than any other Australian actor of his period, while also appearing in television plays. He has enacted Colonel Henniker on stage, screen, television, and wireless.

Allan Cuthbertson says, without deep regret, that he seems "to have settled down as a film character actor, mainly as a modern nasty, a sort of symbol of the sneering Englishman". He was, until *Carrington V.C.*, a poised actor in romantic comedies, and a skilled *farceur*. His early desire to be a Shakespearian did not prevent him from twice turning down invitations to join the Stratford-on-Avon Company because of film engagements, which have taken him to many parts of the world.

Among films in which he has played supporting rôles, or starred, were: *Double Cross* (Donald Houston, Fay Compton); *The Man Who Never Was* (Clifton Webb, Gloria Grahame); *A Novel Affair* (Sir Ralph Richardson); *Yangtse Incident* (Richard Todd); *The Chimney Sweep* (Louis Hayward); *Barnacle Bill* (Sir Alec Guinness); *Law and Disorder* (Michael Redgrave, Robert Morley); *Ice-cold in Alex* (John Mills, Anthony Quayle); *I Was Monty's Double* (John Mills); *Room at the Top* (Laurence Harvey, Simone Signoret); *The Devil's Disciple* (Burt Lancaster, Kirk Douglas, Sir Laurence Olivier); *The Survivor* (Jack Hawkins); *The Guns of Navarone; Freud; The Informers; Mouse on the Moon; The Running Man; Seven Days to Dawn; Survival; Stranglers of Bombay*; and *The Boys*.

Although Allan Cuthbertson welcomes experimentation

247

in the theatrical sphere he believes it must have a sane basis. *Avant-garde* anti-theatre of the *x* equals *o* school—of whom foremost exponent is Samuel Beckett—inclines him, as it does intelligent professional players, to the *derrière-garde*. Harold Pinter he finds sometimes effective, but fundamentally empty. He admires Robert Bolt as a playwright; Sir John Gielgud, Dame Edith Evans, and Sir Laurence Olivier as players.

His hobbies are walking, music, theatre-going, books, and paintings. He has, indeed, become an avid collector of Australian paintings. This may be partly because of a nostalgia for Australia, its people, and particularly its sunny beaches which—despite a strong affection for England—he still misses. His favourite reading is theatrical biography.

Bettina Welch, who was born in Wellington, New Zealand, on March 21, 1921, came to Sydney after leaving school. In 1941, while playing an *ingénue* in David Martin's presentation of *Charley's Aunt* at the Minerva Theatre, Sydney, she was taken up by J.C.W.'s, and put under contract for four years, to be trained meantime as a straight actress. This gesture, at that era of Australia's theatrical decline, was extraordinary, and the treatment—of a beginner in the straight category—unique. J. C. Williamson's have often enough invested in the training of musical comedy possibilities, rarely in the mere actress.

During 1944 she starred for The Firm in *Claudia* on a tour of New Zealand, in *My Sister Eileen* (Melbourne), in *Reunion in Vienna*, and played Elvira in Noël Coward's *Blithe Spirit* during a season which ran for eighteen months from December 1944.

Tall and red-haired, a striking actress in brittle, *toujours gai*, whisky-soda-and-french-windows comedies, she played smoothly in a number of such works: 1948, in a trio of one-act plays by Noël Coward, supporting Cyril Ritchard and Madge Elliott; 1949-1950, with Robert Morley in

248

Edward, My Son; 1951, in *Harvey*, which starred Joe E. Brown, the American comedian with the kangaroo-pouch mouth; 1952, in *Private Lives*, at the Palace Theatre, Sydney, again with Cyril Ritchard and Madge Elliott; 1955, in *Hit and Run*, a revue at Phillip Street Theatre, Sydney, with "Buddy" Charles Tingwell, an Australian who had done well in England on the more frivolous bypaths of theatre, and Gordon Chater, an Englishman who had done well in Australia, particularly in revue. In 1956 Bettina Welch toured for eighteen months, for J. C. Williamson's, with Googie Withers and John McCallum, in *Simon and Laura* and *The Deep Blue Sea*. In 1958 she appeared in *Double Image*, with Emrys Jones.

At the Independent Theatre, Sydney, in 1959, she played Maggie in Tennessee Williams's *Cat on a Hot Tin Roof*; and during 1960, after spending six weeks at Alice Springs for the filming of the television series *Whiplash*, toured Australia and New Zealand with Robert Helpmann in *Nude with Violin*, one of the most inferior of Noël Coward's more inferior plays. In 1961 she made appearances in two televised plays, *Suspect*, and *Shadow of the Vine*. In 1962 she was once again in revue at Phillip Street Theatre (*Out on a Limb*), and once again on tour with Googie Withers, in *The Constant Wife*, through New Zealand. In 1963 Bettina Welch shored up Martine Messager in *Shot in the Dark* at the Theatre Royal, Sydney. She describes her hobbies as reading and cooking.

Diana Perryman was born "practically", she says, "in the proverbial theatre basket. My mother was in the chorus of *The Merry Widow* . . . gradually receding to the back row . . . until six weeks before 'the event' ". The event was in Melbourne, on November 19, 1924. Both her mother and father worked with The Firm for years; her father was also on the Tivoli Circuit. Diana Perryman, therefore, changed schools frequently, sometimes at six-week intervals. She was not, however, a stage child, her only appearance when young being in a walk-on part, at the age of ten, in *White Horse Inn,* on a J.C.W. tour.

It was not until she was working as a secretary in Sydney that she began to study dramatic technique with Doris Fitton's night classes at the Independent Theatre. From being an understudy she worked her way to leading rôles. These included Jessica in John Alden's *Twelfth Night* at the Independent Theatre, 1945; Courtney in *Invisible Circus* (by Sumner Locke-Elliott), produced by John Carlson, 1946; and Peter in Frederick Blackman's production of *Soldier's Wife* (Rose Franken) at the Minerva Theatre, Sydney, 1946.

During 1947 she played the Daughter in *Six Characters in Search of an Author,* and Linda Manners in *Awake, My Love* (Max Afford), both produced by Doris Fitton; and Lucy Lockitt in *The Beggar's Opera.*

In 1948 she played leads in two plays directed by Harry Adams at the Independent Theatre—Edna in *The Dough-girls* (Joseph Fields), and Bess in *They Walk Alone* (Max Catto). Her portrayal of Lavinia in a Doris Fitton production of *Mourning Becomes Electra* received special commendation from Sir Laurence Olivier and Vivien Leigh.

A versatile actress, Diana Perryman had some interesting assignments throughout 1949 and 1950: The Witch of Endor in Honegger's *King David* (Sir Bernard Heinze) at Sydney Town Hall; the title rôle in Wilde's *Salome* (Raoul Cardamatis) at the Independent Theatre; Claire in Elmer Rice's *Dream Girl* (Fifi Banvard) at the Minerva Theatre; the Dark Witch in *Dark of the Moon* (Doris Fitton) at the Independent; Sarat Carn in Charlotte Hastings's *Bonaventure* at the Theatre Royal, Sydney; and Ella in the play based on Robert S. Close's banned book *Love Me, Sailor,* which was presented in a tent.

After *Bonaventure* (1951) Diana Perryman spent four years overseas, working as air hostess with a private charter company, and touring the British Isles, Europe, Scandinavia, the Mediterranean countries, North Africa, the Middle East, and Southern Rhodesia. She did not, during these four years, set foot on a stage.

In 1955 she was back in Sydney at the Independent Theatre as Beauty in Peter Ustinov's *The Love of Four Colonels* (May Hollinworth), and Georgie in Odets's *Winter Journey*, produced by Nigel Lovell. During 1956 and 1957 she toured Australia and New Zealand as Mabel Crosswaite in *The Reluctant Débutante*, with Ursula Jeans and Roger Livesey, and the Australians John Meillon and Fenella Maguire. She received Melbourne's Erik Kuttner Award for Acting in 1960 for her performance in William Rees's production of *Two for the Seesaw*, at the Sydney Theatre Royal, and the Comedy Theatre, Melbourne. The Erik Kuttner Award is annually made to a player chosen by a panel of critics. Among other stage successes were her Millamant in *The Way of the World* (1960); the title rôle in Noël Rubie's *Phaedra*, an adaptation of Racine's *Phèdre* (1961); and Julia in *Shadow of Heroes* (1962). In 1963 she played a number of parts in the Phillip Street Theatre revue *Do You Mind?*

She has played leading parts in television plays—*Other People's Houses, Scent of Fear, Corinth House*, and *I Have Been Here Before*; and in the serials *Autumn Affair, The Story of Peter Gray*, and *Purple Jacaranda*.

In 1961 she was married to Dr Kenneth James Whiteley of the University of New South Wales. She has an interest in archaeology.

Keith Michell was born in Adelaide, South Australia, in December, 1926, and spent most of his boyhood at Warnertown, near Port Pirie. He was educated at Port Pirie High School. In preparation for his intended career as an art teacher he studied at the Adelaide Teachers' College, the School of Arts and Crafts, and the Adelaide University. He became an art teacher at Adelaide High School. He appeared in a number of the productions of the amateur Playbox Company under the direction of Lloyd Prider, and took parts in plays produced for the Australian Broadcasting Commission by Stafford Dyson. When Sir Laurence Olivier was on tour in Australia in 1947, Dyson recommended the young and handsome Michell for an audition. It was successful. He was granted admission to the Old Vic. Drama School in London. Sustained by family aid, his own young-man savings, and the proceeds from the sale of some of his paintings, he was able to afford the Old Vic. School for two years.

By 1950 he had acquired sufficient skill to be drafted into the Young Vic. Company which toured England and Europe. From that time on he has been seen on the stage in Great Britain, Europe, America, Australia, and New Zealand. In 1951 he played Charles the Second in *And So To Bed*, at the New Theatre, London; in 1952-1953, he took the parts of Orlando in *As You Like It* and Hotspur in *Henry the Fourth*, during the Stratford-on-Avon Company's Australian tour.

In 1954, back in England, he played at the Stratford Memorial Theatre as Petruchio in *The Taming of the Shrew*, Theseus in *A Midsummer Night's Dream*, Troilus in *Troilus and Cressida*, and Tybalt in *Romeo and Juliet*. At the end of 1954 he went to New Zealand to play in Christopher Fry's *The Lady's Not For Burning* with the New Zealand Players' Company.

During the Stratford season of 1955 he played Macduff to Sir Laurence Olivier's Macbeth, Master Ford in *The Merry Wives of Windsor*, and Orsino in *Twelfth Night*. By 1956 he had advanced further, and played, with the Old Vic. Company, in London, Antony in *Antony and Cleopatra*, Proteus in *Two Gentlemen of Verona*, Benedick in *Much Ado About Nothing*, and Aaron in *Titus Andronicus*. In the same year he played the title rôle of *Don Juan* at the Royal Court Theatre, Sloane Square.

In 1958 Keith Michell began a lengthy association with *Irma la Douce*, in the parts of Oscar and Nestor. Throughout

1958 and 1959 the play was firmly settled in London at the Lyric Theatre; in 1960 and 1961 it was equally firmly based at the Plymouth Theatre, Broadway, New York.

When Michell returned to the London stage in 1962 it was as leading man in *The Art of Seduction*. Later in the year he played Don John in *The Chances,* the opening play for the Chichester Festival Theatre. Michell, who had been cast in the part by Olivier, was stimulated by the whole occasion, of which he said, "It is always thrilling to do something no one living has done. *The Chances* hadn't been seen in living memory, although the part had been played often by the great Garrick, and is a magnificent one. To crown it all, the new theatre is the most exciting I have ever played in." In *The Broken Heart,* another production of this important opening season, he played Ithocles.

His appearances on television, for the B.B.C., I.T.V., and in New York, have been many and of high standard: Professor Henry Higgins in *Pygmalion* (B.B.C., 1956); the Man in *Act of Violence* (B.B.C., 1956); Rudolph in *The Mayerling Affair* (B.B.C., 1956); Gaston in *Traveller Without Luggage* (I.T.V., 1959); Paul in *The Guardian Angel* (I.T.V., 1959); Hector in *The Tiger at the Gates* (I.T.V., 1959); dual rôles in *The Great Impersonation* (New York, 1960); *Oedipus* (New York, 1961); Heathcliff in *Wuthering Heights* (B.B.C., 1962); *Loyalties* (B.B.C., 1962); and Clarrie in *The Shifting Heart* (I.T.V., 1962). He found "a new kind of freedom, and a fund of forgotten resources" in playing a character from his own country. As do many Australian actors and actresses who have been forced to be short-time or committed expatriates, he pines for opportunities to do more theatre and film work in Australia.

In 1963 he played in Tyrone Guthrie's *The Bergonzi Hand,* and in the I.T.V. series of incidents from Shakespeare's Roman Plays. The series was called *The Spread of the Eagle.* Michell played the Mark Antony of *Julius Caesar,* virile and in the ascendant, and the Mark Antony of *Antony and Cleopatra*, the sunset Antony perishing in flames of poetry. In August 1963 he went to New York to star in Anouilh's *The Rehearsal*. In April and May 1964 he was in Australia with Googie Withers, Joan MacArthur, Raymond Westwell, and Jeannette Sterke (Michell's actress wife) to present *The First Four Hundred Years*, a selection of scenes from Shakespeare's plays. This presentation was timed to be in the nature of a celebration of the four hundredth anniversary of Shakespeare's birth.

Keith Michell married Jeannette Sterke in 1958. They have two children, Paul and Helena. A crammed theatrical career has not made him neglect his first love, and he has held two one-man exhibitions of his paintings in London, the first in 1960, the second in 1962. Works of his were hung at the Australian Artists in London Exhibition held in Australia in 1962.

George Fairfax was born in Melbourne on April 4, 1928, and perhaps inherited his desire to act from his mother, who had acted over the air. He was educated at Caulfield Grammar School, and proceeded thence to the Melbourne University to study law. It was here, under the guidance of Keith Macartney and Joy Youlden, that his interest in drama awakened and quickened. At the age of eighteen he made his début in the title rôle of *Macbeth*, with the Melbourne University Dramatic Society. After two years and two terms of law, he abandoned it for the theatre and its branches. He began with the Little Theatre, South Yarra, Melbourne, founded in 1931 by Hal Percy and Brett Randall. Among the many plays in which he appeared were *First Born*, in which he played Moses, Douglas Stewart's *Shipwreck*, in which he played the Pastor, *Trespass*, *The Golden Lover*, *Now*, *Barabbas*, and *The Gentle People* with George Pravda. Concurrently with his stage appearances he acted in broadcast plays.

Meantime, a desire to produce plays was steadily becoming more intense. In 1954, under the aegis of the British Council, he went to England to attend training courses for producers in Stratford-on-Avon and in London. While there, he acted in B.B.C. plays; and acted and produced with the Ashford Repertory Company in Kent.

In 1956 the Melbourne Little Theatre invited him back as producer. By then the Little Theatre had been rebuilt and reorganized. Later it was renamed St Martin's Theatre. In 1958 George Fairfax was appointed manager-director. Since then he has acted little, but has produced an average of six plays a year for St Martin's. He continues, however, to appear in television plays when time permits, and on the stage, as he did in *The Chairs* (Ionesco), and in Dylan Thomas's *Under Milkwood*. In 1958 he won the Erik Kuttner Award for Acting, for his performance in *The Caine Mutiny Court-Martial*.

His productions include *Relative Values, The Wooden Dish, The Bad Seed, The Keep,* Friedrich Dürrenmatt's *The Physicists,* and *The Playboy of the Western World.*

He is married, and has a daughter born in 1959, and a son born in 1962.

Ron Haddrick was born in Adelaide on April 9, 1929. His early experiences were with amateur groups. From these he graduated to professionalism in plays for the Australian Broadcasting Commission in Adelaide. He was able to become a freelance actor playing parts not only for the A.B.C. but also for commercial stations. When Anthony Quayle and Diana Wynyard were touring Australia with the Shakespeare Memorial Theatre Company from Stratford-on-Avon, in 1953, Haddrick was given an audition by Quayle, and was thereupon invited to join the famous company for the 1954 season at Stratford-on-Avon.

During his five years with the company, he ascended the theatrical slope piecemeal. Throughout 1954 he was no more than a spear-holder doing walk-on parts—the normal first season pattern of Stratford-on-Avon stage training. In 1955 he played small parts such as the First Murderer in *Macbeth*, with Sir Laurence Olivier as Macbeth, and Keith Michell as Macduff; in 1956 he appeared as Charles the Wrestler in *As You Like It*. He also played Hubert in *King John*, and Lucilius in *Julius Caesar*; in 1957, Marcellus in *Hamlet*, Montano in *Othello*, and Tubal in *The Merchant of Venice*; and, in 1958, Tybalt in *Romeo and Juliet*, Antonio in *Twelfth Night*, Horatio in *Hamlet*, and Helicanus in *Pericles, Prince of Tyre*. At the close of the 1958 season, Ron Haddrick played Tybalt, Horatio, and Antonio in the three plays which the Stratford-on-Avon Company took on tour to Leningrad and Moscow, spending two weeks in each city.

Early in 1959 he returned to Sydney, and joined the Trust Players for that year's season, which incurred a loss of £18,899. Of this total, *Julius Caesar*, in which Haddrick played Brutus, and which opened only at the Elizabethan Theatre, was responsible for £8,979. *Man and Superman*, in which he was John Tanner, and *The Long Day's Journey into Night*, in which he was Jamie Tyrone, opened at the Elizabethan but also went on tour.

During the 1960 season the Trust was able to bump up its losses to £31,637. During this season Ron Haddrick played, at the Elizabethan Theatre, Newtown, and Her Majesty's Theatre, Brisbane, the parts of Heracles in *The Rape of the Belt*, Nat Miller in *Ah, Wilderness!* (loss £6,382), and the Fourth Tempter in Eliot's *Murder in the Cathedral*, which was the Trust's contribution to the Adelaide Festival of Arts. He was Monsewer in Brendan Behan's one almost articulate and worthwhile essay in playwriting, *The Hostage* (loss £8,827); and played Morell, the clergyman, in Raymond Menmuir's production of *Candida* (loss £4,619).

In September 1961, after playing Alf Cook in *The One Day of the Year*, Haddrick returned to England to play the same part in the same play, which was presented at the Theatre Royal, Stratford East, under a Trust arrangement with Gleneagles Productions Limited, and Laurier Lister. The play, by Alan Seymour, was a lopsided and petulant attack on Anzac Day, and was hardly a success in London.

Early in 1962 Ron Haddrick returned to Australia, to play Jacko in Russell Braddon's *Naked Island*, and Huysen in Douglas Stewart's *Shipwreck*, both at the Union Theatre, Sydney, and Dunois in *Saint Joan* for the Trust's presentation of Zoe Caldwell to Adelaide Festival of Arts audiences.

In 1963 he played Gayev in Anton Chekhov's *The Cherry Orchard* and the Ghost in *Hamlet*; in 1964 he was John Worthington in *The Importance of Being Earnest*. These three plays were presented at the Old Tote Theatre, Sydney.

Side by side with his stage appearances, Ron Haddrick did plays, serials, poetry readings, and documentaries for the British Broadcasting Commission when in England, and for the Australian Broadcasting Commission and commercial broadcasting stations when in Australia. Some of his rôles have been those of Joe in *Close to the Roof*, Dr Redfern in *The Outcasts*, Petruchio in *The Taming of the Shrew*, Dyson in *A Dead Secret*, Adam Suisse in *The Stranger* (a television serial of great triteness in which Owen Weingott and John Faassen also appeared), and Dave Ruben in *Reunion Day*.

Ron Haddrick, who is six feet tall, and has hazel eyes, admits to no fanciful hobbies or untoward recreations. Before first going overseas in 1953 he used to play A Grade cricket in Adelaide: in 1952 he played in three Sheffield Shield matches for South Australia.

He was married at Stratford-on-Avon in 1956 to Lorraine Quigley, whom he had known in Adelaide. They have a daughter, Lynette, born at Stratford-on-Avon in 1957, and a son, Gregory, born in Sydney in 1960.

John Bluthal was born in Poland (Galicia) on August 12, 1929, and was brought to Australia, at the age of nine, in

R

1938. He received his secondary education at the University High School, Melbourne.

He was interested in the stage from boyhood, and at thirteen appeared in the Yiddish Theatre, Melbourne.

At the Melbourne University he took the Drama Course, and acted with the university's Marlowe Society. In Chekhov's *The Seagull* he played Treplev; in George Bernard Shaw's *Pygmalion* Freddy Eynsford-Hill; and Benjamin in Johan August Strindberg's *Easter*. Shaw's *Arms and the Man* had long ago been musicalized as *The Chocolate Soldier*; at this stage, 1947, *Pygmalion* had not been distorted into *My Fair Lady*, a popular musical comedy. "My Fair", of course, implied cockneyfied "Mayfair".

Side by side with characterizations for the Marlowe Society, John Bluthal was playing extra-murally with the New Theatre, Melbourne, as Cléante in Molière's *Le Malade Imaginaire*, as Dr Benjamin in Clifford Odets's *Waiting for Lefty*, and as the Brown Priest in Sean O'Casey's *The Star Turns Red*. The New Theatre had political attachments.

Egged on by ambition, Bluthal was barely twenty when, in 1949, with his University Drama Course lessons, and a salmagundi of amateur parts as stock-in-trade, he sailed for England. While his hopes of scaling the theatrical barricades were scarcely realized, he did go through some ill-paid experiences which were of value. Between 1949 and 1952 he appeared, for example, in a variety comedy act, and also in a pantomime, both of which wearily and relentlessly toured the provinces. In London, he played with the Unity Theatre Company as Yasha in Marc Blitzstein's *The Cradle Will Rock*, and in Old Time Music Hall revues.

In 1952, back in Australia, he played in *The Square Ring* for the Arrow Theatre Company, Melbourne, and in the same play at the Princess Theatre. After appearing in *As Black as She's Painted*, also at the Princess, he signed a three-year contract with the Tivoli Circuit.

If one examines the performances of Jewish entertainers

at any level—Danny Kaye, Melvyn Douglas, Tony Curtis, Edward G. Robinson—there is observable, no matter how the one differs from the other, a common current of nervous energy, a controlled edginess, an over-emotionalism that, at its worst, produces lush sentimentality, at its best, comedy. Bluthal, growing older, perceived that comedy was the safer, more lucrative bet.

His next eight years in Australia were an interesting tangle of engagements and appearances: variety; *Zip Goes A Million*; appearances with intransigent entertainers of the calibre of Alan Jones, Michael Bentine, and Mel Torme; television; Lehar's *Land of Smiles*, at the Empire Theatre, Sydney; the pantomime *Cinderella* at the Elizabethan Theatre, Sydney; the revues *Bats* and *The Birthday Show* at the Phillip Street Theatre, Sydney; the plays *Sabrina Fair*, and *Bus Stop* at the Independent Theatre, Sydney; broadcasting sessions with Dick Bentley, with Michael Bentine in *Three's a Crowd*, and with Spike Milligan in *Idiot Weekly*. Bluthal produced his own amusing five-minute series *Who?* on television; as well as devising, producing, and starring in *Gaslight Music Hall*.

In 1960 he once more sailed for England with his wife, for in 1956 he had married a contralto singer, Judyth Ann Barron. Fortified by his earlier English experience, and by eight years of Australian experience, he was engaged, after an audition lasting five minutes, to play Fagin in Lionel Bart's *Oliver!* at the New Theatre, St Martin's Lane, London. He played this part for eighteen months. Curiously, it was a part J. C. Williamson's would not cast him in.

He played in B.B.C. television plays and Armchair Theatre; with Michael Bentine, for B.B.C. TV, in the comedy series *The Square World*; with Sid James, Eric Sykes, and Tony Hancock on television; and returned to the stage in 1963, at the Duke of York Theatre, London, to enact six rôles in *The Bed-Sitting Room* with Spike Milligan.

He appeared in two English films, *Mouse on the Moon*, and *Doctor in Distress*.

John Bluthal, with other performers of his generation who have needed to become expatriates, agrees with older men such as Robert Helpmann that the theatre in Australia is largely in the hands of charlatans. As other younger men do, he resents having to earn his living outside his own country. This is partly on his own behalf, partly because he would like his two daughters to be brought up in a country which has one of the highest standards of living—materially, that is—in the world.

Rod Taylor, born in Sydney in 1930, had early yearnings to be an artist, and towards that end studied at the East Sydney Technical College. Meantime, he acted with amateur groups. In 1954 he co-starred with Robert Newton in the technicolor Cinemascope film *Long John Silver*, based on Kylie Tennant's book for children, his performance earning the critics' vote of Actor of the Year. This fillip to ambition decided him to attempt London. *En route* he went to Hollywood, where he was cast in *The Virgin Queen* (1955) for Twentieth Century-Fox. Since then he has gained a reputation for sterling work in other films: *The Catered Affair* (1956), *Separate Tables* (1958), *Ask Any Girl* (1959), *The Time Machine* (1960), *The Birds* (1962), *The V.I.P.s* (1963), and *Sunday in New York* (1963).

Trader Faulkner, born at Mosman, Sydney, on September 7, 1931, was christened Ronald Faulkner. He was nicknamed Trader, after Trader Horn, because he bartered his father's whisky for marbles at the age of seven. His father, John Faulkner, an inventor, had acted in Australian silent films between 1915 and 1929. Some of these were: 1920, *The Breaking of the Drought* (Golden Wattle Films), with Charles Beetham, Rawdon Blandford, Marie la Varre, and Trilby Clarke; 1928, *The Far Paradise* (M.C.D. Productions), with Marie Lorraine, Paul Longuet, and Gaston Mervale; 1928, *Tanami* (Seven Seas), with Wendy Osborne and David Wallace.

His mother, Sheila Whytock, had been a ballerina in the Diaghilev Company, had danced with Pavlova, toured South America, and been *première danseuse* at the Metropolitan Opera House, New York, in the heyday of Enrico Caruso, Feodor Chaliapin, Beniamino Gigli, and Amelita Galli-Curci.

Trader Faulkner was educated by Jesuit priests at St Aloysius and Riverview Colleges, Sydney, but required a crammer to pass his Leaving Certificate. He had a succession of jobs: scrub-clearing, life-saver at the Queenscliff Surf Life-Saving Club, Sydney, clerical work for Lever Brothers, and working in the A.B.C. music record library. This last job gave him a useful knowledge of music, and led to his meeting Peter Finch who, with John Wiltshire and John Kay, had begun the Mercury Theatre venture which was attracting the more dedicated players frustrated by the shallow broadcasting productions in which they earned their living. Peter Finch advised Faulkner to take up speech-training with Bryson Taylor. Fired with enthusiasm, Faulkner began to study anything that might somehow lead theatrewards. *Anything* included training with Ardini, an acrobat who had worked beside Peter Finch in the period when he toured with George Sorlie's tent shows. During 1947, 1948, and 1949, his technique as an actor improving, Faulkner played an increasing number of rôles in broadcast plays.

His stage début in 1948, at the Minerva Theatre, King's Cross, Sydney, was as Reid the cockney boy in *The Guinea Pig*. His performance was a subtle and moving one, and was followed by an impressive appearance as the juvenile lead in Eugene O'Neill's *Ah, Wilderness!* with Lou Vernon in the cast, and Fifi Banvard directing. Already interested by his début in *The Guinea Pig*, J. C. Williamson's were convinced by Faulkner's second appearance that a brilliant young actor was available, and he was given a leading part by The Firm in *Fly Away, Peter* at the Comedy Theatre, Melbourne. From Melbourne he returned to Sydney to play Dr Caius in John Alden's production of *The Merry Wives of Windsor* at the Independent Theatre. Tyrone Guthrie considered the nineteen-year-old Faulkner's performance so admirable that he sent him immediately to London.

He arrived in London in May 1950, and was snapped up —in September he went to New York to play on Broadway Richard Burton's London rôle in Christopher Fry's *The Lady's Not For Burning*. John Gielgud and Pamela Brown were the stars.

From then on his career has been a successful and varied one, and also a more than usually individualistic one, with his ebullience impelling him into exotic situations.

In 1951 he appeared in three English films; in 1952 he travelled to Bermuda with Edmond Knight and Nora Swinburne in Anouilh's *Ring Around the Moon* to play the twins' rôles which Paul Scofield had performed with *panache* in London. In 1953 he played Henry the Fifth and Romeo for the Bristol Old Vic. Company; and in 1954 in Peter Hall's second West End production, *Blood Wedding*, at the Arts Theatre, London, and then, in the same play, at the Playhouse Theatre, Oxford.

The year 1955 found him at Stratford-on-Avon for the Laurence Olivier and Vivien Leigh season, which was lightly sprinkled with other Australian players—Keith Michell, Nancye Stewart, Ron Haddrick, and Kevin Miles. Faulkner played Sebastian in *Twelfth Night*, Malcolm in *Macbeth* (Keith Michell played Macduff), Fenton in *The Merry Wives of Windsor*, Goth in *Titus Andronicus*, and the First Courtier in *All's Well That Ends Well*.

In 1956-1957 he appeared in Anouilh's *Waltz of the Toreadors* at the Criterion Theatre, London. He developed an enthusiasm which became a quasi-obsession, and was to

have an effect on his later career. He began to study flamenco
dancing. He became wonderfully proficient. It requires, one
supposes, no peculiar ability or superhuman training to become proficient enough to do this form of Andalusian dancing in London cabarets, or even on the television programme
Chelsea at Nine, both of which Faulkner did; it is unusual
for an Australian actor to have gained enough skill to be
invited, in 1958, at the Coliseum, London, and again, in
1961, at the Royalty Theatre, London, to dance solo with the
company of the world-famous flamenco dancer, Antonio.
He danced well enough to earn the publicly uttered praise
of Antonio. Trader Faulkner did his study in Madrid, Seville,
and with the gipsies in Granada. After four years he gave
a display of dancing before Carmen Amaya, Queen of the
Gipsies, on the stage of King's Theatre, Edinburgh, in 1961.
She found his mastery of intricate gipsy rhythms so impressive
that she recommended him to the renowned teacher of
flamenco dancing, Antonio Marin, of Madrid, with whom
Faulkner acquired more polish. As well, he studied the
Spanish language, and to some purpose, as will appear.

In January 1961 the Associated Rediffusion Television
Company starred Faulkner opposite Beatrix Lehmann in
Somerset Maugham's *The Mother*, which was set in Seville.
The engagement required him to act, do flamenco dances,
and to arrange the dances for the fiesta scenes in the play.
Later in 1961 he was at the Playhouse Theatre, Oxford, star-
ring with two other Australians, Leo McKern and Diane
Cilento, in Henri de Montherlant's *Queen after Death*.
Although Faulkner's time-consuming passion for things
Spanish suffered no diminishment, his appearances on stage,
screen, and television were not curtailed.

During 1961 he played ten different parts in the television
series *Richard the Lion-Heart*: Prince John, Philippe Auguste
of France, Ubaldo (a Saracen mercenary), a monk, the
Alchemist of Rouen, Marcel (a Breton pirate), a French

tailor, a fop, Elias (a village yokel), and a royal pretender to the English throne.

Throughout 1961, 1962, and 1963 he also appeared in television plays: *The Exiles, The House in Paris, Promenade, Web, Four Just Men, Mr Denning Drives North, A Killer Walks, Twenty-four Hours in a Woman's Life, Richard the Third, Macbeth*, and *The House of Lies* with Zena Walker playing the inscrutable Madeleine Smith, and Faulkner the French lover, Emile, whom no one was able to prove she murdered.

During 1962 he acted in two B.B.C. television plays, *A Piece of Ribbon*, and *The Amateurs* (one of the Maigret series); danced in the flamenco fashion at the Feria in Seville, and at the Rocio in the province of Huelva; and began translating Spanish plays into English. His first two translations were *Sirena Varada*, by Alejandro Casona, and *Three Top Hats*, by Miguel Mihura.

In 1963 he continued translating other, more important works, all by Antonio Buero Vallejo: *In the Burning Darkness, The Writing in the Sand*, and a play dealing with the return of Ulysses to Ithaca and his wife Penelope, *The Weaver of Dreams*. In the same year he was co-featured with Mai Zetterling, Keenan Wynn, and Ronald Howard in a J. Arthur Rank Organization film, *The Bay of San Michel*; played the lead, Josset, in another Maigret episode, *A Man Condemned*, for B.B.C. TV; and on May 31 was married in Chelsea to a model, Bobo Minchin.

Dinah Hilary Shearing was born in Sydney. She spent several years of her childhood in England, and then returned to her native city.

Since her earlier ambitions tended towards making a career of singing and painting, she studied singing at the Sydney Conservatorium, where Dr Edgar Bainton and Sir Eugene Goossens gave her encouragement. Painting she studied at the East Sydney Technical School—the National

Art School of Sydney. Thus trained she was able to work for six months as a display artist in a Sydney shop.

Seeking useful experience she took a small rôle in an amateur production at the Conservatorium. Her appetite for acting was whetted. Soon she was appearing in May Hollinworth's productions at the Metropolitan Theatre, Sydney. In 1945 she was in May Hollinworth's presentation of *Country Wife*, and played Viola in *Twelfth Night*. Eleven years later, in 1956, she was to play Viola for an Australian Elizabethan Theatre Trust tour.

Her first broadcasting work was with Peter Finch and Thelma Scott in *The Mariner*. In 1952 she won the Macquarie Award for the best performance of the year on wireless, in *One-Way Street*.

Since 1952 she has played with a number of reputable companies. A dark-haired and handsome woman, she has a malleable voice of fine tone. Her most important engagements have included:

In 1952 she played for six months in John Alden's production of *King Lear*, and also in *Amphitryon 38* at the Independent Theatre, Sydney. Her next play, with Bruce Stewart and Audrey Teesdale, was Christopher Fry's *A Phoenix Too Frequent*, produced by John Kay at the Phillip Street Theatre, Sydney. She has since played twice in this play for the A.B.C., and once on television for A.B.C. TV.

During 1956 she toured the Commonwealth for the Australian Elizabethan Theatre Trust as Viola in *Twelfth Night*, and as Lydia Languish in *The Rivals*. Later that year, she had the lead in *Bell, Book and Candle* at the Theatre Royal, Hobart, and toured Tasmania in the same absurd play. Back in Sydney she supported Paul Rogers, an English actor, in *The Relapse*.

In 1957 she played Maria Bianchi in Richard Beynon's *The Shifting Heart*. In 1959 she joined the Elizabethan Trust Players to appear in leading rôles in *The Slaughter of St Teresa's Day* (Peter Kenna), *Julius Caesar, Fire on the*

Wind (Anthony Coburn), Shaw's *Man and Superman,* and Eugene O'Neill's *Long Day's Journey into Night.* After the Sydney season the Trust Players took the five plays on tour. Of her performances Hugh Hunt, a superior but ineffectual element, English, in the Australian Elizabethan Theatre Trust's pyramid of Englishmen and prodigal theorists, opined that Dinah Shearing was "beginning to act with truth", a thing she considered she had been doing for some pre-Hunt years. She does admit to a greater difficulty, however, in acting middle-aged women of about fifty with truth than in acting really old women. For the Trust's second season in 1959 she played in Benn Levy's *The Rape of the Belt,* and in Eleanor Witcombe's Christmas play *Smugglers Beware,* which lost £6,328.

She played in T. S. Eliot's *Murder in the Cathedral,* with Robert Speaight, an English actor, during the Adelaide Festival of Arts for 1960. Her husband is Rodney Milgate, an actor and amateur painter. They have an only son, Adam.

Diane Cilento was born in Toowoomba, Queensland, in 1932, second youngest of six children. Her father, Dr Rafael West Cilento (later Sir Rafael), was a noted specialist in tropical diseases, her mother was an eminent gynaecologist.

In 1946, when Diane Cilento was fourteen, the family went to New York, where her father had a post with the United Nations Organization. At fifteen she saw her first play, and became feverishly enamoured with the notion of becoming an actress. She therefore took ballet lessons at Carnegie Hall, and a course of study at the American Academy of Dramatic Art. She joined the Barter Theatre Company in Virginia. She worked backstage in odd jobs: prompter, property mistress, and electrician; she played small parts; finally, she went on tour with the company through the Southern and Mid-Western States of America. At eighteen she went to London, and studied for two terms at the Royal Academy of Dramatic Art before returning to Australia with her parents.

In Brisbane she saved from her earnings as a shopgirl and a bit-part player on the A.B.C. until she could return to London and the Academy. To keep herself in London she took a succession of jobs: serving in a wine-shop, selling theatre programmes, doing walk-on parts with the Mills Circus Troupe, and waiting on table at Olivelli's Soho restaurant.

By 1953, her course at R.A.D.A. completed, she played at the Mercury Theatre, London; at the Library Theatre, Manchester, where she was a noticeable Juliet in *Romeo and Juliet*; at the Arts Theatre, London, in Alec Clune's production of *Arms and the Man* and James Bridie's *Tobias and the Angel*. Critic John Barber, reviewing *Arms and the Man*, wrote, "She is like a lick of flame. She is the one girl I would queue in the rain for, just for the flash of her smile." This leaning was shared by others: in 1954, she was given the leading rôle with Sam Wanamaker and Renée Asherson in Clifford Odets's *The Big Knife* at the Duke of York's Theatre, London.

The impact she made in *The Big Knife* led directly to an £11,000 contract with Sir Alexander Korda to make six films in five years. In 1954 she made two—*Wings of Danger*, with Kay Kendall, and *Passage Home*, with Peter Finch.

In 1955 she made three others, none of them of much value dramatically: *The Angel Who Pawned Her Harp*, with Felix Aylmer; *The Passing Stranger*, in which she was a waitress in a wayside eating-house; and *The Woman for Joe*, in which she was a fairground employee. In February 1955 she married a young, out-of-work Italian, Andre Volpe, at a Kensington register office. This marriage persisted, legally, until October 1962. It was, nevertheless, rather a misalliance for, long before 1962, Volpe had returned to his family in Rome.

In April 1955 she co-starred with Michael Redgrave in

Tiger at the Gates. When this play transferred from the West End to Broadway her performance won The Critics' Choice Award as the Best Actress of the Year, and the Daniel Blum Award. In 1955 she also played Helen of Troy in Christopher Fry's translation of Giraudoux's *The Trojan War Will Not Take Place.* Critics were not unanimously in approval of her interpretation—she played Helen as a sluttish girl who did not care for men.

The year 1957 was one of diverse incidents for Diane Cilento, and had its sombre troughs as well as its glittering crests. She played the Tweenie—most desirable and delectable of rôles for any actress—in *The Admirable Crichton,* opposite Kenneth More as the Robinson Crusoe butler. In March she began work on her first musical play, *Zuleika,* an attempt to resurrect theatrically, with melody, Max Beerbohm's novel *Zuleika Dobson.* Diane Cilento, who had been working and playing hard for years, had the sort of emotional *crise* called a nervous breakdown, and was found in her hotel room at Oxford with her wrists slashed. When *Zuleika* went to London she was not in the cast, but was holidaying in Spain. She returned from Spain to star, as a more glamorous creature than she had hitherto played, in the film *The Truth About Women;* also to appear as Anna in *Anna Christie* for B.B.C. TV, opposite the Scots actor, Sean Connery, whom she later married; and to play the leading rôle in *Less Than Kind* at the Arts Theatre, London. Towards the end of this up-hill-and-down-dale 1957 she returned to Australia to have her first child, a daughter, Giovanna, who was born in December.

Before leaving Australia for America in 1958 she played in an A.B.C. broadcast of *Bell, Book and Candle.* In May 1958 she had an attack of virus pneumonia in New York, where she had gone to play in *The Disenchanted,* a play based on Schulberg's novel. She withdrew from the cast.

Among her assignments of the next several years were: *Jetstream,* an English film, 1959; Tennessee Williams's

Orpheus Descending, at the Royal Court Theatre, Sloane Square, 1959; and, in July of 1959, on Broadway, the part of Ellie in Shaw's *Heartbreak House*, with Maurice Evans. Brooks Atkinson, the New York *Times* drama critic, called her voice, in this play, "hard, tough, and wearing".

In 1960, still on Broadway, she starred in Felicien Marceau's *The Good Soup*; in November she played the amateur harlot, Julie, in Strindberg's *Miss Julie*, at the Lyric Theatre, Hammersmith; in December the professional harlot, Sadie Thompson, in Somerset Maugham's *Rain* for B.B.C. TV.

In 1961 she played *Queen after Death* at the Playhouse, Oxford, with Leo McKern and Trader Faulkner; made the film *The Full Treatment*; in April played a small part in Jean-Paul Sartre's *Altona* at the Royal Court Theatre, Sloane Square; and in September worked in the film *I Thank a Fool*, with Peter Finch. She appeared also in a limited season of Pirandello's *To Clothe the Naked*, at the Playhouse, Oxford. Not only did she play Ersilia Drei, the nursemaid who committed suicide; she had translated the second act from Italian into English. This chore, and a kind of sisters-under-the-skin feeling for Ersilia, inspired her to make her own full translation of the play, to set up the financial and artistic side of the production, and to act Ersilia, in London. The presentation lost much money. In December 1961, on a visit to Australia, she revealed that, Pirandello having failed her, she had plans to have D'Arcy Niland's *Call Me When the Cross Turns Over* filmed, hoping thus to recoup her losses in a venture that could not be anything but commercial. She said, "Doing *Naked* was sheer torture. I have spent my career doing what are called 'artistic' and 'serious' rôles. I've done all that. Now I want to entertain."

As though to support the New Me ("I am making myself over in so far as I want to appeal to the general public more than I used to"), Diane Cilento's next rôle, in February 1962, was in Elaine Dundy's comedy *My Place*. In May she played in Françoise Sagan's *A Castle in Sweden*, and, also, in 1962, acted Mollie in the film *Tom Jones*, opposite Albert Finney.

In October 1962 she and Andre Volpe were divorced; in December 1962 she married Sean Connery in Gibraltar; in January 1963 she had her second child, a son, in Rome.

Other films she has made have been *Stolen Journey* and *The Naked Edge*.

Zoe Caldwell was born in Melbourne in 1934, daughter of a plumber. Her interest in expressing herself on a public platform began early. At the age of twelve she played Slightly in *Peter Pan*. At seventeen she was making her initial appearances for the Union Theatre Repertory Company, Melbourne, under the direction of John Sumner. From this group with its bias on the give-'em-what-they-want side she moved to the newly founded and pretentious Australian Elizabethan Theatre Trust Company, Sydney.

She made her Sydney début as Second Woman of Corinth in the Trust's presentation of a cheapjack, "modernized for the common moron" translation of Euripides's *Medea* by an American, Robinson Jeffers. Medea was played by Dame Judith Anderson, who had escaped Australia over a third of a century before, and had last appeared in her home continent as Iris March in Michael Arlen's *The Green Hat*, deliberately wearing unfashionable black stockings with an otherwise opulently fashionable wardrobe. *Medea*, inaugurating a pattern the Trust was doggedly to adhere to, made an expensive Commonwealth tour, and a meagre profit of £2,742. Albeit meagre, it *was* a profit. Later attempts to herd shrewd Australians together in "a theatre of Australians by Australians for Australians" were scarcely so successful. An English actress in a tinpot English farce—Margaret Rutherford in *The Happiest Days of Your Life*—lost £18,501. An American's production of an Irishman's work—Professor Norman Philbrick's production of *Saint Joan*—

lost £14,000. Australians at play were more successful in the seeming competition for The Greatest Loss of the Year— an ill-constructed musical comedy, *Lola Montez*, lost £31,581. The Elizabethan Opera Company in its 1958 season was even more successful and, with presentations of *Peter Grimes, Lohengrin, Fidelio, Carmen,* and *The Barber of Seville,* achieved a loss of £68,998. Dr H. C. Coombs, Chairman of the Board of Directors, said lightly, "Adverse results of this kind are to be expected in the theatre from time to time." From time to time!

The profit-making *Medea* had its Australian première at the Albert Hall, Canberra, on October 5, 1955. It was directed in mediocre fashion by Hugh Hunt. In the cast were Doris Fitton (the Nurse), Alistair Roberts (the Tutor), Ailsa Grahame (First Woman of Corinth), John Alden (Creon), James Bailey (Aegeus), Peter Kenna (a Slave), and Maree Tomasetti (a Woman Attendant), The costumes were designed by William Constable. So was the scenery, later sold for £100.

In 1956 the Trust's Drama Company was composed of Clement McCallin, Leonard Teale, Ray Lawler, Ethel Gabriel, Peter Kenna, Gordon Petrie, George Ogilvie, Dinah Shearing, Madge Ryan, Diana Davidson, Zoe Caldwell, Maree Tomasetti, Jacklyn Kelleher, Gay Benjamin, James Bailey, Alistair Roberts, Ken Warren, Malcolm Robertson, Lewis Luton, Norman Coburn, and Ron Denson.

As a member of this permanent company, Zoe Caldwell toured in 1956 with *Twelfth Night*—the Trust's first attack on Shakespeare—and Sheridan's anti-romantic comedy, *The Rivals*. Hugh Hunt produced a dull *Twelfth Night*; Elaine Haxton designed settings and costumes. *The Rivals* was produced by Robin Lovejoy who, apparently ambidexterously, also did the costumes and settings.

In 1957 Zoe Caldwell was on tour again, this time with Paul Rogers in *Hamlet* and *The Relapse*. Her unusual attack on the eternally difficult part of Ophelia disconcerted many of the ill-trained and out-of-practice audiences, and all but the two or three perceptive journalists attempting dramatic criticism in Australia.

After the 1957 season the Trust, which not only imported expensive talent, but magnanimously exported local talent at great expense, assisted Zoe Caldwell out of the company, and out of Australia, to England and Stratford-on-Avon.

In 1958 she signed a contract with the Stratford-on-Avon Company, which guaranteed her nine months' work at £9 a week. She lived in a small cottage at the village of Tiddington, about a mile from Stratford, on the banks of the Avon River; grew her own vegetables; baked her own bread; let Sir Laurence Olivier clip her hedge; and did walk-on parts without uttering a syllable until the last play of the season. This was *Pericles*, in which she spoke two lines of dialogue.

Her contract was renewed, and she went on the company's tour to Leningrad and Moscow, playing in *Hamlet, Twelfth Night*, and *Romeo and Juliet*. In 1959, her second season with the Stratford-on-Avon Company, and now twenty-five years old, she skyrocketed from making mute entrances and exits to articulate leading rôles, playing Cordelia to Charles Laughton's Lear, Bianca to Paul Robeson's Othello, and Helena in *All's Well That Ends Well*, with Dame Edith Evans as the Countess. In spite of the skilled and over-shadowing antics of ageing and well-kippered troupers—Laughton, Robeson, Dame Edith Evans—Zoe Caldwell was vivid and electric enough to stir the newspapers and periodicals into kindliness of an ego-warming sort. The *New Statesman* wrote: "Miss Caldwell promises to be the best Shakespearian actress of the decade." Both the *Sunday Times* and the *Observer* had her on their Best Actors of the Year lists.

Sir Tyrone Guthrie, who had produced her in these plays of the 1959 season, followed the next moves in her flowering career when she went to the Royal Court Theatre, Sloane Square, to play Isabella in Middleton's *The Changeling*, directed by Tony Richardson; and to co-star with Mary Ure and Robert Shaw in Oscar Lewenstein's production of Ionesco's *Jacques,* in which she played Jacqueline. She appeared also in several television plays. During her eighteen months at the Royal Court she found the atmosphere highly stimulating. "I was", she said, "able to learn new things, yet still retain my basic Australianness. Too often, Australian players are tempted to sink their nationality, and thus lose their identity in a new environment. They are worse actors because of it."

Sir Tyrone Guthrie now snapped her up to star in a six months' season in Canada, at Stratford, Ontario, and at Winnipeg and Manitoba. She was the first Australian to be invited to the Stratford Festival. Her most distinguished performance was as Rosaline in *Love's Labour's Lost.* For Canadian television she played in *The Lady's Not For Burning,* and George Bernard Shaw's *The Apple Cart.*

This Canadian visit over, she went to Australia to appear for the Elizabethan Theatre Trust in an affected and badly scrambled production of *Saint Joan* by Norman Philbrick, an American professor. This calamity was launched at the Adelaide Festival of Arts, 1962, and taken on tour.

In July 1962 she appeared in the part of a young woman in *The Ham Funeral,* an attempt at trick play-writing by Patrick White, an English-cum-Australian novelist adored by cultural cliques. The production, by John Tasker, lost a mere £3,884. In September 1962 Zoe Caldwell appeared in another meretricious Trust-Tasker production of another meretricious White exercise in theatric writing, *The Season at Sarsaparilla,* for the Adelaide University Theatre Guild and the Union Theatre Company, Melbourne, which helped inflate 1961-1962 Trust losses to £197,041 but did not deflate its dog-like faith in further unholy and spendthrift alliances of White and Tasker.

In February 1963 Zoe Caldwell left for America to play a four months' season with Sir Tyrone Guthrie at the newly built Guthrie Theatre in Minneapolis. Before leaving for

S

America and the future she said much about Australian theatre. She said, for example, after calling herself working-class, that the theatre in England was working-class, while the theatre in Australia was "middle-class and middle-aged". This cryptic remark notwithstanding, she did reiterate, at first, that she was anxious to stay and act in Australia, and was perfectly willing to eschew overseas prestige and overseas money to bring this about. Even though an expressed fan of certain branches of English, Canadian, and Russian theatre, she affirmed, publicly and repeatedly, her desire to work in Australia. After playing in *The Ham Funeral* and *The Season at Sarsaparilla* she boarded an aeroplane, and left.

Judith Anne Arthy was born in Brisbane, Queensland, on November 12, 1940. A brilliant student, she became a school-teacher, meantime pursuing an active career with the Brisbane Repertory Theatre, playing leading rôles in *The Crucible* and *Colombe* in 1957. In September 1958, with her blonde hair dyed black, she played Anne in *The Diary of Anne Frank*. Her success in this decided her to work towards being a professional actress. She studied speech under Rhoda Felgate, O.B.E., and embraced every experience that would improve her stage technique, singing in *Patience* (1959), *Iolanthe* (1960), and playing Ophelia to Mervyn Eadie's Hamlet at Brisbane's Twelfth Night Theatre in September 1960. Robin Lovejoy, a producer for the Australian Elizabethan Theatre Trust, impressed by her ability, gave her her first professional part. She abandoned teaching to make her début in the Australian première of *The One Day of the Year* at the Palace Theatre, Sydney, on April 26, 1961, with Ron Haddrick, Reg Lye, and Nita Pannell.

Since then Judith Arthy, for whom a brilliant future has been prophesied by Vivien Leigh, Zoe Caldwell, and astute critics, has done work in many branches of the theatre: with the John Alden Shakespearian Company, the Bobby Limb

Show, as Isobel the child bride in Tennessee Williams's *Period of Adjustment*, in the film *The Nurse's Story*, with Elizabeth Waterhouse and Margo Lee. All this was done in 1961 during which year she began to study dancing with Margaret Barr, and singing with Brigid Clarke.

The year 1962 was also a busy one. She appeared for the Trust in *Shipwreck* (Douglas Stewart), *The Break* (Philip Allbright) at the Union Theatre, Sydney, with Grant Taylor, Alan Trevor, and John Gray; in *Ring Around Rosa*, with Brian James, Muriel Steinbeck, and Neil Fitzpatrick; and in *The Fantasticks*, which ran for four months at the Russell Street Theatre, Melbourne, before transferring to the Perth Playhouse in February 1963.

Other 1963 activities included an A.B.C. TV appearance in *Night Stop*, with George Whaley; a leading rôle in George Fairfax's production of *Write Me a Murder*, with Moira Carleton, at St Martin's Theatre, Melbourne; the part of a WRAAC in the *Australiana* series which was filmed in Madang, New Guinea; and rôles in a season of children's plays produced by Wal Cherry at the Russell Street Theatre.

From September 1963 to February 1964 she understudied Muriel Pavlow in *Mary, Mary*, a J.C.W.'s production which was launched at the Comedy Theatre, Melbourne, before playing Sydney and Brisbane. Also in 1964 she played the co-lead with John Gray in *Continuity Man* (A.B.C. TV), and important rôles in *A Far Country* (St Martin's Theatre), *The Road* (A.B.C. TV with Alexander Archdale, Norman Kaye, and Joy Mitchell), and *The Tower* (St Martin's Theatre, with Madeleine Orr, Judy Barnes, Andrew Guild, Blaise Antony, Norman Kaye, Joy Mitchell, and Rex Holdsworth).

Judith Arthy's realistic and forthright approach to the needs and hazards of a present-day player in Australia does not taint her idealism. She remains dedicated. Her own words are the words of many younger players who resent being forced into expatriatism: "I'm in the theatre because that's the *work* I want to do. Of course, I want to travel overseas, to learn, to experience. But whatever happens I shall return to Australia, for I believe in it and love it, and want to be loyal to it. Although I deplore its cultural apathy, the land and the people have so much to give . . . freshness, frankness, earthiness . . . that it is deserving of something in return, namely, the gifts, the contributions its own talented ones can give it."

CHAPTER NINE

THE SUMMING UP

Minor theatrical trends, a handful of once-notable players, some players at present notable or up-and-coming, and many defunct dramatic companies are not mentioned in this short work. As Australia has produced no playwrights of the power (and staying power) of Ibsen, Chekhov, Strindberg, and Pirandello, even of Pinero, Maugham, Bridie, Barrie, or Rattigan, little can, obviously, be said of them . . . one-play writers are hardly playwrights.

A number of worthy players are merely mentioned *en passant*. On the other hand, certain performers have been given longish treatment because their careers best illustrate some of the devious and curious paths the ambitious have needed to follow—these paths, beset with bizarre organizations, are sociologically more eye-opening than the players themselves. It is felt that personal omissions—often these were an indifferent, lackadaisical, super-modest, or blasé player's fault rather than the willing author's—do not weaken the broad outline. Simplification has, indeed, helped to point up the pattern of progress or retrogression made during this or that era on the stage or the motion picture screen.

Since 1789 (*The Recruiting Officer*) and 1899 (*The Early Christian Martyrs*) much has happened. There has been a succession of results. These have been revealed as logical, or brutally obvious, and sometimes as disconcerting and disheartening. This is, of course, the way of the world, even of the make-believe world. The success of the painted inhabitants of this world owes something to luck, depends much on their talents and stamina, and a great deal on the whims of a canny public. Inevitabilities, however, do occur. Objective conclusions must, unavoidably, be arrived at.

For example, little can be said about Australian films. There have been interesting ones, historically fascinating ones, landmark ones. There has never been, by world standards, a good one. There have been only bad, appalling, rough-as-bags, cheap and nasty, imitation glossy, repetitious or—at best—mediocre ones. Even recent "big" pictures, made in Australia by slick and insensitive overseas companies, and studded with fashionable stars, have failed to record the depth and subtlety and sensitivity and excitement, let alone the surface texture and tone, of a deep and subtle and sensitive and exciting people, and a vivid and kaleidoscopic country.

On the Beach (Lomitas Productions; producer-director, Stanley Kramer); *Summer of the Seventeenth Doll* (Hecht-Hill-Lancaster; director, Leslie Norman); *The Siege of Pinchgut* (Ealing Films; producer, Sir Michael Balcon; director, Harry Watt); and *The Sundowners* (Warner Brothers; director, Fred Zinnemann)—each of these films was, by and large, a failure, and not only because of triteness, anachronism, and crudity of attack. The eye of the camera—which is the focused eye of author, scenario writer, and director—had a marked squint. Intonations were wrong. Values were awry. Nuances were missing. Australians, the world's best-mannered people, are too devious and shrewd, and Australia itself too vast and multi-faceted, to be offhandedly filmed by passing outsiders who can never get closer to interpretation than the corniest of caricatures. Disregarding such "foreign" attempts, one fact horribly emerges: after more than half a century the Future of the Film in Australia is already a thing of the past. However "wealthy" or "sophisticated" Australia becomes, however heavily movie-making is government-subsidized or Jewish-American-financed, however many famous expatriates are expensively re-imported, a freak success or two is all that can be hoped for. The race was lost decades ago.

For Australian theatre, on the other hand, there may be some hope. It is, alas, difficult to see through the dust of rapidly falling standards and steadily collapsing ideals exactly where the hope lies.

At present, Australian professional theatre is shoddy and limited. Because shoddy, it is ill-supported, and only by the shoddy-minded; because limited, it is clique-supported, die-hard-supported, minority-supported. It is, in effect, no longer theatre of the sort that faces all ways with conviction to catch all audiences. The Firm's lukewarm, carbon-copy commercial successes which catch the social sheep, and the night-out-at-the-theatre-on-mum's-birthday celebrants; and the Trust's expensive, High Camp failures which catch no one worth catching—culture-cranks, and shifting-vote demi-intellectuals—are less theatrical in essence than a football match grand final on any drizzly Saturday. A lifesavers' march-past is better theatre, so are the revolting antics of quarter-educated television compères, so is a horse race. One perceives, without any effort, a difference between the Melbourne Cup and *Macbeth*. One also perceives, nevertheless, that each is an entertainment, an escape, a something organized to make time-off-from-the-daily-grind a means of milking a wallet. That the Melbourne Cup is better entertainment, better theatre, than *Macbeth* (or *Charley's Aunt*) as presented in Australia, is not the public's fault. The public will go to what is presented *for* it, not to what is presented at it on a try-out, take-it-or-leave-it basis. However tricky and treacherous, the public is not treacherous to its own built-in needs to be swept off its feet, to its own sensibilities and sen-

279

sitivities which it behoves playwrights (comic, tragic, dramatic, farcical, epic), entrepreneurs, and directors to know about. As part of the public they should know, and work on the fact that a public must not have to make mental or emotional adjustments, or twists in taste, to prepare for entertainment. It must not have to brace itself to tolerate bad *Charley's Aunt* or bad *Cymbeline*.

The Australian public is composed of men and women who love being entertained, and who are willing and well-heeled enough to pay for entertainment . . . but it is not composed of fools. Fools are imperceptive. The Australian public is far from imperceptive. It has an instinctive—and national—wariness of being sold a pup. Anyway, its collective sixth sense has long ago sniffed out the dead body in the wainscot, a decaying body, and a foreign body. Australian theatre can never develop until it is out of the Australia-insensitive hands of non-Australians and non-Australian homosexuals.

The use of homesexuals in the theatre is as old as theatre. As talented heterosexuals do, talented homosexuals rise to various planes of fame: Australia has spawned as proportionately large a band of *Who's Who* homosexuals connected with the theatre as any more time-battered country. This bald truth alarms nobody. What does alarm is that, during the last ten years or more, there have been imported a coterie of *untalented* English homosexuals, English tonks unheard of outside their home country, to dominate sections of the Australian theatrical scene. If one cannot protest against the employment of the Pommy poofter instead of the Aussie poofter, one can record dismay at the employment of fifth-raters who got nowhere near even spear-holding in Drury Lane, yet who are invited to pit a puniness of vision, and a cock-eyed theatrical sense, against the perception of the highly sensitized Australian public. Once again the public is put in the position of rejection which is not its own fault. Neither is the fault the small-time import's for he has been cajoled out of his English shallows by an Australian "Board" or "Committee"—a cabal of cultural busybodies—"to raise the standards of production" in a country which has already driven out its most gifted actors and actresses, thus leaving English directors who were not good enough to make the grade in England to act boss-cocky to those Australians not good enough to make the grade in England.

Homosexuals finished with and aside, there is—if one judges cold-bloodedly from the published evidence—a grave danger in letting non-Australians loose on the Australian theatre. They cannot know what, and whom, they are up against. The case of the Australian Elizabethan Theatre Trust and its successive directors is worth a sentence or so.

Hugh Hunt and Neil Hutchison, both Englishmen from *Whitaker's Almanack* public schools, both well-read, and immensely articulate on theatrical theory, were each in control during a period in which thousands of pounds of taxpayers' money were lost in not reaching thousands of taxpayers. Stefan Haag, a Viennese with an operatic yen, who is enwreathed in dreams and schemes about Sydney's foreseeable white elephant Opera House, was appointed director in 1963. *Australian* Elizabethan Theatre Trust? Who fools whom? If one accepts—though why should one?—that a Mozart season's loss of £36,051 is money well lost on pandering to a grouplet of Mozart fans, should one accept a loss on a season of *Charley's Aunt*? Or should one ask what the Trust is really up to?

Among the painful things learnt by interviewing many of the players whose careers are sketched herein, the most painful were learnt from the younger, more expressive expatriates. Behind their vanity, their braggadocio, their attitude of *sauve qui peut*, and highly strung Australianism lie troubled minds, and some distaste and contempt for the theatrical condition in their own country. Amazingly, there is little bitterness, but they do express pungently their justifiable dismay. They hanker to be back in Australia for personal and nostalgic reasons. Beyond this they feel a deeper need to be working and creating and living as part of the Australian theatre. One and all they denigrate those organizations and individuals not intelligent or far-seeing enough to enthral a public only too anxious to be enthralled.

The professional theatrical scene is empty of vigorous, intelligent, or inspiring leaders. Now that lavish subsidy has proved ineffectual, even as manure for inferior talent, or as mad-money for insipid directors, Australia's one hope lies in the appearance, fully armed and full of fight, of someone with the intensity, the forthrightness, the unfaltering convictions, the broad view, the skill and hard-headedness of the earlier Australians or adopted Australians. What is desperately needed to replace the footling deputies who now disgrace the stage and its environs are people of the mettle and stature of George Selth Coppin, Oscar Asche, Bland Holt, Robert Brough, Allan Wilkie, and Gregan McMahon.

The race may have died out for ever. For the sake of the future of Australian theatre one hopes not.

AUSTRALIAN FILMS

*Films to which no reference is shown are included to make this list comprehensive.

INDEX

[Page numbers in italics indicate main reference.]

Index

Barnes, Frank 152
Barnum, George 118
Barr, Margaret 275
Barr, Pat 228
Barraud, George 229
Barrett, Franklyn 106, 123, 125-6, 153, 170, 188
Barrett, Wilson 134-5
Barrie, James Matthew 64, 81, 110, 222, 277
Barrie, Mona 113, 169, 217
Barriscale, Bessie 151
Barry, Dan 13, *89-90*, 112
Barry, Phyllis du 125
Barry, Roger 209
Barry, Shiel 54, 72
Barrymore, Diana 14, 218
Barrymore, John 14
Bart, Lionel 259
Basehart, Richard 200
Bashford, Ethel 126
Bateman, Zillah 126
Batters the Tinker 13, 15, 30
Bauer, Maxie 138
Bax, Sir Arnold 195
Bayfield, St Clair 71
Beach, Rex 150
Beattie, Joy 195
Beatty, Harcourt 144
Beaumont, Lottie 106
Beaumont Smith Productions 126, 139, 150, 153, 170
Beck, Ron 191
Beck, Sid 214
Beckett, Samuel 119, 193, 248
Bedford, Randolph 102-3
Beerbohm, Max 268
Beerbohm Tree Company 97, 112, 136
Beetham, Charles 125-6, 260
Behan, Brendan 256
Belasco, David 129-31, 141, 166, 222
Bellew, Kyrle 90
Belmore, Bertha 195
Belmore, Daisy 175
Ben Greet Company 114, 140
Benjamin, Gay 271
Bennett, Enid 134, 151, 169
Bennett, Ethel 139
Bennett, Franklyn 204
Benson, F. R. 96-7, 173
Benson Shakespearian Company 96, 140
Benthall, Michael 207

Bentine, Michael 259
Bentley, Dick 189, 221, 244, 259
Bernhardt, Sarah 13, 15, 77, 80, 86, 91, 169
Bert Bailey Company 104-7, 164
Best, Phyllis 111, 218
Beynon, Richard 265
Birrell, Andrew 37
Birtles, Francis 139, 201
Bishop, Kate 63, 93, 158
Bishop, Sir Henry 22
Bjelke-Petersen, Marie 153
Björnson, Björnstjerne 95
Blackman, Frederick 250
Blanc, Bert le 212
Bland, Dulcie 165, 221
Blandford, Rawdon 124, 126, 260
Blitzstein, Marc 258
Blondin 14
Blow, Mark 114
Bluett, Gus 189, 233
Bluthal, John 257-60
Bolitho, Hector 113, 146
Bolt, Robert 248
Bonnar, Mr 28
Booth, Edwin 39, 112
Borden, Olive 154
Borg, Veda Ann 229
Bosch, Hieronymus 187
Boucicault, Dion *fils* 65, 91, 211
Boucicault, Dion *père* 52, 68, 84, 91, 169
Boucicault, Nina 91, 156
Bourke, Sir Richard 21
Bowen, Sir George 66
Boyd, C. 29
Boyd, Mrs C. 29
Bradley, Frank 221
Bradley, Sheila 240
Brady, Alice 137
Bramley, Nellie 93-4, 116, 126, 149, *175-6*, 183, 191, 217
Brampton, Kenneth 126
Brandon Thomas Repertory Company 70, 221
Branscombe, Edward 194
Bray, Harriet (*see* Coppin, Mrs)
Brayton, Lily 15, 97-9
Breamer, Sylvia 15, 151, 221
Brecht, Bertolt 119
Bridie, James 109, 267, 277
Brieux, Eugène 116, 158
Bromley, Ella 221

T

Index

Index

Index

Index

Index

Index

Index

Index

Index

Index